D1268466

MEMOIRS OF A BRITISH AGENT

MEMOIRS OF A
BRITISH AGENT

R. H. Bruce Lockhart

*Introduction, Epilogue and Notes
by Robin Bruce Lockhart*

LONDON
The Folio Society
2003

*Typeset in Sabon with Kabel Heavy display
at The Folio Society. Printed in Great Britain by
Cambridge University Press on Caxton Wove paper,
and bound by them in cloth and printed paper*

CONTENTS

ILLUSTRATIONS

ILLUSTRATIONS

INTRODUCTION

This first book of my father's climbed almost immediately to the top of the best-seller lists on both sides of the Atlantic, and Putnam, the original publisher, was kept busy with reprint after reprint. The critics hailed it everywhere: 'Holds our attention to the last page,' said the *Sunday Times*. 'A far more real personality than Lawrence of Arabia,' wrote the *New York Times*. 'No better picture of the summer of 1918 in Moscow has been or is ever likely to be painted,' thought Arthur Ransome, while Harold Nicolson's view was: 'A book in a thousand . . . exhilarating and unforgettable.' Published in many languages and in numerous editions, 'British Agent' was turned into a film in 1934: with Leslie Howard, Kay Francis and a cast of over five thousand, it was the most expensive movie Warner Brothers had ever produced. They described the book as 'The Greatest Human Document of the Century'. The film itself was praised as 'The Most Important Dramatic Event of the Year'.

My father, the late Sir Robert Bruce Lockhart, KCMG, was born in Scotland in 1887, without a drop of English blood in his veins. It is said that King Robert the Bruce, when dying at the Battle of Bannockburn, asked his friend Sir James Douglas to cut out his heart, lock it carefully in a casket and take it to Palestine for burial. Sir James set off but only got as far as Spain where he became involved in fighting the Moors, in the course of which he threw the casket at them. One legend is that the casket was brought back to Scotland almost immediately, while another is that it was buried in Madrid and returned to Scotland's Melrose Abbey early last century. In 1996, an old casket *was* unearthed at Melrose Abbey, and many believe it to be that of Robert the Bruce but it has never been opened. Whatever the truth of the matter, the descendants of Sir James Douglas changed their name to Lockhart and later added in the name Bruce.

My father's mother was also very much a Highlander – a Macgregor and a member of Rob Roy's clan. Her grandfather, in 1824, had been one of the first two men in Scotland to obtain a licence to distil whisky – although the Macgregors had been doing so without a licence for several hundred years. They made a lot of money from malt whisky before selling out to Distillers Ltd in 1925. My father spent much of his youth on Speyside with his Macgregor relations, having whisky for breakfast, lunch and dinner like his elders. Yet, despite that, the nearby graveyard where many Macgregors are buried reveals that they all lived into their eighties and nineties. My father, although he spent much of his adult life in England, also died in his eighties in 1970. I scattered his ashes in the River Spey opposite the Balmenach (former Macgregor) Distillery, as requested in his will.

After preparatory school where he learnt Greek and Latin, my father obtained a scholarship to Fettes College in Edinburgh, where, in his own words, he 'spent five years in the worship of athleticism'. From Fettes he travelled to Berlin to study German, and then on to Paris to learn French from a Sorbonne professor. The comments of his educators are worth noting. The headmaster of Fettes described him as: 'A boy of exceptional vigour and ability, very quick and alert in mind combining marked literary and historical tastes.' In France, he scored forty-nine out of fifty marks in his six exams. His professor remarked: 'I had many occasions to talk with M. Lockhart and follow his studies. I know that he knows French very well indeed and speaks it fluently and correctly.' The German professor wrote of him: 'His knowledge of German is accurate and fluent and he has an exceptionally pure accent.'

My father returned to Great Britain in the summer of 1908. His father's plans for him to sit an exam for the Civil Service went down the drain when his favourite Macgregor uncle, who owned a number of rubber plantations in Malaya, suggested my father go out there to manage one of them, and in October off he went to Negri Sembilan, via Canada, Japan and Singapore. He fell in love with the country immediately and learnt yet another language – Malay. But he also fell in love with a Malayan princess, ward of the Sultan of Negri Sembilan, who went to live with my father in his bungalow. This created an enormous scandal: not because a white man was living with a Malay girl – which was quite common in those days – but because a Malayan princess had stooped so low as to live with a white rubber planter. Fate, however, intervened, and in 1910 he was forced to return to England having contracted a particularly virulent form of malaria.

It is interesting to note that my father began his literary career in a small way in Malaya, writing short stories which were subsequently published in the *Sphere* magazine under a pseudonym. He also wrote some poems there which I find very beautiful but which have never been published.

On his return to England he stayed with his parents, by then living in Berkshire, and decided to take the advice given to him to sit the Foreign Office exams for the Consular Service. Over sixty candidates registered that year for only four vacancies. My father came top. After a short period in the Foreign Office he was off to Moscow as Vice-Consul in January, 1912.

Before he left England, his parents gave two or three parties for him. At one of these he fell head over heels in love with 'a beautiful Australian girl' called Jean Haslewood Turner from Brisbane. Her grandfather had been the richest man in Queensland. Ten days after their first meeting, they became engaged – a matter of days before my father had to leave for Russia. They were married in 1913, as soon as he had his first leave.

As readers will note, much of my father's early years in Moscow were spent in meeting all the people who mattered in politics, from Tsarist politicians down to men of the Left who were destined to change the world; at the same time he lived a hectic social life with the aristocracy. His wife, who spent some time in Moscow with him, gave a major social party once a week. Champagne and caviare and pretty girls abounded everywhere, and my father, it is fair to say, did not always resist temptation. Apart from upsetting his wife, one of his attachments was so strongly disapproved of by the authorities that in 1917 he was sent home. While he was away, the Bolshevik revolution broke out and peace negotiations between the Russians and the Germans began in Brest-Litovsk.

When back in England he met the leading politicians; with the British Ambassador and staff en route home, the British Government had no means of contact with the Bolsheviks. My father, in view of his extensive knowledge of Russia and Russians, and despite his extramarital relationship, was returned to Russia by Lloyd George with the mission of keeping the Russians at war against Germany. The British Government, ignoring my father's opposite views, felt sure the Bolshevik revolution would collapse. The story of how it didn't, and my father's involvement with that story, you will shortly discover.

*

On October 19th, 1918, the thirty-one-year-old British agent who had been assigned the extraordinary tasks of keeping a revolutionised Russia in the war against Germany and of preventing Bolshevism from spreading worldwide returned to Great Britain. I doubt whether any British agent has ever been assigned such an immense responsibility, before or since. He had been released from the Kremlin in exchange for Litvinov, whom the British had arrested in reprisal for my father's imprisonment – the first 'spy swap'!

Four days later, bevies of cameramen were assembled to photograph my father before he went off to meet Lloyd George and then on to a forty-minute audience with King George V. After he had attended various sessions with the Chiefs of Staff and other Government officials, the Foreign Office gave him nearly a year's leave before sending him to Prague in October, 1919, as Secretary to the British Legation in the newly created Republic of Czechoslovakia.

After nearly three years at the Legation he was transferred, at the request of the Bank of England, to join the Anglo-Austrian Bank to help it and similar Bank of England-fostered European banks establish stability and increase Great Britain's influence in the middle of Europe. Hence my father travelled much to Austria, Hungary, Bulgaria and Yugoslavia – thus increasing still further his stock of foreign languages.

In 1925, my father returned to England, and Lord Beaverbrook, with whom he had made friends in 1918–19, engaged him to run the 'Londoner's Diary' for the *Evening Standard*. His assistants at various times included Malcolm Muggeridge, Harold Nicolson and Randolph Churchill. It was during this period that he wrote *Memoirs of a British Agent*. While remaining a great friend of Lord Beaverbrook's for the rest of the latter's life, he eventually left his employ and went on to write a further thirteen books – all big sellers, one or two of which I myself have updated. In the 1930s he established himself as a pillar of high society who was invited everywhere, becoming a friend of the Prince of Wales, Lord Mountbatten, King Carol of Romania, Anthony Rothschild, Anthony Eden, the Duke of Sutherland and Lady Emerald Cunard among others.

With the approach of World War II, he was warned in early 1939 to be ready, at a week's notice, to proceed to the Foreign Office's Political Intelligence HQ in the countryside outside London, which, with the outbreak of war in September, 1939, he did; he simultaneously became part-time British Representative to the exiled Czechoslovak Government.

Later, having turned down the offer to be head of MI6 – the British secret service – he was appointed head of a new department named the 'Political Warfare Executive'. In this position he supervised the UK Press and radio, technically under the Minister of Information, and all propaganda – overt and covert – against Germany, under the Foreign Secretary; he also liaised with MI6 and the Chiefs of Staff, and dealt with some matters direct with the Prime Minister.

My father and the then head of MI6 were both knighted with the KCMG in January, 1943, and at the end of the war Anthony Eden offered my father an Ambassadorship but he turned this down, stating: 'I have had enough of politicians and the Government.' However, he received a tax-free pension and did the occasional piece of work for the Foreign Office's Political Intelligence Department. This would consist of writing articles which might influence the relations with Great Britain of specific countries. They were not published under my father's name. On the contrary, the Political Intelligence Department obtained (paid?) people well-known in the countries concerned to pretend they had written the articles. My father also made weekly broadcasts to Czechoslovakia.

On my father's death, I was officially advised that most of his covert work would remain Secret for at least a hundred years. I had found many files and documents of his which were clearly very Secret, and some which were at the least Confidential. All the really Secret material I gave to the Foreign Office, together with what I and they considered Confidential; they promised to return the latter to me after thirty years. When the thirty years were up, I asked for the Confidential material back, but despite manifest complaints by me I was told it had 'disappeared'.

Nevertheless, my father's legacy endures. Now, dear reader, turn the page and start reading 'The Greatest Human Document of the Century', or, as the *Daily Express* described it: 'A first-class book sensational enough to satisfy the cravings of the most rabid of spy fans.'

ROBIN BRUCE LOCKHART

EDITORIAL NOTE

St Petersburg

St Petersburg was known as Petrograd from 1914 to 1924, when it was renamed Leningrad. In 1991, after the dissolution of the USSR, it became St Petersburg again.

Dates

Pre-revolutionary Russia used the Julian calendar, which is thirteen days behind the Gregorian calendar adopted by most Western countries. Thus, the revolution of 'October', 1917, occurred in early November by contemporary Russian reckoning, though it is usually referred to as the October revolution. Shortly after the revolution, Russia adopted the Gregorian (new style) calendar.

Kerensky, Kornilov and the Bolshevik Seizure of Power

By the summer of 1917 the Russian army was demoralised as the Germans advanced towards the Russian border. Deserters fled into St Petersburg. General Kornilov, the army's new Commander-in-Chief, informed Prime Minister Kerensky that he intended to lead his troops into St Petersburg to prevent the overthrow of the Provisional Government by Bolshevik insurrectionaries. Kerensky ordered him to resign, and put St Petersburg under martial law, issuing arms to all citizens willing to fight in the city's defence. It transpired that this was unnecessary: when railway workers refused to operate the trains that would have brought the troops into the city, Kornilov abandoned his advance.

Ironically, the crisis facilitated the resurgence of the Bolsheviks, who had suffered a setback in July when an attempted rising had been suppressed by troops loyal to the Government. In the face of the Kornilov threat, many Bolsheviks had been released from prison, or had come out of hiding, and had taken advantage of the Government's issue of arms. From his exile in Finland, Lenin wrote in September: 'History will not forgive us if we do not assume power.' Within a month he was back in St Petersburg. In an almost bloodless coup organised by Trotsky, the Bolsheviks seized control in late October. Their initial grip on power was precarious: in the elections to the Constituent Assembly in November the party won less than a quarter of the seats. Lenin responded by having the Assembly dissolved at gunpoint in January, 1918 – an act which appalled many foreign Socialists. In Lenin's own words, as recalled by Trotsky, it meant 'the liquidation of the idea of democracy by the idea of dictatorship'.

Russian Names

The forms of Russian names transliterated from the Cyrillic to the roman alphabet have been amended according to modern conventions.

PART ONE

THE MOSCOW PAGEANT

People pass. One has eyes. One sees them.

FROM THE FRENCH

My arrival in Moscow coincided with the visit of the British parliamentary delegation, which, on the invitation of the Russian Government, had descended upon St Petersburg and Moscow in that January of 1912. It was an imposing body, headed by the Speaker of the House of Commons. Lord Ampthill, Lord Derby, and Lord Weardale represented the peers, General Sir James Wolfe Murray the Army, Lord Charles Beresford the Navy, and four bishops the Church. There were many others, and altogether the delegation was about eighty strong. Attached to it in the capacity of interpreter was the inimitable and indispensable Maurice Baring.* By the time it had reached Moscow, several of its members had fallen by the way and had returned home. The hospitality of St Petersburg had been too much for them. Now the remaining parliamentarians had to face the far greater ordeal of Muscovite hospitality – an ordeal which I was to share to the full.

On my arrival at the Brest-Litovsk Station I was met by Montgomery Grove, my new chief. He was in full uniform and was just dashing off to the ballet for the gala performance in honour of the British visitors. Instructing the porter how to deal with my luggage, he whisked me into a sleigh, drove me to the Metropole Hotel, pushed a bundle of invitation cards into my hand, and, depositing me with the hall porter, rushed away to keep his engagement.

A little bewildered but full of curiosity I proceeded to examine my new surroundings. The hotel was full to overflowing, and the room reserved for me was on the top floor. Most of my neighbours were women, gaudily painted and gaudily dressed, who, after discovering by exhaustive telephone enquiries both my innocence and my modest purse, lost all interest in this new arrival. In any case, even had they so wished, Vice-Consuls could not compete with the Russian merchants of those days.

As I walked through the hall to the restaurant, my first impressions were of steaming furs, fat women and big sleek men; of attractive servility in the underlings and of good-natured ostentation on the part of the clients; of great wealth and crude coarseness, and yet

* Maurice Baring (1874–1945), writer, journalist and diplomat who was instrumental in introducing Chekhov to the West. He was then a foreign correspondent for *The Times*.

a coarseness sufficiently exotic to dispel repulsion. I had entered into a kingdom where money was the only god. Yet the god of roubles was more lavish, more spendthrift, less harsh, than the god of dollars.

The restaurant itself was a blaze of light and colour. The long high room was surrounded by a balcony on all sides. Along the balcony were gaily lit windows and doors opening into the private rooms – known in Russia as 'kabinets' – where, hidden from prying eyes, dissolute youth and debauched old age trafficked roubles and champagne for gypsy songs and gypsy love. I do my beloved gypsies a wrong. Their morals were better than most people's. They kept themselves for themselves. The mercenary love, to which I refer, was Austrian, or Polish, or Jewish.

The restaurant itself was a maze of small tables. It was crowded by officers in badly cut uniforms, Russian merchants with scented beards, German commercial travellers with sallow complexions and close-cropped heads. And at every table a woman, at every table champagne – bad champagne at twenty-five shillings a bottle. At the hotel end of the room was a high balustraded dais, where an orchestra, resplendent in red coats, crashed out a Viennese waltz with a frenzy which drowned the popping of corks and the clatter of dishes and finally by its increasing furore subdued the conversation. And in a little pulpit all for himself, the Mephistophelean figure of Konchik – Konchik, the leader of the orchestra, Konchik the prince of cabaret violinists, Konchik – by that strange law of nature which decrees that every leader in Russia shall be foreign – the Czech.

As I drank my first glass of vodka and for the first time ate caviare as it should be eaten – on a warm 'kalatch'* – I realised I was in a new world, in which primitiveness and decadence lived side by side. Had an eldritch soothsayer appeared before me and foretold that seven years later I should again be sitting in that hall, that I should be alone, divorced from all my friends and surrounded by Bolsheviks, that in the place where Konchik was now playing Trotsky would be denouncing the Allies in my presence, I should have laughed her to scorn. Yet it was here that in 1918, as the guest of Trotsky, I was to attend my first meeting of the Bolshevist Central Executive Committee and that I was to shake hands for the first and only time with Stalin.

* A warm roll with a handle like a basket.

At that moment, however, all my thoughts were fixed on Konchik. The tumultuous wave of the 'Blue Danube' had died down. From a 'kabinet' had come a command for 'I Do Not Speak to You' – that song once sung by Panina, the greatest of all gypsies. At its plaintive minor chords the room hushed, while Konchik, his eyes almost lost in his fat face, made his violin croon and sob and finally fade away in a whisper of despair and unrequited love.

Poor Konchik. The last time I saw him was four years ago in Prague. He was playing in a small restaurant frequented by soulless diplomats and stolid Czech bourgeois. His savings had been engulfed in the revolution. His last possession was his violin. The mention of Russia brought tears to his eyes.

That first night in Moscow, however, he was a king in a palace of his own, and it was with praiseworthy resolution (alas! I make vain resolutions every time I make a change of surroundings) but with natural reluctance that I dragged myself to bed at eleven o'clock. I was well pleased with Moscow. The clear starlit snow, the crisp, dry cold, the jingle of the sleigh bells, and the strange silence of the snow-banked streets, had stirred my pulses. Now Konchik's music had provided me with a new sensation, blinding me to the defects of a life, which was to put both my health and my character to an impossible test. To be strictly truthful, my early departure from the restaurant was not entirely due to a newly acquired sense of duty. Knowing nothing of Russia, I had assumed that thick clothes would be necessary to protect me from the cold. I had, therefore, invested in the thickest of woollen underwear. As in winter the temperature of the average Russian room approaches that of a Turkish bath, I suffered acute discomfort. After that first night I put these offences away from me and have never worn them since.

For the next three days I lived in a turmoil of entertainment. I did not even see the Consulate. Instead, I followed modestly at the heels of the delegation, lunching now with this corporation, now with that, visiting monasteries and racecourses, attending gala performances at the theatre, shaking hands with long-bearded generals and exchanging stilted compliments in French with the wives of the Moscow merchants.

On the third day this fierce round of festivities was wound up with an immense dinner given by the Haritonenkos, the sugar kings of Moscow. I describe it in some detail because it gives an amazing picture of the Moscow which existed before the war and which will never come again.

The Haritonenkos' house was an immense palace on the far side of the river just opposite the Kremlin.

To meet the British delegates every official, every notable, every millionaire, in Moscow had been invited, and when I arrived I found a throng like a theatre queue struggling on the staircases. The whole house was a fairyland of flowers brought all the way from Nice. Orchestras seemed to be playing in every antechamber.

When finally I made my way upstairs, I was lost in a crowd in which I knew no one. I doubt even if I shook hands with my host and hostess. But at long narrow tables vodka and the most delicious 'zakuski',* both hot and cold, were being served by scores of waiters to the standing guests. I took a glass of vodka and tried several of the unknown dishes. They were excellent. Then an English-speaking Russian took pity on my loneliness, and I had more vodka and more 'zakuski'. It was long past the appointed hour for dinner, but no one seemed to be moving, and presently it struck me that perhaps in this strange country the people dined standing up. I had another vodka and a second portion of reindeer tongue. Then, when my appetite was sated, a footman came along and handed me a card with a plan of the table and my own particular place, and a few minutes later a huge procession made its way to the dining-room. I do not wish to exaggerate. I say truthfully that I cannot remember the number of courses or the different varieties of wine which accompanied them. But the meal lasted till eleven o'clock and would have taxed the intestines of a giant. My immediate neighbours were a Miss von Meck, the daughter of a railway magnate, and Commander Kahovsky, the Russian flag-lieutenant, who had been attached to Lord Charles Beresford.

Miss von Meck spoke excellent English, and under the warm glow of her unaffected volubility my shyness soon melted. Before the meal was half-way through she had given me a lightning survey of Anglo-Russian relations, a summary of the English and Russian characters, a thumb-nail sketch of everyone in the room, and a detailed account of all her own realised and unrealised desires and ambitions.

* Sweetmeats or hors d'oeuvres.

Kahovsky, however, seemed nervous and ill at ease. I was soon to discover why. During dinner he was called away from the room and never returned. The next day I learnt that he had gone to the telephone to speak to his mistress, the wife of a Russian Governor, who lived in St Petersburg. They had been on bad terms for some time, and with dramatic instinct she had chosen this moment to tell him that all was over. Kahovsky had then pulled out his revolver and, still holding the receiver, had put a bullet through his brain. It was very sad, very Russian, very hard on Lord Charles Beresford, and by way of example a little dangerous for a young and highly impressionable Vice-Consul.

Dinner having dragged itself to an end, we again went upstairs to another vast room, where a stage had been erected. Here for over an hour Geltzer, Mordkin and Balashova provided us with a delightful ballet divertissement, and Sibor, the leading violinist of the 'Big Theatre' orchestra, played Chopin nocturnes to us.

What the evening must have cost I do not know. For me it was not to finish until the early morning. After the musical entertainment we danced. As far as I was concerned, it was not a successful experiment, and, strangely enough, in those days the Russians were poor ballroom dancers. Clinging firmly to the friendly von Meck girl, I repaired once more to the dining-room, where a continuous supper was in progress. Here I met my host's son, a young chubby-faced boy, who was still in his teens and who even at that age showed signs of the corpulence of good living. With flushed cheeks he informed us that, after the guests had gone, we were going on to hear the gypsies. We formed a minor conspiracy, collected half a dozen kindred spirits, and at four in the morning set out in 'troikas' – private 'troikas' drawn by magnificent Arab horses – on the long drive to 'Streilna', the kingdom of Maria Nikolayevna.

I can still visualise those 'troikas' standing before the house: the fur rugs; the drivers, with tiny fur-capped heads protruding from the immense folds of their 'shubas',* for all the world like gargantuan golliwogs; the beautiful horses straining at their bits; below us, the ice-bound river lit up like a silver thread by the moon, and immediately before us the ghostly towers of the Kremlin standing out like white sentinels before the starry camp of night.

We took our place – two of us to each 'troika'. The drivers purred

* Greatcoats.

7

to their horses, and in a second we were off. For four glorious miles we tore at breakneck speed through the deserted streets, up the Tver-skaya, past the Brest-Litovsk Station, past the famous night estab-lishment of Yar, out into the Petrovsky Park, until with stinging cheeks and icicles on the drivers' beards we drew up before the miniature crystal palace which is 'Streilna'.

As in a dream I followed the others through the Palm Court, which is the main part of the building, into a large pine-walled 'kabi-net', with a roaring wood fire burning in an open fireplace. The proprietor rubbed his hands and bowed. The head waiter bowed without rubbing his hands. A host of waiters in white uniforms bowed still lower and moved silently to their various tasks. In a few seconds, the room was prepared for the great ritual. We guests sat at a large table near the fire. Before us was an open space and behind it a semicircle of chairs for the gypsies. The wine waiter brought the champagne, and then Maria Nikolayevna came in followed by eight gypsies, four men with guitars, and four girls, with eyes like sloes and sinuous graceful bodies. Both men and women were dressed in the traditional gypsy costume, the men with white-brocaded Russian shirts and coloured trousers, the girls in coloured silks with a red silk kerchief round their heads.

When I met her that night for the first time, Maria Nikolayevna was a plump, heavy woman of forty. Her face was lined, and there was a wistful sadness in her large, grey eyes. In repose she looked an old and lonely woman, but when she spoke the lines in her face van-ished into smiles, and one realised the immense reserves of strength which she could call upon at will. The cynic will say that her task in life was to collect foolish and preferably rich young men, to sing to them, and to make them drink oceans of champagne until their wealth or their father's wealth was transferred from their pockets to her own. Common sense may seem to be on the cynic's side, but there was nothing cynical in Maria Nikolayevna's attitude towards life. She was an artist – in her own way, a great artist – who gave full value for her money, and her kindness and generosity to those who were her friends came straight from the heart.

That night I heard her sing for the first time, and the memory of those great deep notes, which are the secret of the best women gypsy singers, will remain with me until I die. That night, too, I drank my first 'charochka' to her singing. For a novice it is rather a trying ordeal. A large champagne glass is filled to the brim. The gypsy singer places it on a plate and, facing the guest who is to drink the 'charochka', sings the following verse:

> Like a scented flower
> Breathing out perfume,
> Bring the brimming glass;
> Let us drink a toast.
> Drink a toast to Roman,
> Roman our beloved,
> And until he drinks it down
> Pour him out no more.

The last four lines are a chorus, which is taken up with increasing frenzy by the whole troupe. The singer then advances towards the guest whom she is honouring, and holds out the plate to him. He takes the glass, bows low, stands erect, and then drinks the bumper in one draught, replacing the glass upside down on the plate to show that he has not left a drop.

It is an intimate ritual. Only the guest's Christian name is used, and, as there is no Robert in Russian, there and then Maria Nikolayevna christened me 'Roman', which is the Russian equivalent, and Roman or Rómochka I have remained to my Russian friends ever since.

Maria Nikolayevna's art, however, was, as I discovered even then, on a far higher plane than the singing of mere drinking songs. When she sang alone, her voice now passionate, now appealing, then sinking to an infinite sadness, my heart melted. This gypsy music, in fact, is more intoxicating, more dangerous, than opium, or women, or drink, and, although champagne is a necessary adjunct to the enjoyment, there is a plaintiveness in its appeal which to the Slav and Celtic races is almost irresistible. Far better than words it expresses the pent-up and stifled desires of mankind. It induces a delicious melancholy which is half-lyrical, half-sensuous. Something there is in it of the boundless width of the Russian steppe. It is the uttermost antithesis of anything that is Anglo-Saxon. It breaks down all reserves of restraint. It will drive a man to the moneylenders and even to crime. Doubtless, it is the most primitive of all forms of music, somewhat similar in its appeal (may the spirit of Maria Nikolayevna forgive me for this sacrilegious comparison) to the negro spirituals. And it is very costly. It has been responsible for the bulk of my debts. Yet tomorrow, if I had thousands and the desire to squander them, there is no entertainment in New York, Paris, Berlin or London or, indeed, anywhere in the world, which I should choose in preference to a gypsy evening at 'Streilna' in Moscow or at the Villa Rhode in St Petersburg. It is the only form of entertainment which has never bored me and which, if I yielded to the temptation, I know would never fail to charm.

It would be foolish of me to pretend that my appreciation of gypsy music began on that first evening, or rather, early morning at 'Streilna'. Knowing not a word of Russian, I was, in truth, a little bewildered. I did not know my companions well enough to allow a loose rein to my Celtic temperament, and the heat of the room and the sweet champagne made my head ache. I was, therefore, not sorry when at six in the morning the party broke up, and we made our way home. Then it was that I discovered the innate subtlety of the Russian. Both in St Petersburg and in Moscow he has his places of amusement far outside the town – not for any sinister or licentious purpose but merely in order that the drive back may cure him of the after-effects of his carouse. There is no such thing as a pick-me-up in Russia. The crisp, dry winter air is all the tonic that is necessary. By the time I had reached my hotel, I was fit enough to begin the evening all over again.

The Russia of those first three days of my Moscow life is gone for ever. I do not know what has happened to Miss von Meck. In 1930 her father – an old man of nearly seventy – was shot by the Bolsheviks as a dangerous counter-revolutionary. The Haritonenkos are dead. Their son is dead. Their elder daughter now lives in a two-roomed servantless flat in Munich. In 1930 she came over to England to protest to Lord Thomson,* whom she had entertained in Russia, against the purchase of her father's house by the British Government. The house today is the headquarters of the British Embassy in Moscow. It was first confiscated by the Bolsheviks and then sold by them to His Majesty's Government.

The next afternoon, much to its own and everybody else's relief, the delegation left for England. It was to have one more adventure

* Christopher Birdwood, Lord Thomson (1862–1946), military attaché and Chief of Military Commission to Romania 1915–16.

before it quitted Russian soil. As the train, which bore them back to sanity, drew into Smolensk late in the evening, a delegation of Russian clergy, headed by the local bishop, stood on the platform to welcome them. They had come with bread and salt to greet the English bishops. They found drawn blinds and darkened carriages. The unfortunate English were sleeping off the effects of ten days' incessant feasting. The Russians, however, were insistent. They had faced the cold to see an English bishop, and an English bishop they would see even in his nightshirt. At last the train conductor, more terrified by his own clergy than by the prospective wrath of the foreign strangers, woke up Maurice Baring. That great man was equal to the occasion, and the dénouement was swift. Poking his head out of the window, he addressed the clergy in his best Russian:

'Go in peace,' he shouted. 'The bishops are asleep.' And then, to clinch the matter, he added confidentially but firmly: 'They're all drunk.'

If the exotic gaiety of these first three days was enough to turn the head of any young man, the departure of the British delegation soon brought me to my senses. The first sight of the British Consulate was a shattering blow. It was in the Consul's flat in a shabby side-street and consisted of a single room. There was no messenger, no door-keeper. The Consul's maid opened the door and, if she were out, I took her place. Montgomery Grove was a kind and tolerant chief, but he was married, had three children, was without private means, and in an extremely expensive post was shamefully underpaid. He was far poorer than the majority of the local British colony, which was composed mainly of Lancashiremen engaged in the cotton industry. Fortunately, the work was not very arduous. Every morning from ten to one I sat in the little ante-room, which was the Consular office. Its sole furniture consisted of two desks, a bookcase, a safe, a map of Russia and three chairs. If there was more than one visitor, Montgomery Grove fetched another chair from his drawing-room. I sat with my back to my chief, licked stamps, and whacked a typewriter. For the first few weeks I spent most of my time in translating commercial reports from the local German newspaper and in typing out copies of a stereotyped application in Russian for the renewal of the '*permis de séjour*', which was required by every foreigner in Russia and which was furnished by the local Russian Passport Department. We had, of course, no clerk. Such Russian correspondence as was necessary was done by Montgomery Grove. Before I had been six weeks in the Consulate I was tipped by a fat Russian merchant for opening the outside door for him. Fear of hurting his feelings made me pocket the twenty copecks.

I had seen much of official life in the Malay States.* Even the young cadets had their punkah-wallahs, their clerks, their uniformed messengers. They sat, too, in luxurious offices and maintained a dignity which was respected by the whole business community. In Moscow the representative of the British Empire was housed in surroundings of which a Malayan Sanitary Board inspector would have been ashamed. Montgomery Grove, who had been a dashing and good-looking officer in an Indian cavalry regiment, must have felt his position keenly. He was not in a position to entertain the rich

* See Introduction, p. xii.

Muscovite merchants and made no attempt to do so. He carried out his duties without complaint, was a pillar of the local English church, and steered a careful and on the whole skilful course through the rough waters of local British sectional interests and jealousies.

To myself the complete insignificance of my own position was a salutary lesson in humility, and, once I had recovered from the first shock, I accepted the situation with resignation and even managed to derive amusement from it. I had, of course, to leave my hotel. In those days a Vice-Consul with a salary of £300 a year could not afford to live at the Metropole, and the week I spent there cost me more than my first month's salary. Moreover, it was essential for me to learn Russian. Indeed, in the absence of an interpreter, Montgomery Grove could not go on leave until I did. I therefore transferred myself, body and baggage, to the bosom of a Russian family. Here, I must confess, I had an extraordinary stroke of luck. Every year half a dozen English officers came to Moscow to study Russian for their interpreter's examination. To meet their needs a certain number of Russian families specialised in teaching Russian. Most of them were squalid middle-class homes with nothing to recommend them in the way either of comfort or of intellectual uplift. By good fortune, the one family which had a vacancy at the time of my arrival was the Ertels, and to the Ertels by the grace of God I went.

Madame Ertel, the head of the house, was the widow of Alexander Ertel, the well-known Russian novelist and a friend of Tolstoy. She was a plump and rather delicate little woman of about fifty, very intellectual, with a keen interest both in literature and in politics, fussy in a crisis, but a born teacher. She had a large flat with an excellent library on the Vozdvizenka. The other inmates of my new home were her daughter, a dark-eyed temperamental young girl more like an Italian than a Russian, her niece, tall, good-looking and English in appearance, an Armenian student called Reuben Ivanovich (his surname, like Michael Arlen's,* I can never remember), and a wondrously old lady, who was known as 'babushka' (grandmother), who rarely spoke, and who appeared only at meal times. Into this new and modest existence I plunged myself with my

* The author Michael Arlen (1895–1956), who was born Dikran Kouyoumdjian in Bulgaria of Armenian parents, and was naturalised British in 1922. Best known for his novel *The Green Hat* (1924).

usual enthusiasm and my genius for adaptability. My afternoons
were my own, except on rare occasions, and I devoted them exclu-
sively to the study of Russian. Every day I had a lesson from
Madame Ertel and her daughter, and under their skilful tuition I
made rapid progress. They did their best, too, to make me one of
the family, and, although I feel that at times I must have been a sore
trial to them, we never exchanged an unpleasant word.

This was a wholly delightful and instructive period of my Russian existence. Long before I had mastered enough Russian to take
part in the general conversation, I suspected that the Ertels were bitterly opposed to the Tsarist form of government, and that their
sympathies were with the Cadets* and Social-Revolutionaries.† As
my Russian improved (in four months I could speak with considerable fluency), my suspicions were confirmed, and the knowledge
that I was living in an anti-Tsarist stronghold gave a new thrill to
my life and an added zest to my Russian studies. The thrill became
almost a fear when one day over evening tea I was introduced to a
woman whose husband had been shot during the 1905 revolution. I
mentioned this episode to Montgomery Grove, who shook his head
gravely and warned me to be careful. Nothing untoward, however,
happened to me through this association. Later I was to realise that
all the Moscow 'intelligenzia' shared the Ertelian view.

The Ertels, in fact, were typical representatives of the intelligentsia. When at ten o'clock every evening they assembled round
the samovar, they would sometimes sit far into the night discussing
how to make the world safe by revolution. But when the morning
of action came they were fast asleep in bed. It was very harmless,
very hopeless, and very Russian. But for the war and the antiquated
inefficiency of the Russian military organisation, the Tsar would
still be on his throne.

Let me create no false impression. My Russian friends were not
obsessed by revolution. Politics, in fact, were reserved for special
occasions such as unhappy political anniversaries or some outra-
geous political sentence in the Russian courts. At other times the
conversation was stimulating and instructive.

* Constitutional Democrats, the party of the liberal intelligentsia.
† A mix of extremist and moderate radicals who emerged from the Populist
movement. Led by Kerensky, they constituted Russia's strongest party until
the Bolsheviks seized power after the 1917 revolution.

Many writers came to the house: old friends of the late M. Ertel; young men with plays to read and novels to place; painters, musicians, actors and actresses; and, much impressed, I worshipped at the feet of all of them. It was at Madame Ertel's that I first met Olga Knipper, the widow of Chekhov and the leading Moscow tragédienne. It was Madame Ertel who first took me to see a Chekhov play performed by the Moscow Art Theatre players in that sober, solemn theatre where applause was forbidden and where a late arrival was shut out for the whole act.

During this period my life was divided into two watertight compartments: one, Russian and unofficial, and the other official and mainly English. My own preference was for the Russian and unofficial. Occasionally, I dined out at the houses of local British residents. More rarely I attended an official banquet at the German Consulate-General. I paid a few formal calls on my Consular colleagues, and once or twice a week I went to the local British Club at the Hotel National. Of the rich Russians, whom I had met during the visit of the British delegation, I saw nothing. Very soon I discovered that of Society with a big S in Moscow there was none. There was a small handful of nobles, who kept entirely to themselves. The rich merchants formed a group of their own. The intelligentsia were accessible, but only to those who were brought into their circle. Outside their business relations the English and the Russians remained severely apart.

Many of the local English, in fact, regarded the Russians as good-natured but immoral savages, whom it was not safe or proper to introduce into their home circle. It amused me to see Madame Zimin, a Moscow millionairess, lunching every Sunday and playing bridge with her three husbands – two ex, and one real. It showed a tolerance and an understanding which at that time were beyond the range of Western civilisation. The English wives, however, held up their hands in pious horror.

My introduction to the English colony was not very happy. Almost the first Englishmen I met were two brothers called Charnock. Both were Lancashiremen and both were connected with the cotton industry. At the time, Harry, the younger brother, was managing director of a large cotton mill at Oriechovo-Zuevo in the province of Vladimir.

Now Oriechovo-Zuevo was one of the storm-centres of Russian

industrial unrest, and as an antidote to vodka drinking and political agitation among his factory hands Charnock had instituted 'soccer' football. His factory team was then champion of the Moscow League.

Through some confusion with my Cambridge brother* the rumour had already gone round the British colony that I was a brilliant footballer. Without waiting to enquire whether 'rugger' or 'soccer' was my game, the Charnocks invited me to join the 'Morozovtsy', which was the name of their factory team. Always ripe for adventure, I accepted. A few hours later I discovered that there was a British team in Moscow for which I was expected to play. The president of the club did his best to persuade me to change my mind, but, having given my word, I was not prepared to go back on it.

At first there was some feeling against me, but I never regretted my decision. Later, when I came to know these North-countrymen better, I realised what splendid fellows they were. As for the Charnocks, they have remained my firm friends ever since, and I have always counted my football experiences with the Russian proletariat as a most valuable part of my Russian education. I fear the experience was more profitable to me than to my club. I was, in fact, hardly worth my place. Nevertheless, these league matches were great fun and excited immense enthusiasm. At Oriechovo we played before a crowd of ten to fifteen thousand. Except by foreign teams we were rarely defeated. Certainly, Charnock's experiment was a complete success. If it had been adopted in other mills, the effect on the character of the Russian working-men might have been far-reaching.

In my Russian football career I had only one exciting episode. This was in Moscow, when my factory team were playing the German champions. In an encouraging spirit of fair play the Russian Football Association had invited a German to referee. The Germans were considerably bigger than our men and used their weight with unnecessary vigour. In particular, the German right half was unduly rough towards a young English schoolboy of seventeen – a nephew of Charnock and a brilliant footballer – who was playing outside-left to me. When the German had bowled him over most unfairly for the fifth or sixth time, I lost my temper and addressed him in lan-

* One of the author's brothers, Rufus, played rugby for Cambridge and Scotland.

guage which I admit I should never have used in England. In a trice the referee was on my tracks.

'Be careful,' he said in excellent English. 'I heard what you said. If you use language like that again, I'll send you off the field.'

The words I had used were not so very bad. They were an invocation to the Deity to blast the German and to consign him to the nethermost depths of hell. But for a moment I shuddered. Like a flash I saw headlines in the English Press: 'British Vice-Consul Sent off the Field for Foul Language', and I apologised abjectly and profusely. I told the referee my fears after the game.

'If I'd known who you were,' he said with a laugh, 'I should have had you off without a warning.'

During those first months of preparation there was one other influence which affected my life. This was my friendship with George Bowen, a young 'gunner', who was studying Russian at the expense of the War Office. On the whole, I saw little of the military interpreters. Bowen, however, was an exception. He was a sandy-haired, little man, very serious and intelligent, but possessed of a quiet humour which rarely misfired. We became great friends and dined together at least once a week, when we found relief from our labours in comparing the idiosyncrasies of our Russian teachers. He was a hard worker and, as we made a kind of gastronomic competition out of our Russian knowledge (whoever was first 'stumped' by a word in the menu paid for the dinner), our association did little harm to our Russian studies.

By June we had both been six months in Moscow and were able to talk together with considerable fluency – and inaccuracy – in 'pidgin' Russian. With characteristic self-consciousness we did not practise these exercises in the streets, but reserved them for the seclusion of the parks and forests. We lived frugally and modestly, and only rarely did we permit ourselves to depart from the rigid economy which under Bowen's influence even I had learnt to practise.

There were, however, lapses. One digression in particular nearly brought disaster in its train. In July my chief and his family had departed to the 'dacha' – a kind of summer bungalow outside the town, whither all Russians, except the poorest, repair in order to escape the torrid heat of the Moscow summer. My family had gone to the country leaving me alone in the flat. Bowen was '*en villégiature*' with his family also in a 'dacha'. I was lonely and miserable but still firm in my newly-found asceticism. Then one afternoon George Bowen walked into my flat. The sky was like ink. A storm was rolling up from the south and the heat, which had melted the pavement to a soft pulp, was stupefying. With flushed face George threw his hat on my bed and sank into a chair.

'I'm fed up,' he said. 'This dacha existence has defeated me. We have five grown-ups and three children in four rickety rooms. The walls are as thin as paper. The bugs stop me sleeping. The dog is sick daily in my room. Vasili Vasilievich snores and today I caught Maria Petrovna picking sprouts out of the dish with a hairpin. I'm through with Puritanism. Tonight, I'm going Berserk!'

At that moment the storm broke, and for three-quarters of an hour the lightning played fireworks round the blue and golden cupolas of the Kremlin. In the flooded streets the trams stood motionless like ships riding at anchor. The thunder shook the house to its foundations.

We closed the windows and, coatless, lay back in our chairs. The sweat poured down George's face in streams. My head ached. It was an hour of bitter agony not unmingled with fear.

Then suddenly the skies cleared and the sun came out. Quickly we opened the windows. A delicious freshness came from the monastery garden opposite. The trees, which an hour before had been parched and white with dust, were now radiantly green. The streets resumed their normal bustle. The trams moved, and we moved with them.

Very deliberately we laid our plans. George should stay the night with me. We should dine at the Hermitage.* Later we should go to the Aquarium. No expense should be spared.

Cheque-book in hand, we walked down to Muir and Mirrielees – the Harrods of Moscow – and handed in our cheques. Each was for £25 – a month's salary for me and more for the rarely reckless George. With trepidation we watched the cashier's face. Hitherto, we had never cashed more than £10. He paid without a moment's hesitation. In those days the credit of British officials abroad was still unassailable.

Happy and irresponsible, we drove into the beautiful summer gardens of the Hermitage. We chose our sterlet† from the fish-tank fountain. We dined as young men generally do dine, recklessly, incon-

* The most popular restaurant in Moscow among the wealthy.
† A small sturgeon.

gruously, sampling all the unknown Russian dishes and drinking more vodka and champagne than were good for us. Our extravagance commanded a new attention from the white-robed waiters, while in our honour Krysh, the sleek Jewish violinist, played all his English repertory to us. The dinner was a prolonged one, and we finished up with cigars and Napoleon brandy at ten roubles a glass. The brandy was not good; certainly, Napoleon never tasted it. But fools must learn their lesson by experience. In my case the lesson was well mastered. Since that day Napoleon brandy has never tempted me.

It was at the Aquarium a few hours later that the great adventure befell us. This vast open-air amusement park was presided over by a negro called Thomas – a British subject with whom the Consulate was frequently at variance over the engagement of young English girls as cabaret performers. The entertainment he provided consisted of a perfectly respectable operetta theatre, an equally respectable open-air music hall, a definitely less respectable verandah *café-chantant*, and the inevitable chain of private 'kabinets' for gypsy-singing and private carouses. We had strolled into the *café-chantant* rather late and, taking the best box, had settled down to watch what even in our exalted state seemed a dreary performance. The rapid succession of talentless singers and dancers, who showed themselves on the stage for two minutes, smirked, and then rushed off to the dressing-room to change and join the tables below, soon wearied us, and even the 'Macaroni Man',* who drank incredible quantities of champagne in an incredibly short space of time, failed to relieve the gloom which was rapidly descending on us. Then suddenly the lights in the hall were dimmed. The band struck up an English tune. The curtain went up, and from the wings a young English girl – amazingly fresh and beautiful – tripped lightly to the centre of the stage and did a song and dance act. Her voice was shrill and harsh. Her accent was Wigan at its crudest. But she could dance, as Moscow had never seen an English girl dance. The audience rose to her. So did two young and suddenly refreshed Englishmen. The head waiter was summoned. Pencil and paper were demanded, and then after bashful meditation – it was a new experience for both of us – we sent a combined note inviting her to join us in our box. She came. Off the stage she was not so beautiful as she had seemed ten minutes before. She was neither witty nor wicked. She had been on the stage since she

* A popular comedian.

was fourteen and took life philosophically. But she was English, and the story of her career thrilled us. I expect our shyness and our awkwardness amused her.

We were not allowed to enjoy our conversation without interruption. A waiter brought in a note and handed it to our guest. She read it, begged to be excused for a minute, and left the room. Presently, we heard high words outside the door – a male cockney voice predominating. Then there was a scuffle and a final 'blast you'. The door opened and was hurriedly shut, and with flushed face our Lancashire lady returned to us. What was the matter? It was nothing. There was an English jockey – a mad fellow, always drunk, who was making her life a burden and a misery. We expressed our sympathy, ordered more champagne, and in five minutes had forgotten all about the incident.

We were not allowed to forget for long. An hour later the door was again thrown open. This time Thomas himself appeared, followed by a policeman. Outside the door was a mob of waiters and girls with scared faces. The negro scratched his head. There had been an accident. Would Missie go at once. The English jockey had shot himself.

Suddenly sobered, we paid our bill and followed the girl to the shabby furnished rooms across the road where the tragedy had taken place. We were prepared for the worst – scandal, possibly disgrace, and our almost certain appearance as witnesses at the inquest. For both of us the matter seemed terribly serious. In the circumstances the best course seemed to be to take Thomas into our confidence. He laughed at our fears.

'I will make that ol' right, Mistah Lockhart,' he said. 'Bless yo' heart, the police won't worry you – or the English Missie either. They'm shore used to tragedies like this, and this one has been coming for a long time.'

He was right. Indeed, to anyone who was not a political suspect, above all, to anyone who had some official rank, the Russian police showed a deference, which, if generally reinforced by the concrete of hard cash, was not without its advantages. Still, some days were to elapse before our fears were finally allayed, and it was with grim forebodings that I awoke the next morning – or rather the same morning – to hear George Bowen splashing in his bath and crying to the Heavens to tell him who was the fool who said: 'Joy cometh with the morning.'

In that summer of 1912 I had the good fortune to see the Emperor twice – a rare opportunity in Moscow, for the Tsar of all the Russias seldom visited the ancient capital. The city had too many tragic memories for him, and the horror of the shambles of the Khodynka Field, where at his coronation celebrations hundreds of peasants were crushed to death, was ever present in his mind. Moscow, too, was the centre of radicalism and, as such, was anathema to the Empress. On the first occasion, the Tsar came to unveil the statue to his father, the Emperor Alexander III. It was a strictly official cere-mony, attended only·by the nobles, the military and civil heads of departments, and a selected number of the leading merchants. I remember the visit for two reasons: first, because for weeks before the Moscow police had pestered us and, indeed, all the Consular Corps with idiotic questions regarding the political reliability of our various nationals who lived anywhere near the route along which the Emperor was to pass, and, secondly, because on his way to the Kremlin the Tsar stopped at the spot where the Grand Duke Serge had been murdered,* and knelt down alone on the cobbled stones and prayed. I could not help wondering what thoughts must have flashed through the mind of this least-to-be-envied of monarchs, as he knelt on the spot where the human débris of his uncle had once stained the ground. Boris Savinkov, who had planned the Grand Duke's murder, was then in exile. He was to come back again in 1917, to become Minister of War in the Kerensky Government, to seek refuge once more in exile on the advent of the Bolsheviks, and to return finally on that sinister and still unexplained mission, when he cast his lot with the present rulers of Russia only to throw himself or to be thrown to his death from a Kremlin window close to the spot where the Grand Duke met his fate.

The occasion of the Emperor's second visit was the centenary of Borodino† and the liberation of Russia from the yoke of Napoleon. This time the celebration was a national one and strikingly impressive in the demonstration of loyalty it aroused. Never have I seen a finer

---

* One of the many assassinations perpetrated by the extremist wing of the Social-Revolutionaries between 1901 and 1905.
† A village some seventy miles west of Moscow where Napoleon fought the Russians during his 1812 campaign. Although the Russians were ultimately defeated, Napoleon's Grande Armée suffered grave casualties. Shortly after, at the onset of winter, Napoleon retreated from Moscow with catastrophic results.

body of men than the Cossack troops who formed the Emperor's bodyguard. Well may the pre-war foreign military attachés be forgiven for overestimating the military power of Russia. Yet the real symbol of Russia's strength was the frail bearded figure with the strange, wistful eyes, who rode at the head of his troops and whose feeble shoulders seemed incapable of supporting the mantle of autocracy which, like a shroud, hung over them. Even on that day, when revolution was far from most men's minds, the Tsar inspired pity and sympathy more than admiration. An Imperial visit was an ordeal which at any moment one felt might end in tragedy, and, as far as Moscow was concerned, everyone breathed a sigh of relief when the suspense was over and the Imperial train had left the city.

When the autumn came, I made another friend, who was to render me great services during my apprenticeship in Moscow. This was Michael Lykiardopoulos, the talented secretary of the Moscow Art Theatre. 'Lyki' was a strange, lovable creature; one-third Greek, one-third Russian, and one-third English. His secretarial duties gave him a fixed salary. His real work in life was as a translator. He had real literary flair, an excellent Russian prose style, and a quite remarkable knowledge of eight or nine European languages. He knew most of the great writers of Europe and had translated their best works into Russian. It was through him that I first met H. G. Wells, Robert Ross, Lytton Strachey, Granville Barker, Gordon Craig, Aleister Crowley, not to mention numerous hangers-on of literature, who came to Moscow to worship at the shrine of Russian art. In his spare time he acted as ballet critic for one of the leading Moscow newspapers. He knew everyone in the literary, artistic, and dramatic world of Moscow, and, through him, many doors, which otherwise would have remained closed, were opened to me.

Poor 'Lyki'. During the war he ran our propaganda department in Moscow under my supervision – and ran it very well. His temperament was far too volatile to give any value to his political judgement. A Russian defeat depressed him almost to the point of suicide. The smallest victory drove him to the other extreme. Towards the end of 1915, when he had made up his mind that Russia was irretrievably ruined, he made a hazardous journey on our behalf into Germany, travelling as a Greek tobacco merchant and bringing back with him a mass of valuable information and a new optimism. The revolution finally destroyed all his hopes, and before the Bolsheviks had made their coup d'état he withdrew to Stockholm and eventually to England. Like many Russian liberals he became a violent reactionary and spent most of his energy in writing anti-Semitic articles for the English Press. He was a born journalist, living only for the day, but his loyalty and his kindness to his friends were wonderful, and of all my Russian friends (in spite of his mixed nationality I can never regard him as anything but Russian) he is the one whom I miss most. He died in London in 1924.

At the end of my first year in Russia I returned to England to be married. Looking back on this experiment from a disappointing and disillusioned middle age, I find my conduct in the highest degree reprehensible. I had neither money nor position, and my prospects held out nothing more than a dreary and penurious career in the worst-paid service in the world. My wife was an Australian called Turner. Her grandfather had been the richest man in Queensland. On her father's death misfortune had overtaken the estate, and her mother was unable to allow her more than a hundred or two a year. My wife herself, who was delicate, had been brought up in England and Switzerland. All her friends were rich or well to do. She herself had been used to a life of luxury. To ask a girl, who had been brought up in this way and who was then only twenty-one, to share with me a life of poverty in a semi-barbarous town like Moscow was an effrontery for which there is no excuse. It is a tribute to her courage that she was able to adapt herself so quickly to a situation which imposed so many hardships upon her. My marriage was a contract from which I alone reaped any benefit.

Had I taken stock of myself at that time, I should have seen a young man of twenty-five, broad-shouldered and broken-nosed, with a squat, stumpy figure and a ridiculous gait. The young man's character was a curious mixture of Lockhart caution and asceticism and Macgregor* recklessness and self-indulgence. Hitherto, the Macgregor had held the whip hand over the Lockhart, and perhaps his chief failing had been an all-too-Celtic tendency to confound licentiousness with romanticism. Such accomplishments as he had – a good memory, a facility for languages, and a capacity for sudden bursts of hard work, were largely nullified by a lazy tolerance, which always sought the easiest way out of any difficulty, and by a fatal disposition to sacrifice the future for the cheap applause of the moment. In short, a still unformed and unattractive young man, whose self-consciousness at moments amounted almost to a disease. Had anyone told him that five years later he would be head of an important British mission at a crucial moment in his country's history, he would have smirked, put his head on one side, and blushed with modesty.

* The family name of the author's mother: see Introduction, pp. xi–xii.

This, I submit, is an accurate picture of myself as I was at the end of 1912. With marriage, however, my life changed, and I made a serious effort to conform to the conventionalities of my new state. The result was wholly beneficial. My night-life was cast off, and a round of irksome social duties took its place. Intercourse with the British colony now became an obligation, and, as we were entertained, so we entertained in return. I found, however, a new zest for work. I continued my Russian studies and, until my wife learnt the language, I had to run the small flat we had taken, give orders to the servants, and superintend the household accounts. I read twice as much as when I was a bachelor. My knowledge of Russian was now tolerably good, and there was the whole field of Russian literature to explore. I began, too, to write for the English newspapers not so much from any internal urge as from necessity. The money was needed in order to supplement our scanty income, and after a little practice I found it not difficult to earn. I re-wrote and sold the short stories I had written in Malaya.* I became a fairly regular contributor to the *Morning Post* and the *Manchester Guardian*, both of which newspapers were then interested in sketches of Russian life, and I found a ready home for more serious articles and even for short stories in the numerous British reviews which then flourished. These literary efforts were written under a pseudonym (in those days diplomats and consuls were not allowed to write), but in my first year as a free-lance journalist I earned nearly £200, and by the time the war came and put a stop to these activities, I was making a steady £25 to £30 a month.

Nor did marriage interfere with my Russian friendships. On the contrary, it extended them. 'Lyki' was a constant visitor to our flat and requited our hospitality by bringing us into contact with the wide orbit of his own literary, journalistic, and artistic world. At the end of my first eighteen months in Russia I knew most of the leaders of the Moscow intelligentsia.

This contact, necessitating as it did the constant discussion of politics, gave me my first interest in foreign affairs. Through the Charnocks and other Englishmen connected with the cotton mills, I kept my finger on the pulse of industrial unrest. To complete my equipment as an intelligence officer there remained only the nobility, the merchants – and the British Embassy – to conquer. With the

* See Introduction, pp. xii–xiii.

Embassy in St Petersburg we had practically no contact. The German Consul-General might see his Ambassador once a month. French Consuls-General might reasonably hope to finish their careers as Ministers. But between the two British services there was an impassable gulf which has not been satisfactorily bridged to this day. Political reports from Moscow were not encouraged. Commercial queries were positively discouraged. In the archives of the Moscow Consulate there is – or was – a letter from a certain British Ambassador, which we used to pull out in moments of disgruntledness and which ran as follows: 'Dear Mr ——, Please remember that I am not here to be bothered with questions about trade.'

The inadequate equipment of the Moscow Consulate was not only a subject of grievance to the unfortunate Consular officers. It attracted the attention of British visitors, who were not slow to notice that, of all the Great Powers, Great Britain was the only one which was not represented by a Consulate-General. Invariably they expressed disgust, returned to England, and did nothing. There was one exception. One wintry afternoon in 1913, when I was alone in the Consulate, there was a ring at the door. I sprang to my feet and admitted an elderly, well-dressed man with a beard who handed me his card. His name was Tennant, and, although I did not realise it at the time, he was a relation of Mr Asquith, who was then Prime Minister. I took him into our dingy little room.

'Can I see the Consul or the Vice-Consul?' he asked.

'The Consul is out,' I replied. 'I am the Vice-Consul.'

He breathed heavily. The trudge up the three flights of stone stairs had shaken his wind.

'Is this all the British Consulate?' he asked at last. I told him it was. His chest heaved. His eyes flashed. Then with a great growl came his comment:

'More like a water-closet than a Consulate.'

He invited me to lunch with him the next day. At luncheon he asked some pertinent questions. He made no promises, but, when he went away, I had a feeling that this time something was going to happen.

The weeks, however, passed into months, and gradually I abandoned hope. When the summer came, we shared a 'dacha' with the Groves – a large, roomy wooden house at Kosino beside a lake where there were boats to row and pike and perch to catch. This risky experiment opened with a tragedy. My wife had bought a new toy – a pedigree French bulldog, called Pipo, who afterwards achieved immortality by being painted by Korovin. Naturally, she took him to the 'dacha'. Although in the Moscow flat he was as good as gold, his first night in the country was a disaster. The train journey must have upset his delicate constitution, for in the middle of dinner he forgot himself in the most offensive sense, and the carpet, a new investment of the Grove family, was irreparably ruined. Men are singularly ineffective on these occasions, and for the rest of that meal Grove and I kept our eyes firmly glued to the table. In spite of this inauspicious overture, the 'dacha' concert turned out better than might have been expected. By the morning Mrs Grove's very just anger had evaporated. With tearful eyes my wife begged for her dog. Pipo himself was profuse in his apologies. And Pipo remained.

With Pipo we had one more adventure, which might have ended disastrously for him and which for us had unpleasant consequences. Close to the lake there was a holy pool, where pilgrims from far and wide used to bathe in the hope of being cured of various diseases. One evening, when my wife was out walking, she passed the pool and with a natural modesty hurried away from the mass of naked bodies which sought relief from its stagnant waters. Pipo, however, was a gregarious animal and in a minute he was splashing wildly among the pilgrims. There was a shriek from the pool. At first my wife thought the bathers were playing with the dog, and she continued placidly on her way. Then the shriek grew into an angry roar, and the dog came tearing down the path with twenty naked figures in hot pursuit. My wife picked up her skirts and ran. Fortunately, the 'dacha' was close at hand. Fortunately, too, I was at home. For five minutes I harangued the nudities from the 'dacha' steps, and in the end my argument, backed by silver roubles, prevailed. More roubles had to be expended on the priest for the re-purification of the waters, and altogether the adventure was more costly than amusing. At first, too, I was afraid lest the outraged bathers might wreak their vengeance on the dog, and for some days Pipo had to be kept on a chain. In this, however, I did the Russians an injustice. Having made their peace, they bore no malice, and, as in future nothing would induce the dog to approach within a hundred yards of Siloam Lake, no harm resulted.

Three years later economic duress forced us to sell him. He was a valuable dog, and he went to a millionaire's house. What his ultimate fate was I do not know. He was an aristocrat and must, therefore, have hated revolutions. I fear that, like Gorky's Great Dane, he may have been eaten by a starving population.

That summer, too, Sir Henry Wilson* visited Moscow, and I dined with him and Colonel Knox, our military attaché, at the Hermitage. Even in those days Sir Henry was fully alive to the dangers of the European situation and had summed up all the possibilities in his far-seeing mind. In considering the relative strength of the European Powers, he had worked out all his facts to the smallest detail. In his opinion the French army was fully equal to the German. If ever it came to war, the Russian army would be the extra weight which would load the scales overwhelmingly in France's favour. Sir Henry was not the only expert whose judgements were to be rudely shattered by the tornado of 1914.

At the beginning of July came the repercussion to the Tennant visit. It came, too, in the form of what Fleet Street calls a bombshell. Moscow was elevated to a Consulate-General with a largely increased office allowance. The Groves were transferred to Warsaw, and Charles Clive Bayley, formerly HM Consul at New York and a scion of a family famous in Indian history, was appointed to reign in their stead. I shed a sympathetic tear over the departure of the Groves (they had been very kind to us) and with new hopes and new ambitions made ready to welcome my new chief.

* Sir Henry Hughes Wilson (1864–1922), Director of Military Operations at the War Office 1910–14.

Charles Clive Bayley was then in his fifty-second year. He was a big, florid man with pouches under his eyes. The eyes could both twinkle and flash. Such hair as he had left was fair. His body was rather too heavy for his legs and, when he coughed or laughed, the veins stood out on his forehead. As he always laughed at his own stories, of which he had an inexhaustible fund (in two years I never heard him repeat himself once), I was in constant apprehension lest he should die of apoplexy. He wore an eyeglass and had a presence and a proper sense of his own importance.

He could speak neither French nor German. But he had served for ten years under Sir Thomas Sanderson in New York and knew all there was to know about running a Consular office. He combined what the Americans call 'drive' with dignity, and no man could take liberties with him.

What was more important he had private means and was prepared to spend his own money on maintaining his position as Consul-General. He took a large flat for himself in the most fashionable street in Moscow and leased an adequate office for the Consulate-General on the first floor of a new house close at hand. He engaged an experienced clerk, two typists and a general factotum and commissionaire called Alexander Nechaev, who, as a former Russian civil servant, knew every short cut, legal and illegal, through the red-tape maze of Russian bureaucracy. In the eyes both of the Russians and of our Consular colleagues we acquired a new prestige. Alexander saw to that. He at once invested Bayley with the title of an Excellency, and within a month of his arrival every department, both civil and military, in Moscow knew through the agency of the devoted Alexander that the new British Consul-General was a man whose favour was worth courting and whose wrath was vastly to be feared. On occasions Alexander overplayed his hand and, when we caught him using the Consular seal in order to further his own personal ends, Bayley exploded. It required all my tact and all my pleading to prevent the old scoundrel's immediate dismissal. A man who at a minute's notice could wangle a visa after office hours or a sleeping berth to St Petersburg, when the Wagon-Lits office had been sold out for days, was not to be lightly discarded, and in the end Bayley relented.

Both in the office and outside it Bayley did his best to live up to the rôle for which the wily Alexander had cast him. All his life he had done himself well, and he knew how to entertain others. His wife, who was born a Ricardo, backed him up to the best of her ability. She was a kind, little woman, very shy and very English, but very hospitable and always willing to put herself out to promote her husband's interests. The Russians sat up and took notice. They ate the Bayley dinners. They liked the Bayley cocktails which I imagine he was the first man to introduce into Moscow. Almost they were prepared to take him at Alexander's estimate.

A few rays of this new glory were reflected on me. In the office Bayley drove me hard. Speaking no languages, he was dependent on my services for much of his information. On the other hand, he taught me how to run an office, how to handle all kinds and conditions of men, and how to coax or bully the various departments of the Foreign Office at home. 'If you can't get things by asking politely, you must make yourself a nuisance,' he used to say. He lived up to his own precepts, 'kowtowing' to no man, and, if necessity arose, making himself a nuisance both to the Foreign Office and to the Embassy. To my astonishment I discovered that, by taking a high hand, he enhanced his own reputation. His stock rose. He went to St Petersburg to see the Ambassador and came back with a mandate to inspect the other Consulates in Russia. In spite of a 'peppery' temper (as a young man he had been on the Gold Coast and had acquired a liver) he was a splendid chief, and such merits as I ever possessed as a Consular officer I owe entirely to his training. Outside the office he was like a father to me, and I was never separated from him. At his house I met scores of people, whom otherwise I should never have known, and whose friendship was afterwards to be of the greatest service to me during the war. Under Bayley's tutelage I developed from a shy and ignorant youngster into a self-reliant and tolerably efficient administrator.

In the spring of 1914 I had an amusing experience, while I was in charge of the Consulate-General during one of Bayley's tours of inspection. One Saturday afternoon I was summoned to the telephone by the Pristav* of the Tverskoi district. Two Englishmen – a naval doctor and a chief petty officer – had been arrested for shoplifting. I put on my coat and hurried round to the Pristav's

* A police inspector of a district; generally an ex-army officer.

Lubianskaya Square, Moscow, at the turn of the century. *Below,* the
restaurant of the Metropole Hotel, 1908

Harry Charnok's Morozovtsy football team. The author stands third from the left. *Below left*, the author, *c.*1915, and, *below right*, 'Lyki' – Michael Lykiardopoulos, Secretary of the Moscow Art Theatre house. The Pristav – a bullet-headed, pimply-faced man with a military moustache, was polite but obdurate. The two men were under lock and key. They had been caught red-handed. He was having tea in his private apartment, when I called, and did not seem to relish my intrusion. At my request, however, he sent for the protocol and read it to me. On their own showing the two men had been sent out from the Tyne on a warship, which was being delivered to China, and, having completed their mission, were returning to England via the Trans-Siberian railway. During the four hours' stop in Moscow they had gone into a shop, had picked out some handkerchiefs, some socks, and a birchwood cigarette case, and had put the goods in their pocket. Then, just as they were about to produce the money to pay for them, they had been seized by a shop detective. It was not a very plausible story. The evidence of the shop detective and of the policeman who had been called in to make the arrest was damning. The detective swore that he had watched the petty officer slip the cigarette case into his pocket with all the skill of a professional thief.

The only point in the men's favour was that between them they had about £80 in English notes, and the total value of the goods found on them was less than £3. I made great play of this anomaly and also of the fact that a misunderstanding might have arisen over the language difficulty. I requested an interview with the two men.

My eloquence, however, was vain. The Pristav smiled condescendingly.

'You have your duty to do, Mr Consul,' he said. 'I have mine. It is a bad case.'

There seemed nothing for me to do except to retreat. At this moment a good-looking young man burst into the room.

'Papa,' he said excitedly, 'we've won.'

Then he saw me, stared confusedly for a moment, rushed forward and shook me warmly by the hand.

'Mr Lockhart,' he said, 'you don't remember me. I played against you last year. I'm the centre-half of the Union Club.' His face glowed. He dashed back to his father. 'Papa, this is Mr Lockhart, who used to play for the Morozovtsy – the best team in Russia. He must have tea with us.'

The Pristav frowned and then smiled.

'Forgive me,' he said. 'In discussing our business, I forgot all about tea.'

He rang the bell, ordered more cups and some vodka, and, as we sat and pledged each other, the boy told us the story of the after-noon's match. The Pristav listened in silent admiration. Obviously, he doted on his boy. I, too, sat on, hoping for an unexpected dénoue-ment to my own problem. When the boy had finished his recital, he turned again to me:

'And what are you doing here, Mr Lockhart?'

The father blushed.

'Mr Lockhart has some official business to discuss with me. I think you had better go.'

When the boy had gone, there was an awkward silence. Then the Pristav cleared his throat.

'Mr Consul,' he said, 'I have been thinking over this case. I am convinced that you are right and that a British naval doctor with £50 in his pocket would not steal a few worthless handkerchiefs. The devil of it is that the goods were found in both the men's pockets. If only all the goods had been in the gunner's pockets and we could call the doctor as witness, the case would not be so difficult.'

He scratched his shaven head. Then he pushed the bell.

'Send me the policeman who made the protocol on this English case,' he ordered.

The policeman appeared – a stout, honest fellow conscious of having done a good day's work and expecting to be praised.

'Did you make this protocol?' asked the Pristav.

'Yes, sir.'

'Did you find the goods in the pockets of both men?'

'Yes, sir.'

'Are you quite sure?'

'Yes, sir,' said the policeman.

'Think again,' roared the Pristav in a voice of thunder.

The policeman blenched but made the same answer. Even for a Russian he was slow in the uptake.

The Pristav returned to the charge.

'Do you think that a naval doctor, an officer of the English fleet, would steal a pair of socks and a handkerchief?'

The policeman shuffled.

'Yes, sir – I mean, no, sir,' he stammered.

'Fool,' growled the Pristav. 'What do you mean? Do you mean that you found all the goods in the petty officer's pocket and nothing in the pockets of the doctor.'

This was said very slowly and deliberately, every word being punctuated with a tap of a large ruler on the table.

This time even the policeman understood.

'Yes, sir,' he whispered hoarsely.

The Pristav tore up the protocol.

'Go,' he said. 'Draw up a new protocol at once and don't let me catch you out in inaccuracies again.'

He turned to me with a sheepish grin.

'That's all I can do,' he said. 'The case will have to go before the magistrate. I warn you there will be trouble over the detective who is a pig-headed fellow and who in any case is paid by results. But at any rate you have now a witness for the defence. The rest depends on you. I can release the doctor at once.'

Football has its uses. I thanked him profoundly, begged him to send the doctor round to my flat, and rushed off to enlist the services of Alexander Wilenkin, the Consular lawyer.

That same evening we laid our plans. The naval doctor stuck to his story that they had intended to pay for the goods, and Wilenkin, who knew England almost as well as he knew Russia, saw his way clear. The petty officer would have to stand his trial. The doctor's evidence would be valuable, but the chief witness for the defence was to be myself. This was Wilenkin's plan of campaign.

At once I raised objections. I was doubtful about the propriety of a British Consular officer appearing in a case of this kind. In any case I did not see how I could be of assistance.

'Leave it to me, my dear-r Lockhart,' said Wilenkin in his guttural Jewish accent. And I did.

Wilenkin, who belonged to a rich Jewish family, had the reputation of being the best-dressed man in Moscow, and in his defence of the two Englishmen clothes played an important part.

On the Tuesday we all appeared before the examining magistrate, Wilenkin and I, complete in morning coats, striped trousers, monocles and top hats. Our entry into the squalid, crowded court made a sensation.

The case opened badly. The shop detective gave his evidence with overwhelming effect. The petty officer, dirty and unshaven after three days in prison, made an unfortunate impression on the bench. Wilenkin's speech, however, was a masterpiece. Basing his defence on the fact that the two men were well supplied with money, he pointed out the improbability of two such distinguished members of His Majesty's Navy risking their careers for the sake of a handkerchief and a pair of socks. Englishmen were, admittedly, queer people. They washed. They had a preference for clean linen. What more natural than that they should profit by their stay in Moscow to permit themselves the luxury of a wash and a clean handkerchief. The detective had erred on the side of eagerness. Finally, the matter had a profound political aspect. England and Russia were now friends – almost Allies. One day – how soon no one knew – they might be fighting side by side. Had the magistrate weighed in his mind the deplorable effect a miscarriage of justice might have on the present happy state of Anglo-Russian relations? *Autres pays, autres mœurs*, and in order to demonstrate that English customs were different from Russian he had brought into this court a very busy man – the acting British Consul-General.

I stepped forward with all the dignity I could muster and took the oath.

'Is it quite a common occurrence in England for respectable people to enter a shop, pick up an article off the counter and put it in their pocket before they have actually paid for it?' asked Wilenkin.

'Yes.'

'Have you done it on occasions yourself?'

'Yes,' I answered without a blush.

The petty officer left the court without a stain on his character. But that night every newspaper in Moscow came out with large headlines: 'British Consul in Moscow swears that in England shoppers may put goods in their pocket before paying for them!'

My reputation, however, survived this sarcasm. I was beginning to know my Moscow.

This was merely a minor achievement for Wilenkin. In peacetime regarded by most people as a fop, he proved himself a lion of Judah in the war. He was, in fact, the bravest Jew I have ever met. He was one of the first Russians to enlist as a volunteer. By his physical courage as much as by his intelligence he rose from the ranks to be a junior officer. He won the St George's Cross for bravery in action.

Bemonocled and clean-shaven in his civil life, in war he grew a magnificent beard and mustachios. When the first revolution came, he threw himself heart and soul into the task of persuading his men to continue fighting. His skill as an orator raised him to the dignity of Vice-President of his Army Soviet,* and it was he who brought back to St Petersburg the troops which suppressed the first Bolshevik attempt at a coup d'état in July, 1917. After the Bolshevik revolution of November, 1917, he threw in his lot with Savinkov and had a hand in almost every counter-revolutionary plot against the new régime. His indifference to danger amounted almost to foolhardiness, and on several occasions I warned him of the risks he was running. In July, 1918, he was arrested in Moscow as a counter-revolutionary. He was one of the first victims of the official terror, when, as a reprisal for the attempt on Lenin's life on September 1st, 1918, the Bolsheviks shot seven hundred of their political opponents.

Throughout the spring and early summer of 1914 my life ran on active and pleasant lines. I had sufficient work to keep me out of mischief. My interest in Russia and things Russian was amounting almost to a mania, and my ambition to make myself the best-informed Consular officer in Moscow was well on the way to fulfilment. My pride was pleasantly titillated, when the Austrian Consul-General borrowed our annual report (written mainly by me) in order to paraphrase it as his own. In the past he had always conferred this honour on his German colleagues. If I showed any disposition to 'let up', a judicious mixture of praise and exhortation from Bayley kept my nose to the grindstone. It has been my fate in life to be the willing horse of various masters. My pleasures were few – a little tennis, an occasional game of billiards, and an odd weekend in the country. Yet I was not unhappy. My home life was peaceful and undisturbed. Obviously, if I was the last person any woman should have married, marriage was good for me.

In June, 1914, I had another surfeit of official entertainment. Admiral Beatty and a picked selection of the officers of the First Battle Cruiser Squadron paid an official visit to Moscow. The youthful appearance of the youngest admiral since Nelson nearly led to my official undoing. Dressed in uniform and cocked hat, I had been sent

* An elected local, district or national council, originally formed by workers during the 1905 revolution.

by Bayley to meet the train and to welcome Beatty on the platform. It was my first encounter with the Navy, and I knew less than nothing of the distinguishing marks of the different ranks. On the platform I found the Prefect, the Governor, the general commanding the Moscow district, and other Russian officials to whom I should have to introduce the British admiral. The train drew up, and out of the special carriage stepped a brisk young man who looked no older than myself and whom I naturally supposed was Beatty's flag-lieutenant. I stood waiting for the emergence of the great man himself, and there was an awkward pause. It was ended very quickly by my supposed flag-lieutenant.

'How do you do?' he said. 'I'm Beatty. Introduce me and tell me whom I shake hands with first.'

I went hot and then cold. When I told him afterwards of my embarrassment, he laughed and took it as a compliment.

In my own defence I must admit that the Russians were equally astonished by Beatty's youthfulness.

The visit was a tremendous success. Beatty's officers, who included Admiral Halsey, Admiral Brock, and several other captains, whose names were to become household words during the war, went down with the Russians like a dinner. Their clean-shaven, red-cheeked faces brought a breeze of health and vigour into the parched atmosphere of the Moscow summer, and Beatty's square jaw and the jaunty angle at which he wore his cap gave a lasting joy to the Moscow caricaturists, who were only too glad to have this opportunity of contrasting the efficiency of the British Navy with the shortcomings of their own. The climax to a whirlwind triumph came with Beatty's speech at a dinner given by the town in a large marquee in the Sokolniki Park. After a succession of dreary orators the English admiral arose, and in a voice which would have carried through a gale, delivered a speech which stirred the sluggish Muscovites to an extraordinary display of emotion. Never before had they seen an admiral who had not a beard down to his knees. The military strength of Britain might be insignificant, but the British Navy was the real thing. Today, I often wonder why Lord Beatty has never gone into politics. That voice of his would wake even the sleepers in the House of Lords. It was a first-rate performance, and his visit did much to enhance British prestige.

Then came tragedy – swift as an eagle in its descent and pitiless in its consequences. On June 28th the Archduke Franz Ferdinand was murdered, and, however secure London may have felt, Moscow realised from the first moment that the red sun of war had already risen. It was at this time that a tragedy occurred in my own family. In June my wife had been expecting a child. I had wished to send her home and had written to my grandmother in the hope that she would provide the necessary financial assistance. The reply had been stern and uncompromising. She herself had given birth to her first child under a bullock cart in New Zealand. A woman's place on those occasions was by her husband.

The doctor recommended to my wife was a German called Schmidt – a kind and gentle old man who was long past his best. I had misgivings and wished to employ a Russian. The English women in Moscow, however, were strongly prejudiced against Russian doctors. Schmidt spoke English, and my wife liked him.

The crisis came on June 20th and lasted all through the night. Inexperienced as I was, I soon realised that the birth was complicated. It was one of the hottest nights I have ever known in Moscow or anywhere else, and for hours on end I stood at the open window in the drawing-room, smoking cigarette after cigarette and trying to keep my mind a blank. At three o'clock Schmidt came into the room. The sweat, streaming from his face, had dripped on to his white overalls.

'It is difficult,' he gasped, 'very difficult. I must have another doctor.'

He gave me the number, and I rushed to the telephone. Hours seemed to pass. Again I resumed my stand at the window, listening for the sound of the 'droschke'* wheels on the cobbled streets. After several false alarms the doctor arrived – a young man, whose efficient manner inspired me with a new confidence. Then he disappeared into the bedroom, and again there was an immense silence. At five o'clock all was over. Katja, the cook, tiptoed across the room, her apron up to her eyes. Then the young doctor came in.

'The mother is alive,' he said gravely. 'The girl will not live.'

Very quickly he told me the details. The birth had been difficult. There had been great exhaustion, and they had had to use instruments. The first instruments had been defective. If he had been summoned sooner . . .

* A horse-drawn carriage.

'The child is dead?' I whispered. He nodded.

In a dream I ordered coffee and biscuits for the doctors. In a dream I saw them off at the door. Then I sat down to wait for the morning. At seven o'clock my mother-in-law came in and took me into the room which would have been our nursery. The child was lying in a cot. They had dressed her in the clothes which for months past my wife had been making for her. Her eyes were open. There was not a mark on the little waxen face. She looked so fresh and sweet that it was impossible to believe that she was dead. The little cap which covered her head concealed the fatal bruise.

Mechanically I went about the tasks of the day. I telephoned to Bayley to tell him what had happened. I called on the chaplain to see what could be done about the burial, and in the afternoon I walked down to the Sadovaya to order the tiny coffin. As I passed the Hermitage, a street-woman accosted me. I walked past, and she came back to me. Silently I handed her five roubles; for a moment our eyes met; then she turned and ran. I think she thought I was mad.

Two days later I made the long 'trek' out to the German cemetery, carrying the coffin on my knees. The sun beat down pitilessly from a cloudless sky, but I never felt the heat. An Englishman of seventy was being buried, and it was among strangers that I stood, while the chaplain read the burial service and the two coffins of the man who had lived his full life and of the nameless child were lowered into their common grave . . .

All through that burning July, while my wife lay in danger, first of her life and then of her reason, I toiled at the Consulate-General, striving to kill my thoughts with a surfeit of work. And, as the days passed, the tension of the Russian people grew, until gradually it swelled into an angry murmur. Why was England hanging back? As July broke into August, scores of people telephoned daily to know the reason and, not receiving satisfaction, grumbled and threatened. Through the long white days troops in full marching kit tramped through the streets, singing their plaintive songs and leaving a cloud of dust in their trail. The heart of Russia was on fire with war.

On the morning of Wednesday, August 5th, I set out as usual on my short walk to the Consulate-General. At the street corner opposite the office a crowd of demonstrators impeded my progress. A band was playing, and raucous voices were calling for the Consul-General. Suddenly a man in the crowd recognised me. 'Way for the

British Vice-Consul,' he roared. Strong hands passed me over the heads of the crowd to the entrance, while a thousand voices thundered: 'Long live England.' A bearded student kissed me on both cheeks. England had declared war on Germany. Another day's delay, and the demonstrators would have smashed our windows.

PART TWO

WAR AND PEACE

Eine grosse Epoche hat das Jahrhundert geboren, aber der grosse Moment findet ein kleines Geschlecht.

[The century has given birth to a great epoch, but the great moment finds a petty generation.]

GOETHE

My recollections of those first war months in Moscow are remarkably vivid, although today in the light of after-events they seem more like a strange dream than an actual experience. The contrast between 1914 and 1932 is too great. I have to shut my eyes to recall the enthusiasm of those early days. There in the patchwork of my memory I see again those moving scenes at the station: the troops, grey with dust and closely packed in cattle-trucks; the vast crowd on the platform to wish them Godspeed; grave, bearded fathers, wives and mothers, smiling bravely through their tears and bringing gifts of flowers and cigarettes; fat priests to bless the happy warriors. The crowd sways forward for a last handshake and a last embrace. There is a shrill whistle from the engine. Then, with many false starts, the overloaded train, as though reluctant to depart, crawls slowly out of the station and disappears in the grey twilight of the Moscow night. Silent and bare-headed, the crowd remains motionless until the last faint echo of the song of the men, who are never to return, has faded into nothing. Then, shepherded by the gendarmes, it files quietly out into the streets.

I come away with a hopefulness which overrides my better judgement. Here was a Russia which I had never known – a Russia inspired by a patriotism which seemed to have its roots deep down in the soil. It was, too, a sober Russia. The sale of vodka had been stopped, and an emotional religious fervour took the place of the squalid intoxication which in previous wars had characterised the departure of Russian soldiers.

Among the bourgeoisie there was the same enthusiasm. The wives of the rich merchants vied with each other in spending money on hospitals. There were gala performances at the state theatres in aid of the Red Cross. There was an orgy of national anthems. Every night at the opera and the ballet the Imperial orchestra played the national hymns of Russia, England, France and Belgium, while the audience stood at attention in a fervour of exalted patriotism. Later, especially when the number of Allied hymns assumed the dimensions of a cricket score, the fervour evaporated, and the heavy-paunched Muscovites groaned audibly at an ordeal which lasted over half an hour. But in those early weeks of 1914 Russian patriotism had much on which to feed itself. The beginning of the war, indeed, was all Russia, and, as the news of each Russian advance was made public, Moscow gave itself up to a full-throated rejoicing. If there were pessimists at that moment, their voice was not raised in the market-place. Revolution was not even a distant probability, although from the first day of the war every liberal-minded Russian hoped that victory would bring constitutional reforms in its train.

In St Petersburg, it is true, these early Russian triumphs invoked covert sneers at the failure of the Franco-British effort. In drawing-rooms one heard whispers about English faint-heartedness, and pro-Germans spread slimy rumours about England's determination to fight until the last drop of Russian blood. In Moscow, however, the tongues of the slanderers were silent, and enthusiasm for the Russian victories was tempered by a generous sympathy for the difficulties of France and England.

Indeed, as far as Russia was concerned, the heart of the alliance was in Moscow. If ever Bayley or I appeared in public, we received an ovation. At the 'Bat'* Nikita Baliev would come before the curtain, point us out, and say: 'Tonight we have with us the representatives of our Ally, England.' The band would then play 'God Save the King', and the whole audience stood up and cheered. We pretended to be bored by these unaccustomed attentions, vowed to each other that we would avoid them in future, and returned as frequently as discretion permitted. There is no limit to the vanity of the very great, and Bayley and I were only two very ordinary mortals.

On September 10th we attended in full uniform a gala performance at the theatre in honour of the capture of Lemberg by the Russians. I went with sadness in my heart. The German armies were on the Marne, and the fate of Paris hung in the balance. My brothers were in France, and here was I taking part in the celebrations of a Russian victory. Inside the theatre the uniforms of the officers made a brilliant setting to the jewels and costly dresses of the women. The play was a Russian adaptation of Rostand's *L'Aiglon*, and Bayley and I shared a box near the stage and directly opposite the box occupied by the French Consul-General. During the first act the Frenchman was called away. He remained absent for some time. When he came back, his manner was agitated. Then the curtain fell, but the lights did not go up. In an instant the atmosphere became

* A well-known nightspot.

44

electrical. 'The Russians had won another victory. They had captured 100,000 prisoners. They had taken Przemysl.' In the darkness rumour ran riot. Then the footlights went up again; the orchestra filed into their places, and a young girl of eighteen, the daughter of the President of the French Chamber of Commerce, came on to the stage. With her white dress, her face free of all make-up, and her glorious golden hair, she looked like the Angel Gabriel. In her trembling hands she held a slip of paper.

The audience hushed itself in an expectant silence. Then, quivering with emotion and nervousness, the girl began to read: 'The following official telegram has just been received from French headquarters.' She stopped as if her tongue were chained. The tears streamed down her face.

Then, in a shrill crescendo, she read the message: '*Je suis heureux de vous annoncer victoire sur tout le front.* – Joffre.'

The lights blazed up. The girl ran wildly off the stage, and in a storm of cheering the orchestra struck up the 'Marseillaise'. Bearded men kissed each other. Women smiled and wept at the same time. Then, as the orchestra broke into the chorus, a miracle happened. From the gallery above came the tramp of marching feet, and four hundred French reservists, singing in a glorious unison, took up the refrain. They were leaving for France the next day, and they sang the 'Marseillaise' with all the passionate ardour of their Latin temperament. It was epic. It was the last occasion on which Russia was to feel supremely confident about the outcome of the war.

The capture of Lemberg had softened the grim defeat of Tannenberg.* But the Tannenbergs were to be repeated, and, although the Russians were to hold their own against the Austrians almost to the end, it was already clear that they were no match for the Germans. Tannenberg, in fact, was the prelude to the Russian revolution. It was a message of hope to Lenin. It gave a handle to the hidden army of agitators in the factories and in the villages and, by destroying the pick of the Russian officers, it undermined the war-spirit of a people who by nature and by the exigencies of the Russian climate have always been incapable of any sustained effort.

Certainly, the transition from optimism to pessimism was not accomplished in one stage and, if on the Russian front there never

* The Russian advance into East Prussia in August, 1914, was halted by a German counter-offensive at Tannenberg.

was the same immobility as in France, there were long periods of monotonous inactivity.

The decline in morale was, in fact, gradual, and, as it became clear that the war was to be a long one, life stabilised itself. In Moscow, which was far removed from the front, the spirit of the bourgeoisie was by no means discouraging. There was, it is true, little attempt to economise or to make sacrifices. There was no sentiment of public opinion against shirkers, and '*embusqués*' could find security in a Red Cross organisation without fear of being handed a white feather. Theatres and places of amusement flourished as in peace-time, and, although the proletariat and the peasantry were deprived of their alcohol, no such restrictions were imposed on the well-to-do classes. To replenish their private stock of wine they required a permit, but, as the cost of living rose and since Russian officials were badly paid, permits were easily obtainable. In restaurants the only difference was that one drank one's alcohol from a teapot instead of from a bottle. As control became more lax, even the pretence of the teapot disappeared.

On the other hand, an immense and extremely valuable work was done by the so-called public organisations, represented by the Union of Cities and by the Union of Zemstvos,* in providing the Army with a whole network of hospitals and factories. Without this aid, the Russian military machine would have broken down far sooner than it did. Yet, instead of stimulating this patriotic effort and encouraging the public organisations in every way it could, the Russian Government did its best to hamper and curtail its activities. It may be said that the public organisations were politically ambitious, that they were honeycombed with liberalism and therefore a menace to the autocracy. Admittedly, both the Cities Union and the Zemstvos Unions were controlled by liberals, who had a deep suspicion of St Petersburg. Admittedly, too, their headquarters were in Moscow, and Moscow was never popular with the Emperor. But, in the beginning at any rate, their enthusiasm for the war was single-minded, and the political aspirations, which came later, were the direct result of a policy of perpetual pinpricks. It was the tragedy of Russia that the Tsar, dominated by a woman who was obsessed with the one ambition to hand down the autocracy unimpaired to her son, never took the public organisations into his confidence. The fact that grad-

* Local councils in rural areas.

A new recruit for the Russian army taking leave of his family. *Below*,
Tsar Nicholas II blessing troops prior to their departure for the front

Kiev street scene, early 1900s.
Left, Grigory Rasputin

ually Moscow became more absorbed in the internal political struggle than in the war itself was mainly the result of the Tsar's fatal obtuseness. And, although his loyalty to his Allies remained unshaken to the last, it was his failure to harness the loyalty of his own people which eventually cost him his throne.

For me personally that first winter of 1914–15 was a period of sadness relieved only by incessant hard work. My wife had made a slow recovery from her illness. Her nerves were shattered, and she was forced to enter a Russian sanatorium – an experience which did her little good and which, had I known more about Russian sanatoria, I should never have allowed her to undergo. We gave up our flat, and in the period of looking for a new one took over a furnished flat from some English friends who had gone to England. My days and frequently my nights were entirely absorbed by Consular work, which the war had more than trebled. In particular, the blockade and the manifold regulations controlling imports and exports involved an immense amount of ciphering, most of which I had to do single-handed. Moscow, too, had become an all-important political centre, and, as Bayley relied almost entirely on me for his political intelligence, my time was fully occupied. Another difficulty in my own case was the want of money. My wife's confinement had been expensive. With the new importance of our position our social obligations had increased. The business community – and Moscow was the chief commercial city of Russia – was prospering exceedingly from the lucrative war contracts, which were being handed out lavishly, and with the increased cost of living which this prosperity brought in its train we were left at a sore disadvantage both towards the Russians and towards our own English colony. Moreover, the war had put an automatic end to my earnings from journalism. I was not permitted to write about the war. The English newspapers were interested in nothing else.

A pleasant relief to the monotony of our existence at this time was the visit of Hugh Walpole,* who arrived in Moscow shortly after the outbreak of the war, and who remained with us for some months. He was a frequent visitor to our flat, and his cheery optimism was a godsend to my wife. At that time he had written several books, including *Fortitude*, and already had his feet well planted on

* Hugh Walpole (1884–1941), novelist. He became godfather to the author's son Robin.

the ladder of success. He was, however, entirely unspoilt, could still blush from an overwhelming self-consciousness, and impressed me more as a great, clumsy schoolboy, bubbling over with kindness and enthusiasm, than as a dignified author, whose views were to be accepted with awe and respect. With the exception of Bayley we took him to our hearts, and he repaid our friendship with a sympathy and kindness which have never failed. With Bayley he was less successful. Bayley, who was then a sick man, was a cynic and an autocrat. He mistrusted enthusiasts. Still more did he dislike contradiction. Hugh, whose enthusiasm for everything Russian knew no bounds, liked argument and had views of his own. He irritated Bayley, and I fancy the irritation was mutual.

When Hugh left us, he went to the front as a Red Cross orderly. Later, he became head of the British propaganda bureau in St Petersburg. From the first he had made up his mind to make the best of Russia. Certainly, Russia got the best out of him. His adventure at the front produced *The Dark Forest*. His experiences in St Petersburg inspired *The Secret City*.

My diary shows that at this period I went out little and that such spare time as I had was spent in reading. In the last fortnight of January, 1915, I read and finished *War and Peace* in Russian. Occasionally I went with Walpole to the ballet and to the circus. It was with Hugh, too, that I first met Gorky – at Nikita Baliev's 'Bat'. In those days the 'Bat' was the favourite haunt of literary and artistic Moscow. Its performance did not begin until after the theatres had ended and many actors and actresses went there to sup as much as to see the performance. The 'Bat', in fact, started as a kind of club of the Moscow Art Theatre, Baliev himself having been a member of the company and failed to make good in that severe school. Today, his troupe is as well known in Paris, London and New York as ever it was in Russia, but to my mind the performances have lost much of the delicious intimacy of those early Moscow days, when there was no gulf between player and audience. Baliev, incidentally, is an Armenian and belongs to what was once a rich family.

Gorky made a deep impression on me as much by his modesty as by his talent. His eyes are extraordinarily expressive, and in them one can read at once that sympathy with human suffering which is the dominating influence on his character and which in the end was to drive him, after a long period of opposition, into the arms of the

Bolsheviks. Today, Gorky writes more bitterly against the bourgeoisie and against the moderate Socialists than the most violent 'Chekist'* in Moscow, but in spite of these literary outbursts I refuse to believe that he has lost that fundamental kindness which in the past he never failed to show to any case which deserved his pity. No one who has ever seen Gorky with children, with animals, and with young authors, will ever credit him with the power to inflict harm or suffering on any of his fellow creatures.

It was at the 'Bat', too, that I first met Chaliapin.† An hour before I had seen him at the opera in *Boris*,‡ a part in which he is and looks every inch a king with the manners of a great aristocrat and with hands which seemed to belong to some ancient Doge of Venice. The whole thing was a trick – a marvellous example of that dramatic art which, as Stanislavsky always used to say, could have made him the greatest actor in the world, had he chosen to abandon his singing for the drama. Off the stage the man was still a peasant, with a peasant's appetite and the huge, strong hands of a son of the soil. In those days Gorky used to tell a good story of Chaliapin. In their youth the two men were tramping the Volga district in search of work. At Kazan a travelling impresario was looking for local talent to supplement his chorus. He wanted a tenor and a bass. Two poorly clad applicants entered his ramshackle office and were given an audition. The impresario took the tenor and rejected the bass. The tenor was Gorky. The bass was Chaliapin.

Moscow, always much more anti-German than St Petersburg, was a perfect cesspool of rumours of pro-German intrigues in high places. One entry in my diary in February, 1915, runs as follows: 'Today an officer telephoned to ask when England was going to rid Russia of "the German woman".' This, of course, was a reference to the Empress, and my own comment was: 'This is the third time that this kind of thing has happened this week.' It was to happen still more frequently as the months passed. To this period, too, belongs the most popular Moscow story of the war. The Tsarevich is seen crying in the corridor of the Winter Palace. A general, who is leaving the palace after an audience, stops and pats the boy's head.

* A member of the Cheka, the Bolshevik secret police.
† Feodor Chaliapin (1873–1938), bass singer and actor.
‡ *Boris Godunov* by Modest Mussorgsky, first performed in St Petersburg in 1874.

'What is wrong, my little man?'

The Tsarevich replies, half-smiling, half-crying:

'When the Russians are beaten, papa cries. When the Germans are beaten, mama cries. When am I to cry?'

Stories of this kind were repeated all over the country and did immense harm both among the industrial proletariat and the peasantry. Moscow, in fact, lived on stories and rumours, and, if the spy-hunting mania was never as bad as in England and in France, there was considerable persecution both of the Jews and of the Russians of German extraction. Not all the stories, however, were concerned with the shortcomings of the autocracy. The German Kaiser received a considerable share of the wit and sarcasm of the Muscovite humorists. Many of them are too coarse for print. Others have been told before. One, however, is, I think, new to English readers. In the winter of 1915 the Kaiser visited Lodz and with a view to placating the local population made a speech. His audience was, of course, mainly Jewish. As they listened to him, they heard him refer, first, to the Almighty and the All-Highest, then to God and himself, and finally to himself and God. When the speech was ended, the leading Jews withdrew into a corner to discuss the situation.

'This man will do for us,' said the Chief Rabbi. 'He's the first Christian I've met who denies the Holy Trinity.'

How strange and unreal these stories sound today. Then, however, they were the stock-in-trade of every gossip and the staple entertainment of every salon.

I have said that Bayley was a sick man. Lack of exercise – always the curse of the Moscow winter – and overwork had undermined his health, and in April, 1915, he made up his mind to return to England and to undergo the operation which for some time he had been told was necessary. With characteristic kindness he insisted on my taking a week's leave before his departure. It was the last real holiday I was ever to have in Russia and I enjoyed every minute of it. Leaving Moscow still bound in the grip of winter, I went to Kiev, the cradle of Russian history and the Holy City of the Orthodox Church. When I woke up after my night in the train, I looked out on green fields and delicious white cottages glistening in the warm sunshine. My travelling companion, an officer, who was returning to the front, greeted me with a smile. 'You will like Kiev. You will find a better atmosphere here than in Moscow, let alone St Petersburg.' In the exuberance of my spirits I was prepared to believe anything. Actually, he spoke the plain truth. Although full of wounded, Kiev had far more war-spirit than Moscow. Indeed, right up to the revolution, the nearer one came to the front, the more optimistic was the prevailing sentiment. All the best of Russia (with, admittedly, some of the worst elements) was in the trenches. It was the rear, and not the front, which let the country down.

As we drew near to Kiev, we stopped for some considerable time at a wayside station. A train, carrying Austrian prisoners, was stranded in a siding. The prisoners, apparently unguarded, had slipped out of their cattle-trucks and were sprawling about on some woodpiles, enjoying the first warmth of the southern sun before continuing their long 'trek' to Siberia. Poor devils. They looked as underfed as they were wretchedly clad. In Moscow the news of the capture of so many thousands of prisoners had always filled me with a fierce exultation. Here, face to face with the unfortunates themselves, I had only one thought. Snodgrass, the American Consul-General, who was in charge of German interests in Russia, had given me a graphic account of the terrible conditions of the Russian prison camps, and with a deep pity in my heart I wondered how many of these poor fellows, some, doubtless, happy to be captured and ignorant of the fate that lay ahead of them, would ever see their homes again. Then, as I stood at the open window looking at them much as a visitor studies a new animal in the zoo, one of the prisoners began to sing the Intermezzo from *Cavalleria Rusticana*. He was a Croat, and the spring had warmed his heart, bringing him memories of his Dalmatian home. He was sublimely unconscious of our train-load of Russians. He was singing to please himself, and he sang as though his heart would burst. I do not know who he was. Probably he was a tenor from the Zagreb opera. But the effect of his voice in that tiny station with its background of green fields and orchards was magical. His fellow prisoners stopped their pebble-throwing. The Russians in our train rose from their seats and stood in silent admiration at the windows. Then, when he had finished, Austrians and Russians combined in one spontaneous outburst of applause, while from the carriages a hail of cigarettes, apples and sweetmeats descended on the prisoners. The singer bowed gravely and turned his head away. Then the whistle went, and we passed on our way.

I arrived at Kiev about midday on Good Friday and spent the afternoon wandering about the town and looking at the churches, of which there are almost as many as in Moscow. Then, tired and rather lonely, I went to bed at nine o'clock. The next day I was up betimes. The sun was streaming into my room, and I was determined to make the best use of my temporary freedom. I am an American in my passion for sightseeing, and I 'did' Kiev with all the thoroughness of the typical American tourist. After Moscow it was a relief to find hills and a real river. The fine weather had brought the whole of the town into the streets, Russians doing their Easter shopping and Jew shopkeepers catering for their needs. For, in spite of its churches, Kiev is almost more Jewish than Christian. Everyone seemed to be smiling. The news from the Austrian front, for which Kiev was the base, was still good. Przemysl had fallen only a few weeks before, and in the prevailing optimism I felt happier than I had felt for months.

After luncheon I took a 'droschke' and drove to the Vladimir Hill, where I left my driver and climbed up to look at the view. In England or in America private enterprise would have built a hotel or a sanatorium here. The Russians have put up a statue to St Vladimir, who stands overlooking the Dnieper with a great cross in his hand. The Dnieper itself is a noble river – far more imposing than the Volga and totally unlike any river I had ever seen. After more than three years in a plain without hills and without sea I found it more soul-satisfying than perhaps I should today.

Then I drove down to the suspension bridge to have a look at the town from the plain. For, strangely enough, while Kiev itself is built on a cluster of hills, all around the country is as flat as the plain round Moscow. The white-roofed steamboats were already plying on the river. The trees were just coming into bloom. The lilac was out, and by the roadside buttercups were growing in profusion. By its position overlooking the river Kiev reminded me of Quebec, and, if Quebec has perhaps the finer site, the picturesqueness of the Kiev architecture is more than sufficient compensation.

In the evening I went to Saint Sofia to attend the midnight service. In Moscow my visits to the Russian church had always been on such official occasions as the Emperor's birthday or name-day. Always I had been in uniform and had stood among the elect on a square shut off from more humble worshippers. Here at Kiev I was one of a crowd so dense that several people fainted. In spite of the discomfort, I remained to the end, took part in the procession, and shared in the emotional uplift of the vast congregation of peasants and pilgrims.

The pilgrims, pleasantly picturesque at a distance, were assembled in force, and on Easter Monday I went to see them at the famous Kiev Lavra, which with the Troitse-Sergievsky monastery near Moscow is the most celebrated holy place in Russia. So warm was the sun that I had to go back and take off my waistcoat. When I arrived at the monastery church, a service was going on, and thousands of soldiers were drawn up on the square outside. Pilgrims – bearded old men with limpid eyes and wizened-up old women – were picnicking everywhere. In the church itself I found an aged philosopher in a corner contentedly munching a loaf of black bread. He seemed supremely happy. From the church I went to the catacombs – cold and unimpressive subterranean passages containing the bones of forgotten saints. In front of each coffin was a collecting box by which sat a priest, and, as the footsore pilgrims clumsily inserted their copecks, the priest leant forward over the relics of the dead saint and chanted: 'Pray to God for us.' With a shudder I ascended into the sunshine and went out to a grassy plot on the cliff-edge. Here three blind beggars, sitting about three paces apart, were reading aloud the Gospel with varying degrees of success. One, a young man of not more than twenty-five, was wearing a soldier's uniform. If he had lost his sight in the war, how had he learnt the Braille system so quickly? If not, why was he wearing a soldier's uniform? I did not disturb his peace of mind by asking an indiscreet question, preferring to regard him as a living member of that holy Russia which in those early days of the war had evoked the emotional sympathies of my own countrymen.

Further along the bank a gypsy with a fortune-telling parrot was doing a lucrative trade with the soldiers. The parrot was a well-trained bird and could give its customers the correct change up to about thirty copecks. What with the necromancers and the priests, most of the soldiers and the pilgrims must have gone away with empty pockets. What was left went to an old harpist who, to his own accompaniment, sang Caucasian folk-songs in a wheezy voice. It was all very peaceful, very harmless and very orderly. Both pilgrims and soldiers had in a contented mind a full reward for their outlay.

In Kiev I had no adventures; yet the memory of the week I spent there remains more clearly fixed in my mind than any other incident in the war. Perhaps it was the spell of the sunshine, or perhaps the contrast with the excitement of my Moscow life, which has left me with so lucid an impression of this episode. Certainly, prolonged excitement can become as monotonous as the most vegetable existence, and in the next three years exciting incidents were to tax my memory to its utmost capacity.

As I left Kiev, the weather broke, and the rain descended in torrents. The station was a desert of depression, and, as I looked back over the railway-bridge, I felt grateful that the town had put on its gayest colours for my special benefit. Yet my heart was weighed down with the thought that I was leaving the south, the sunshine, and the smiling, laughing Ukrainians for the cold and cruel north. I did Moscow and the Great Russians an injustice. When the collapse came, Kiev was to be the centre of the worst atrocities of the revolution and the Ukrainians the perpetrators of the most brutal outrages.

On the return journey I had one minor adventure, which was due to Russian carelessness or to Russian indifference to accepted Western conventions. I had to share a sleeper with a lady. She was charming and within the first hour had told me her life story. She had been a famous singer and, having amassed a considerable fortune, had married a Guards officer. After six years of married life he had shot her in a fit of jealousy. The bullet had penetrated her neck. Since then she had been unable to sing. In her company the hours passed unnoticed, and it was late before I retired to rest. There was, however, no romance about the meeting. Although she carried her years well, she must then have been over sixty.

Soon after my return to Moscow Bayley went to England on sick-leave, and at the age of twenty-seven I was left in charge of what was rapidly becoming one of our most important posts abroad.

His departure neither exalted nor depressed me. I had acted for him before when he was absent on tours of inspection. I expected him back within a month. I was merely carrying on during his temporary absence.

Events, however, were to prolong my period of responsibility. From Kiev I had returned to a Moscow full of rumours and depression. Things were going badly on the German front. The Russian advance into Austria had been checked. The heavy counter-attacks had already begun, and refugees were streaming into the city and taxing its housing resources to the utmost. From my Socialist acquaintances I had received disquieting reports regarding discontent and disorders among the new conscripts in the villages. The wounded did not like going back. The peasants objected to their sons being taken away from the fields. My English friends in the provincial textile factories had become increasingly anxious about the Socialist agitation among the workmen. It had become anti-war as well as anti-Government. In Moscow itself there had been bread riots, and the Assistant-Prefect had been stoned. Sandetsky, the Commander-in-Chief of the Moscow district and a gruff old patriot, who hated Germans, had been removed from his post, and Prince Yusupov, the father of the young prince who later was involved in the Rasputin murder, had been appointed Governor-General in his place. The only reason for Sandetsky's dismissal, it was rumoured, was an excess of patriotism. The Empress, whose work for the wounded was untiring, had given icons to the Russian soldiers and money to the German and Austrian prisoners. True or untrue as this report may have been, Sandetsky had protested against the mollycoddling of prisoners in high quarters and had been disgraced. The atmosphere was unhealthy. Confidence in the Russian arms had given way to a conviction of German invincibility, and in every section of the Moscow population ruled bitter resentment against the alleged pro-German policy of the Russian Government. The famous Russian steamroller which English imagination had invented had broken down. Incidentally, it was one of the stupidest comparisons ever coined.

Obviously, the situation called for action, and I sat down and completed two tasks on which I had been working even before Bayley's departure. One was a long report on the industrial unrest with a first-hand account of the aims of the Socialists. The other was a political report on the situation in Moscow. It was pessimistic in tone and hinted at the probability of serious riots in the immediate future. Then, with some trepidation, I sent them off to the Ambassador. I received a personal letter of thanks with a request that political reports should become a regular feature of my work.

My prediction of trouble received startling confirmation within a fortnight. On June 10th vast anti-German riots broke out in Moscow, and for three days the city was in the hands of the mob. Every shop, every factory, every private house, owned by a German or bearing a German name, was sacked and looted. The country house of Knop, the great Russo-German millionaire, who more than any man had helped to build up the Russian cotton industry by importing English machinery and English managers, was burnt to the ground. The mob, mad with drink, which it had procured from the wreckage of some German-named wine merchant, showed no mercy. It cared nothing that its victims were Russian subjects and in many cases men who, in spite of their names, could speak no German. At Zündel's, a factory in the worst industrial area, the German-speaking manager, terrified into firing on the mob, was killed on the spot. I went out into the streets to see the rioting with my own eyes. For the first twenty-four hours the police could or would do nothing. Fires broke out in many quarters of the city, and, if there had been a wind, the disaster of 1812 might have repeated itself. On the Kuznetsky Most I stood and watched, while hooligans sacked the leading piano store of Moscow. Bechsteins, Blüthners, grand pianos, baby grands and uprights, were hurled one by one from the various storeys to the ground, where a high bonfire completed the work of destruction. The crash of falling woodwork, the cruel tongues of flame, and the raucous yelling of the mob swelled into a terrifying discord, which even the troops, who had been called out, were at first unable to quell.

On the third day, after some shooting, the authorities were able to restore order. But, for the first time since 1905, the mob had felt its power. Its appetite for disorder had been whetted.

In this holocaust a considerable amount of British property had been damaged, and I therefore called immediately on the Prefect and on Prince Yusupov, the Governor-General, to make my official protest. I found the unfortunate Prefect in a state of collapse. He knew that he would be held responsible – as indeed he was. He was superseded within twenty-four hours. Prince Yusupov, as one of the richest landowners in Russia, was in a different situation. He was bitterly opposed to what he called the pro-German 'brakes' in St Petersburg and he was inclined to take the view that the riots would have a salutary effect on a lukewarm Government.

Shortly afterwards Prince Yusupov went on leave and never resumed his post. The account of his dismissal or, as he called it, his refusal to return is amusing. Soon after the riots he gave a dinner to General Klimovich, the new Prefect, and to Count Muraviev, the Governor of the province of Moscow. Two days later Dzhunkovsky, the Assistant Minister of the Interior and the head of the secret police, rang up Muraviev from St Petersburg and said to him:

'Two days ago you dined with Yusupov.'

'Yes.'

'You had sterlet and chaud-froid of partridge.'

'Yes.'

'You discussed the merits of Moscow and Petersburg women.'

'Yes.'

'You drank a Mouton-Rothschild of 1884.'

'Yes,' said the astonished Muraviev, 'but how the devil do you know all this?'

'Why,' replied Dzhunkovsky, 'Klimovich has just sent me in a full report.'

Muraviev repeated the story to Yusupov, who exploded angrily, said he was not going to be spied upon by his assistant, and swore he would not return to Moscow until Klimovich was kicked out.

Klimovich remained, and Yusupov never returned.

The origin of the Moscow riots is still shrouded in mystery, but I have always held the view that the Moscow Governor-General was greatly to blame in that he first tolerated what he apparently thought was to be a healthy anti-German demonstration and did not intervene until the situation had become highly dangerous.

As a result of this deplorable affair I received a request from the Ambassador asking me to come to St Petersburg to see him. Looking back across the years, I find it hard to recapture the thrill which this message gave me. Vice-Consuls, even acting Consuls-General, were not summoned every day to be consulted by Ambassadors. For one awkward moment I wondered if in any respect my handling of affairs had been remiss or if in any way I could be held responsible for what had happened. I decided the question in my own favour and consolidated my growing store of self-confidence. I took the precaution of calling on Michael Chelnokov, the Moscow Mayor and my best friend in Russia, to collect the latest political information. Then, packing my bag, I set out for the station, where the indispensable Alexander had 'wangled' me a sleeper to myself.

Although I had been three years in Russia, it was my first visit to St Petersburg. It was also the first time I was to see Sir George Buchanan. Although today I have a hate of all towns, a city which is new to me rarely fails to touch some side of my emotions. In one sense St Petersburg did not disappoint me. It is, in truth, a far more beautiful city than Moscow, and the view – especially the winter view – from the British Embassy, which has or had a noble site on the river opposite the fortress of Peter and Paul, is almost fairy-like in its beauty. But even in summer, in the season of the white nights, St Petersburg always seemed to me cold and grey. Beneath its lovely exterior its heart was chill. Never at any time did it inspire me with the same friendly affection as Moscow.

On my arrival in the early morning I drove to the old Hotel de France, made a careful toilet, breakfasted, and then walked across through the Palace Square to the Embassy. I had a feeling of uncomfortable apprehension as if I was about to visit my dentist. As a Scot I sometimes try to cure my inferiority complex towards the English by a simulated contempt for their intellectual shortcomings. In the presence of foreigners I am a lion of self-confidence. The blustering swagger of the Americans only increases the sense of my own importance. Russians always make me feel that I am a 'grand seigneur'. But the meek arrogance of an Englishman's modesty reduces me to the level of an awkward gawk. I imagine that this inferiority complex, which now cramps me more securely than ever, dates from that day when I first entered the portals of the British Embassy.

As I made my way up one side of the broad double staircase, at the top of which the Ambassador used to receive his guests and on which three years later the unfortunate Cromie* was to be shot down and trampled to death by Bolshevik soldiers, I felt like a schoolboy going to interview his headmaster. I turned to the left and was shown into a kind of ante-room which opened out of the corridor. Here I was met by Havery, the Chancery servant – a wonderful character, who had all the Englishman's contempt for foreigners and whose penchant for grumbling was equalled only by his kindness of heart. I was given a chair and was told to wait. As the minutes

* Captain Francis Cromie (1882–1918), British naval attaché in St Petersburg.

passed, the anticipated pleasure which my visit had aroused in me gave way to an increasing trepidation. The only member of the Embassy staff whom I knew was Colonel Knox, the military attaché. He was out. The Ambassador had fixed no time for my interview. Obviously, everyone was very busy. Perhaps I should have telephoned to ascertain the hour of my appointment. I became nervous and ill at ease. An ultra-sensitive nature has been my curse all through life. It – and it alone – is responsible for that reputation for calculated insolence which I acquired – most undeservedly – during my official career and which, later, was to cause a very high official in the Foreign Office to stigmatise me as an 'impudent schoolboy'. Never has this sensitiveness frozen me into such unnatural impotence as during that long-drawn-out quarter of an hour in Havery's ante-room.

At last, a large white door with an iron bar across it opened, and a tall, athletic, and extremely good-looking man of about thirty came out. It was 'Benji' Bruce, the Head of the Chancery and the inevitable and indispensable favourite of every Ambassador under whom he has ever served. Telling me that the Ambassador would see me in a few minutes, he took me into the Chancery and introduced me to the other secretaries. Later, I was to know them better and appreciate their merits, but my first impression was of a typing and telegraph bureau conducted by Old Etonians. At uncomfortably close quarters in a large room, blocked with tables, sat half a dozen young men busily engaged in typing and ciphering. That they did their task well, that 'Benji' Bruce could type as fast as any professional typist and cipher and decipher with astonishing speed is beside the point. Here was a collection of young men, all of whom had had thousands of pounds spent on their education, who had passed a difficult examination, yet who, in the middle of a great war in which their special knowledge might have been used to their country's advantage, were occupied for hours on end in work which could have been performed just as efficiently by a second-division clerk. This system, now fortunately abolished, was typical of the want of imagination which reigned in Whitehall during at any rate the first two years of the war. Any side-show mission – and in Russia there must have been a score – could command an almost unlimited supply of money from the Treasury. The professional diplomats, who, whatever their shortcomings may have been, knew their job better than the amateurs, were left to carry on as in peacetime, not because of any danger of secrets being divulged, but merely because this system had been in force for generations and because, in the Chief Clerk's department in the Foreign Office, there was no one with sufficient elasticity of mind or force of character to insist on its being altered. No wonder that, after the war, many of the younger diplomats, weary of this senseless drudgery, sent in their resignations. Bruce was a case in point. A man of strong and attractive personality, an excellent linguist, and a firm disciplinarian with a real genius for organisation, he ran his Chancery with remarkable efficiency. If a trifle obstinate as becomes an Ulsterman, he served his various chiefs with passionate loyalty. When he resigned soon after the war, the Foreign Office lost perhaps the best-equipped of its younger diplomats.

After I had kicked my heels in the Chancery for twenty minutes, Havery came in and announced that the Ambassador was free. As I entered the long study, in which afterwards I was to have so many interviews, a frail-looking man with a tired, sad expression in his eyes came forward to meet me. His monocle, his finely chiselled features, and his beautiful silver-grey hair gave him something of the appearance of a stage-diplomat. But there was nothing artificial about his manner, or, indeed, about the man himself – only a great charm and a wonderful power of inspiring loyalty, to which I yielded at once.

His whole manner was so gentle that my nervousness left me instantaneously, and for an hour I talked to him, telling him my fears and my anxieties about the situation, the shortage of munitions, the subterranean propaganda against the war, the growing discontent of every class of the population with the Government, the murmurs against the throne itself. He showed some surprise. 'I thought the atmosphere in Moscow was much healthier than in St Petersburg,' he said rather sadly. Indeed, it was, but I guessed that up to this point he had rated Moscow patriotism too highly. I had shaken a faith that perhaps was never very strong.

I was asked to luncheon and was introduced to Lady Georgina, the Ambassador's wife. She was a woman of strong likes and dislikes, which she made little attempt to conceal, and for some months she never failed to greet me, whenever I came to St Petersburg, with the remark: 'Here comes the pessimistic Mr Lockhart.' In every other respect, however, she showed me nothing but kindness, and, although I never quite overcame my original awe, I counted myself among the fortunates who enjoyed her favour. To Sir George himself she was everything that a wife should be, watching over his health with tireless zeal, running his house like clockwork and never failing in that passion for punctuality which in the Ambassador amounted almost to a mania. She was a big woman, and her heart was in proportion to her bulk.

This is no place in which to give an account of Sir George Buchanan's work in Russia, but I should like to pay my tribute to the man himself. Every British official who was in Russia during the war years has had inevitably to face the criticism which failure brings in its train. And in British eyes the collapse of Russia in 1917 was the greatest of all failures. The tendency, therefore, to seek scapegoats among their own countrymen is strong. Sir George Buchanan's name has not escaped the calumniators either in England or in Russia. I have heard Ministers of the Crown declare that with a stronger British Ambassador the revolution might have been avoided. There are Russians who with the basest ingratitude have accused Sir George Buchanan of having instigated the revolution. Both criticisms can be dismissed as wholly ridiculous. Indeed, the Russian accusation is a particularly cruel and baseless slander, which, to the shame of London society, has been repeated without contradiction in London drawing-rooms by Russians who have enjoyed British hospitality in high places. It is a form of vilification which no personal sufferings can justify or ever excuse. Sir George Buchanan was a man whose every instinct was opposed to revolution. Until the revolution came he always refused to meet and, actually, never did meet any of the men who were responsible for the overthrow of Tsardom, nor did he either personally or through his subordinates give any encouragement to their ambitions. Naturally he would have been lacking in perspicacity, if he had failed to foresee the catastrophe that was approaching, and in his duty if he had been afraid to warn the Russian autocracy of the dangers which he saw threatening it. This difficult task he undertook in a memorable conversation with the Emperor. I saw him just before he went to see the Tsar. He informed me that if the Emperor received him sitting down all would be well. The Tsar received him standing.

The Whitehall assertion that a stronger Ambassador might have

Left, Prince George Lvov, head of the Zemstvos Union. *Below left*, British Ambassador Sir George Buchanan, and, *below right*, Alfred, Lord Milner, a member of Lloyd George's War Cabinet from 1916

Revolutionaries distributing leaflets in Moscow, April, 1917. *Below*, crowds fleeing in an outbreak of violence between Bolsheviks and the Provisional Government outside the Duma in July, 1917 averted the final catastrophe is based on a fundamental ignorance of the traditions of the Russian autocracy. Contempt for foreigners is a characteristic of the English race, but in this respect the attitude of the most insular John Bull is tolerance itself compared with the arrogant indifference of St Petersburg society to the stranger within its gates. With no long lineage and less real civilisation than one might expect from the luxury of its life, the Russian aristocracy lived in a world of its own. A foreign Ambassador was not accepted merely because he was an Ambassador. If he was liked for his own social qualities he was invited everywhere. If not, he was ignored. It was not actual snobbishness. The Russian aristocracy was as hospitable as the other sections of the Russian population. But it made its own selection of the recipients of its hospitality, and frequently its choice was startling in its indiscrimination. During the war years a junior lieutenant in the British Military Censor's office probably went to more parties in high places than all the members of the Embassy put together.

To the aristocracy the complete absolutism of the Tsar was something more than a religion. It was the rock on which its own sheltered existence was built. In its eyes the Emperor was the only real monarch in the world, and for its own sake it was always ready to regard any attempt by foreign diplomats to influence him as an encroachment on the Imperial authority. The most efficient members of the bureaucracy were Baltic barons – a class hidebound even today in reaction. From the first they saw in the war a danger to the autocracy, and England as the home of constitutional monarchy they regarded with deep suspicion. Nor, for all his weakness, was the Emperor himself easily accessible or in any way, except the most tactful, amenable to foreign influence. He would have resented as much as his advisers any attempt by an English diplomat to speak plainly to him.

Sir George Buchanan's task was therefore abnormally difficult. He had to overcome the political prejudice against England which still remained from past differences of policy. He had to take into consideration the peculiar susceptibilities of the ruling class. To suggest that because he walked warily he was a weak man is to underrate his whole character. He had been selected for the St Petersburg Embassy because of the excellent work he had done at Sofia, and I doubt if there was anyone in the British diplomatic service who understood the Slav character better. If not a man of outstanding intellect (he had the Scot's mistrust of brilliance), he had remarkable powers of intuition and an abundant supply of common sense. To Russian cleverness he opposed complete honesty and sincerity tempered with caution. He won the full confidence of Sazonov, the most reliable of the Tsarist Ministers, and by the vast bulk of the Russian population he was regarded as a man whose heart was in an Allied victory as distinct from a purely English victory, and who would countenance no intrigues at the expense of Russia. I say intentionally 'the bulk of the Russian population', for it is a mistake to imagine that Sir George Buchanan was an unpopular figure in Russian society. Except in pro-German circles his admirers among the aristocracy were numerous. It was only after the revolution that the nobility began to murmur against him, seeking in him a scapegoat for their own failure and a cloak for their own loose talk against the Emperor. More than all the resolutions of the Zemstvos and the Cities Unions, more than all the agitation of the Socialists, it was the openly expressed criticism by Grand Dukes and highly placed aristocrats which sapped the authority of the Imperial throne. When the history of Anglo-Russian relations during these fateful years is seen in perspective, future generations will recognise how great was the work accomplished by Sir George Buchanan in helping to keep Russia in the war for as long as she remained. Certainly, I can imagine no greater calamity to the English fortunes than an English Ambassador in St Petersburg who had tried to play the little Napoleon of Whitehall before the Emperor.

As a chief Sir George Buchanan was delightful – a man in whom all thought of self was submerged in the highest conception of duty. He was worshipped by his staff, and, when he took his daily walk to the Russian Foreign Office, his hat cocked on one side, his tall, lean figure slightly drooping under his many cares, every Englishman felt that here as much as the diplomatic precincts of the Embassy itself was a piece of the soil of England.

If there was one aspect of his character on which I should lay stress, it was his magnificent courage both physical and moral. Physically, he did not know the meaning of the word 'fear'. Morally, he triumphed completely over what I think was a natural inclination to the line of least resistance and faced without a moment's hesitation situations and interviews which were repugnant to him.

To me he was unfailingly kind. Through the insignificance of my own position I was able to see people whom neither he nor other members of his staff could see. I was thus enabled to supply him with information which, provided it was correct, was of some value to him. Many an Ambassador would have taken this information as a matter of course and incorporated what he required in his own despatches. This was not Sir George's way. He not only gave me every encouragement both by letter and in personal discussion, but he also sent my reports home to the Foreign Office – frequently with a covering despatch of approval. As a result, I was given full credit for my work in London and on several occasions received a personal letter of commendation from Sir Edward Grey.* My head went a little higher in the air. I fought more fiercely with the Chief Clerk's department for increased office and personal allowances. But to Sir George I was full of gratitude and of that respectful submission which gratitude should always bring with it. Later, I was to forfeit his goodwill by the anti-intervention attitude I adopted after the Bolshevik revolution. But of all the men I have worked under in my career he was, with the single exception of Lord Milner,† the one who inspired in me the greatest affection and hero-worship, and I am glad that, before he died, I was able to make my peace with him.

* Sir Edward Grey (1862–1933), Foreign Secretary 1905–16.
† Alfred, Lord Milner (1854–1925), High Commissioner of South Africa 1897–1905, a member of Lloyd George's War Cabinet from 1916, Secretary for War 1918–19, and Colonial Secretary 1919–21.

I returned to Moscow well pleased with my reception and greatly encouraged by the Ambassador's request that I was to keep in close touch with him and to come to St Petersburg whenever there was anything important to discuss. Although I said nothing about my visit, the redoubtable Alexander was not so silent, and very soon I found that both with the officials and with the politicians my prestige was considerably enhanced. I expect that on Alexander's lips the story lost nothing in the telling and that in the Governor-General's office and in the headquarters of the Zemstvos and Cities Unions it was broadcast that His Excellency the Acting British Consul-General (Alexander always omitted the Acting) was now going regularly to St Petersburg to consult if not actually to advise His Super-Excellency (in Russia Ambassadors *were* Super-Excellencies) the British Ambassador.

During that summer of 1915 I consolidated my friendship with Michael Chelnokov, the Moscow Mayor and a former Vice-President of the Imperial Duma. Chelnokov, a splendid type of Moscow merchant, grey-bearded, patriarchal, broad-shouldered and, in spite of a game leg, stout-hearted beyond most of his compatriots, was a grand fellow. Although he was twenty years older than myself, we became the closest friends, and through him not only did I come to know intimately all the Moscow political leaders like Prince Lvov, Vasily Maklakov, Manuilov, Kokoshkin, and many others, but I also received copies of the numerous secret resolutions which were passed by such bodies as the Moscow Municipality, the Zemstvos Union, of which Prince Lvov was head, and the Cities Union of which Chelnokov himself was the moving spirit. Sometimes I was even able to obtain in Moscow through the same source copies of secret resolutions passed by the Cadet Party in St Petersburg or of such documents as Rodzianko's* letter to the Prime Minister and to send them to our Embassy in St Petersburg before anyone else had brought them to its notice. These minor successes naturally added to my reputation as a 'news-getter'. Through the Zemstvos and Cities Unions, too, I was of some service to the War Office. The Zemstvos and the Cities Unions, though stupidly hampered by the Government, were the nearest Russian equivalent to our Ministry of Munitions, and from Lvov and Chelnokov I received regularly the

* Mikhail Rodzianko (1859–1924), President of the Duma 1911–17.

latest figures regarding the output of every kind of war material.

During the two and a half months of Bayley's absence I had entrenched myself solidly in Moscow. I had received the thanks of the Foreign Secretary. I was *persona grata* with the war-leaders in Moscow. The Ambassador had sent for me. At the end of July Bayley would return. He would, I felt, be pleased and I should have the satisfaction of knowing that I had done my job well. There seemed nothing more to which I could look forward.

Then, however, came a new crisis. Things had gone from bad to worse on the Russian front. The retreat in Galicia and in the Carpathians did not affect Moscow so much except in the increase of wounded, but the advance on Warsaw was different. For some weeks Polish refugees had been pouring into Moscow. Now on July 19th came a telegram from Grove informing me that Warsaw was being evacuated and that he and the remaining members of the British colony were leaving for Moscow immediately. Three days later he arrived, and on the same day came a telegram from Bayley, informing me that he had been appointed Consul-General in New York and was returning to Moscow at once to pack up. I had no ill will against the Groves. If I had any personal ambitions, I was unconscious of them. But I must confess that this double-barrelled shock filled me with consternation. If Bayley went to New York, Grove obviously would take his place in Moscow, and, quite candidly, after Bayley I did not relish a return to the Grove régime.

On July 30th Bayley arrived, carrying a surprise packet in his pocket. All my apprehensions were ended. Grove was to be transferred to Helsingfors.* I was to be left in charge of the Moscow Consulate-General. Bayley informed me that, on his appointment to New York, the Foreign Office had promptly appointed a new Consul-General to Moscow. Sir George Buchanan, however, had protested, saying that I had done invaluable work and that it would be a mistake to hamper my activities by imposing on me a chief who could not know the situation as well as I did. Bayley told me with genuine joy that the Foreign Office was very pleased with me. I tried to look unconcerned. Although I had done nothing to push my own claims, I was full of remorse about the Groves, who I knew would be bitterly disappointed. But deep down in my heart there was a quiet exultation: 'Not yet twenty-eight and in charge on your own merits

* The Swedish name for Helsinki.

of one of the most important Consulates-General in the war.' A certain amount of self-conceit is good in the young. Except in the case of the ambitious and the brigands it soon gets rubbed off.

For a week I waited hand and foot on Bayley, helping him to clear up, arranging farewell dinners for him, and taking over from him at the Consulate-General. The British Club gave him a splendid send-off, and we had our own formal parting at the Consulate-General, when everybody gave Bayley a gift and was given one in return. I received a massive cigarette case which I have to this day. Alexander wound up a rather trying performance with a speech which undid the last floodgates of even Bayley's emotions. (My lady secretaries were both crying, and only old Fritz, the Lett clerk, remained impassive.) In lyrical language he referred to Bayley and myself as shining examples to all Russians of what an official ought to be and declared his firm intention that, if I were to leave Moscow, he would leave with me. The bathos of Alexander's oratory just put the necessary brake on my own tear-glands. Yet I was full of sadness over Bayley's departure. He had been more like a father to me than a chief. He had been kindness itself to me during my wife's illness. That he was devoted to me and genuinely interested in my advancement, though pleasing to my vanity, did not deter me from listening to the excellent advice which he gave me from the store of his worldly knowledge. I was losing not only a friend but an ally – in a very real sense my only ally in a city of nearly two million inhabitants. Alas! I never saw him again. His advice, which consisted mainly in an exhortation to observe the eleventh commandment so long as I remained an official, fell on stony ground.

The fall of Warsaw* was the culminating tragedy of the disastrous summer campaign of 1915. It was a blow which could not be hidden even from the masses, and naturally there was a great increase of pessimism and peace talk. Men like Chelnokov and Lvov were firm enough; their roots were in the soil. But the professional politicians were excited, and their nervousness spread like a wet fog until it enveloped half the population. Horrible rumours of Russians manning the trenches with nothing but sticks in their hands perco-

* Warsaw fell to the German and Austro-Hungarian forces on August 5th, 1915. Since the Congress of Vienna in 1814–15 the city had been regarded as part of the Russian Empire, and its loss was a severe blow to Russian morale.

lated through from the front to the countryside. Neither the old men nor the young recruits had any stomach for this slaughter, and at factory centres like Ivanovo-Voznesensk there were anti-Government strikes attended in some cases by shooting.

As usual, the authorities devised a counter-irritant for this public excitement. On August 23rd, when the pessimism was at its worst, Moscow hummed with rumours, emanating apparently from official quarters, that the Allies had forced the Dardanelles. In the afternoon a Moscow newspaper came out with large headlines: 'Official: Dardanelles Taken.' Then followed a graphic account of the bombardment of the straits with casualty lists and names of ships complete. On receipt of this news vast crowds assembled in the streets. People knelt on the Tverskaya Square to thank God for this glorious victory. There was a manifestation before the Consulate-General. In vain I tried to tell the mob that the news was false. 'Official communiqué' shouted the newsboys, and in the storm of cheering my voice was lost. Later in the evening the crowd got out of hand, and near the Skoboliev monument there was a demonstration against the police, which ended as usual with a charge of mounted gendarmes.

The next day there was general disappointment at the false report, and, together with my French colleague, I called on the Prefect to demand summary action against the editor and the publishers. He received us with the usual official unctuousness. He had already anticipated our just indignation. He had closed down the newspaper for the rest of the war. We expressed our gratitude in proper terms. After this statement I was surprised to find the paper still continuing to appear, having changed its name from *Evening News* to *Evening Gazette*. In every other respect it was identical with its predecessor. The headlines and the type were the same. The erring editor of the day before had signed the leading article of today.

I fumed and gave the Prefect best. I discovered later that the victory stunt had been operated in connection with the police in order to let the public work off steam.

I do not profess ever to have mastered the psychology of the Tsarist police. I refuse, however, to believe either in its efficiency or in its honesty. The dreaded 'Okhrana' of the Seton Merriman novel was a myth fearful more by its name than by its omniscience. It was an organisation run by bunglers and clever crooks, and in it the bunglers outnumbered the brains by nine to one.

As the autumn advanced, the approaching tragedy of Russia impressed itself more and more on my mind. Worse things were to happen than the fall of Warsaw. Yet the same defect of character, which made the Russian incapable of sustained effort, helped to take the edge off his pessimism. No Muscovite could continue for long to wring his hands. Actually, as blow succeeded blow, local patriotism reasserted itself, and, if in St Petersburg there were few people who believed in a Russian victory, Moscow adopted the slogan that the war could not be won unless the dark influences in the capital were eliminated. From this moment dates the first of the many resolutions demanding a Ministry of national defence or of public confidence. At first these demands were modest enough. Moscow was prepared to accept legitimate Tsarist Ministers – that is, men like Krivoshein, Sazonov, Samarin, Shcherbatov and others, who had no connection with the political parties in the Duma. It would at this stage have been simple enough for the Tsar to have formed a new Ministry, which would have satisfied public opinion, without going outside the usual circle from which he chose his advisers. By giving in time the six inches of reform, which were necessary, he might have saved the yards which a disillusioned country was to take by force afterwards. Those nearest him, however, saw the matter in another light. They told him that any concession now would be regarded as a fatal weakness and that the appetite of the reformers would only be whetted. This was an argument which never failed to convince the Empress, and in consequence the Tsar's reply to those who were working hardest for Russia's victory was to dissolve the Duma, to relieve the Grand Duke Nicholas of his command, and to dismiss Samarin, Shcherbatov and Dzhunkovsky, the three Ministers who at the moment were most popular in Moscow.

The dissolution of the Duma provoked the usual strikes and protests. But the assumption of the Supreme Command by the Tsar himself was the first milestone on the way to Golgotha. It was the most fatal of the many blunders of the unfortunate Nicholas II, for as Commander-in-Chief he became personally responsible in the eyes of the people for the long succession of defeats which owing to Russia's technical deficiencies were now inevitable.

The dismissal of Samarin and Dzhunkovsky was the indirect

sequel of an episode of which I myself had been a silent witness. One summer evening I was at Yar, the most luxurious night-haunt of Moscow, with some English visitors. As we watched the music-hall performance in the main hall, there was a violent fracas in one of the neighbouring 'kabinets'. Wild shrieks of women, a man's curses, broken glass and the banging of doors raised a discordant pande-monium. Head waiters rushed upstairs. The manager sent for the policeman who was always on duty at such establishments. But the row and the roaring continued. There was more coming and going of waiters and policemen, and scratching of heads and holding of councils. The cause of the disturbance was Rasputin – drunk and lecherous, and neither police nor management dared evict him. The policeman telephoned to his divisional inspector, the inspector tele-phoned to the Prefect. The Prefect telephoned to Dzhunkovsky, who was Assistant Minister of the Interior and head of all the police. Dzhunkovsky, who was a former general and a man of high charac-ter, gave orders that Rasputin, who, after all, was only an ordinary citizen and not even a priest, should be arrested forthwith. Having disturbed everyone's enjoyment for two hours, he was led away, snarling and vowing vengeance, to the nearest police station. He was released early next morning on instructions from the highest quar-ters. He left the same day for St Petersburg, and within twenty-four hours Dzhunkovsky was relieved of his post. Samarin's dismissal, which followed later, made a very painful impression. A nobleman of splendid character, he was then Oberprokuror or Minister in Charge of Church Matters and one of the very best representatives of his class. No one but a madman could accuse him of anything but the most orthodox conservative opinions or of any lack of loyalty to the Emperor. Yet every liberal and every Socialist respected him as an honest man, and the fact that the Emperor could thus sacrifice one of his most loyal advisers for a creature like Rasputin was accepted by nearly everyone in Moscow as a complete proof of the Tsar's incom-petence. 'Down with the autocracy!' cried the liberals. But even among the reactionaries there were those who said: 'If the autocracy is to flourish, give us a good autocrat.'

This was the only occasion on which Rasputin came across my path. From time to time, however, I saw the mark of the beast at Chelnokov's house, where the Mayor would show me a short type-written note requesting him to fix up the bearer in a safe and

comfortable job in the Cities Union. The note was signed in an illit-
erate scrawl 'G.R.' – Grigory Rasputin. The requests were invariably
turned down by the sturdy Chelnokov.

With the advent of winter – and in that year of 1915 it came early
– a period of stagnation set in on the front and with it came a lull in
the political discontent. Life went on.

My wife and I dined out six nights in the week. Most days we had
people to luncheon – English officers, generals, admirals, colonels,
captains, passing through Moscow on their way to the headquarters
of the various Russian armies. Once a week my wife had a reception,
and by some innate talent of her own succeeded in making the
wolves lie down with the lambs. She was especially delighted when
she could include a Socialist or two in her bag. Nevertheless, everybody came – from the Commandant of the Kremlin, the Governor,
the Prefect and the generals of the Moscow district (not all of the
generals were well disposed either to the Government or to the local
authorities) down to the rich Moscow millionaires, and the ballet
dancers, the actors and writers, and the shy and rather awkward
politicians of the Left. There were, as far as I remember, no con-
tretemps, although on one occasion Sasha Kropotkina, the daughter
of that fine old anarchist, Prince Kropotkin,* nearly came to blows
with Countess Kleinmichel over the lack of martial spirit in St Petersburg. This mingling of the different sets of Russians in Moscow was
as good for them as it was useful to us. It broke down barriers which
had never been stormed before. It provided us with information of
the most varying character.

That there were Russians whose hearts were still set on victory
was brought home to me in a remarkable manner when my brother
Norman was killed at Loos. I did not receive the news until early in
October. We had been out in the country and were dining with some
Russians at the Hermitage. My wife had gone home to change her
shoes. There she found the telegram and telephoned to me at the
restaurant. It was the first time that the death of someone I loved had
come to me without warning, and in the telephone box I broke
down and cried bitterly. I told my Russian friends what had happened and went home. The next morning nearly every Moscow

* Prince Peter Kropotkin (1842–1921), geographer, writer and anarchist.
Lived in exile in Britain from 1886 until he returned to Russia after the
1917 revolution.

newspaper had a very generous tribute to my brother and to the heavy losses of the Scottish troops, and for days to come I received letters of sympathy from Russians of every class and rank.* Many came from people I did not know even by sight. Most of them ended with an expression of profound conviction of the ultimate triumph of the Allies.

It must not be thought, however, that my life was all tragedy. The strikes, the political discontent, the defeats, stand out today like landmarks in a great plain, but they were not everyday occurrences or even an important part of my daily life. I had my own problems to tackle: committees to attend (the British colony ran various enter- prises for the wounded and the refugees; in addition, there were recruiting committees, war supply committees, etc.) and an immense routine work at the Consulate which, apart from my political work, was a whole-time job in itself. Some of my troubles were humorous; others merely irritating. I could laugh when my wife rang me up at the Consulate to say that the servants had gone on strike or rather refused to enter the flat, because there was an evil spirit, a polter- geist, whose chief offence seemed to be the breaking of valuable plates. Certainly, a rare and precious icon had fallen by itself, and, as my wife took the servants' side, there was nothing for it but to enlist the services of the priest. He came and for the sum of five roubles gave the poltergeist a liberal sprinkling of holy water. The flat was cleansed; the servants returned; and strangely enough, the queer noises and the breaking of plates ceased.

Less amusing were the frequent rows among my Consular staff, which had swollen considerably since the influx of the British refugees from Warsaw. Bayley had left me with a legacy in the per- son of Francis Greenep, a once well-known London lawyer. Always very neatly dressed, he was a fine-looking old man, and his silver hair and his monocle lent distinction to a staff of which I myself was almost the most youthful member. When in the right mood, he had charming manners. His work, too, was punctually and excellently done. But – and it was a big but – his temper was explosive and, as he was always on the look-out for insults, there were many scenes. One day it would be Alexander who had ruffled his dignity. Another time it would be St Clair, the Vice-Consul from Warsaw, who had

* At the next (Russian) Christmas – January 7th, 1916 – the author re- ceived over three hundred Christmas cards, mostly of sympathy.

been attached to me and who, although more Polish than Scottish, had all the pride of the ancient Scottish family to which he belonged. Strange, difficult fellows they were: responsive to emotional appeals, but not to be driven. I expect I tried them highly, and in any case living for months and indeed years on end at high tension in a small office, where one saw the same faces every day, was strain enough to break the strongest nerves, and neither Greenep's nor St Clair's were up to standard. I could manage the rows between the various members of the staff. It was another matter when Greenep's wrath was unloosed on visitors to the office. For his own sake I kept him as much as possible in his own room, but obviously I could not prevent him from entering the main office in the execution of his duties. In a long series of incidents two had serious results. One morning, as I was deciphering a telegram in my own room, I heard an angry altercation from the outer office. Above the general din, I could hear Greenep's voice, trembling with rage: 'Do what you're told, sir, or leave the office.'

I rushed out just in time to prevent my aged hothead from doing physical violence to an English artillery major, who was purple with indignation.

'Are you in charge of this Consulate?' he stuttered to me. 'Then you will give me satisfaction or I'll report you to the Foreign Office. This fellow here has insulted the King's uniform.'

Greenep was standing by the side of the office counter, his finger pointing at the portrait of the King which adorned the wall.

'Take off your hat, sir, in His Majesty's presence.'

He kept repeating his demand in a kind of eldritch refrain. With the help of Fritz, my Lettish clerk, who had been a witness of the whole scene, I sifted out the truth. The officer in uniform had come into the office with his cap on. Greenep, who was passing through, had pointed to the King's portrait and had said politely enough: 'Don't you see the King's portrait, sir? This is not a station waiting-room.' The officer had paid no attention. Greenep had then demanded more peremptorily that he should remove his hat. And then the fur had started to fly.

It was a difficult case. Actually, Greenep was in the wrong in losing his temper. The officer, however, had been tactless. He was inclined to stand on his rights and insisted that, when he came into an office, it was correct for him to keep his cap on. But for his pomposity I should have had no alternative but to dismiss the unfortunate Greenep – a course which I was loath to take, partly because the man was devoted to me and, secondly, because it meant putting him into the street. I tried to smooth down the officer without sacrificing Greenep, but he insisted on his pound of flesh. I refused to give it to him. He left me vowing vengeance. I reported the whole matter to the Ambassador, apportioning the blame equally between the two protagonists and representing the affair as a case of war nerves. I heard no more, and fortunately for me the incident was closed.

More serious was a similar episode in which Greenep affronted Baliev, a rich Armenian and a brother of the famous Nikita. In his spare time Greenep supplemented his income by giving lessons to rich Russians. Baliev was one of his pupils. Apparently there had been some trouble about payment. At any rate, Greenep nursed a grievance. It found its outlet, when one day Baliev came into the Consulate to obtain a visa. Unfortunately, Greenep was again in the main office, and the sight of the rich man, who he alleged had done him out of his hard-earned roubles, maddened him. Once again I had to rush out and make peace. This time, however, the consequences were more serious. There had been witnesses of the incident, and Baliev was determined to take his legal remedy. Luckily, his lawyer was a great friend of our own lawyer and was as anxious as I was to prevent a public scandal. Between us we worked out every possible compromise which would satisfy Baliev's wounded feelings and at the same time save Greenep from dismissal. In the end Baliev agreed to drop all proceedings in return for a public apology to be made in the presence of the Consular staff and of himself and his lawyer. The apology was to be drafted by him.

It was a long one. There were several references to gentlemen and gentlemanly behaviour. It was an unpleasant dose for anyone, and for twenty-four hours Greenep refused to swallow it. I pointed out to him that I could do no more and that if the matter came before the courts there could only be one result. He would have to go.

Finally, he agreed. The apology was typed out, and with the lawyers I arranged the formalities for its delivery. In the main office Fritz and the three lady typists sat like mummies at their desks. On the door side of the counter stood Baliev and his lawyer. I took up my own stand on the office side of the counter. When all was ready, I walked to Greenep's room, brought him up before the counter, and put the apology into his hands. He was in his best suit. His hair was carefully brushed. His monocle was fixed firmly in his eye. His face was like a statue. Only from the trembling paper in his hands could one suspect the suppressed rage.

'Shall I begin?' he said in an ominous whisper. He read through the idiotic document, a rich flush suffusing his cheeks until they became the colour of a turkey's comb, while Baliev, fat and sweating with fear, extracted what satisfaction he could from the English-man's humiliation. When he had finished, Greenep turned one awful glare at his enemy, crumpled up the paper in his hand and with a 'There, you may have your pound of flesh!' strode out of the room.

Today, the scene seems comic enough and, indeed, a trifle undignified as far as my own participation is concerned. But at the time it was a serious business. Indeed, so great was Greenep's capacity for nursing a grievance, that he might very easily have involved the Consulate-General in a scandal or in expensive litigation and, certainly, in ridicule.

There were, however, compensations. In November, 1915, the Ambassador wrote me a letter informing me that the Foreign Office was so pleased with my work that I was to be left in charge of the Consulate-General until the end of the war. I used this letter with great effect in order to improve my financial position, which, with my increased responsibilities, was becoming precarious. For some time I had been conducting a bitter correspondence with the Foreign Office. We were in the middle of a great war. I was being involved in far greater expenditure than ever Bayley had had to face, and I was receiving neither increase of pay nor increase of office allowance. I enlisted the services of the Ambassador on my side. They were given whole-heartedly. Very early on, he wrote to the Foreign Office saying: 'There is scarcely any Consular post of the same importance as Moscow at the present moment. It is the industrial and, in a certain broad sense, the political capital of Russia . . . You will have seen from Mr Lockhart's despatches the excellent work that has been done by that office since Mr Clive Bayley's departure.'

Even Ambassadors, however, cannot disturb the unimaginative routine of the Chief Clerk's department or of the Treasury, and it was not in an obdurate Whitehall, but in the heart of my grandmother that Sir George Buchanan's letter was of service to me. The old lady, thrilled always by success, was delighted by the Ambassador's encomiums. I knew just exactly how to launch my appeal. My brother Norman had supplied the perfect form to all of us, when he was a small boy in his first term at Marlborough. As his birthday approached, he had written to his grandmother as follows:

DEAR GRANNIE,

I hope you are well. I am enjoying school very much. My birthday is next Tuesday. All the boys here have cameras and spend their time taking snap-shots. The weather has been very good, and we have played more hockey than 'rugger'! I am in the fourth form and my housemaster is called Taylor. His nickname is 'Trilby'. He is a parson and he says prayers faster than anyone I have ever heard. I hope you are well, dear Grannie, and that you are not finding Edinburgh too cold. I was first in scripture last week.

Your loving grandson,

NORMAN.

PS I have no camera.

With the right bow in my hands – and this time I had it – I could play a still better tune on this fiddle. I gave the old lady a glowing account of the Scots in Russia and the part the Bruces, the Gordons, the Hamiltons, had played in building St Petersburg and in winning Peter the Great's battles. Had not a Learmont – the very name of her house – provided Russia with her greatest poet? I dwelt on all the famous people I had met. I described the dinners given by my colleagues and by my Russian friends. My PS assured her of my unfailing belief in ultimate victory provided the cost of living could be kept down.

Perhaps in her dreams she already saw me rallying the spent Russians to the attack. Perhaps she was amused by my artfulness in the same way as she had been amused by my brother's hint about the camera. At any rate, just as he received his camera, so I received my cheques – cheques, too, for generous amounts – which relieved my financial embarrassments and enabled me at any rate to keep my end up.

May her soul rest in peace. She was a grand woman and even in the days of my failure she treated me better than I deserved. Without her I should have been completely lost in Moscow – a reflection which I feel sure will not make the members of the Chief Clerk's department sleep less comfortably in their beds. Let them not think I bear them a grudge. The Whitehall game of battledore and shuttle-cock, of vouchers and vouchers for not producing a voucher, has been played ever since the gods were on Olympus. It will be played for all time. On the whole, too, it is played in good temper by both sides. My only complaint is that in wartime the rules of the game should be relaxed.

A workers' demonstration
in St Petersburg, July,
1917. *Right*, Karl
Radek, a member of
the Central Executive
Committee

Leon Trotsky. *Below*, Alexander Kerensky (centre) and others in Moscow, *c.*1917

As 1915 drew to its end, my political work increased. The Allies were now seriously anxious about the Russian situation, and to my other labours was added the task of entertaining and shepherding the various missions sent out by France and England to stimulate the Russians to fresh efforts. Hitherto we had had a small list of more or less regular visitors. They included men like Colonel Knox (now General Sir Alfred Knox), Sir Samuel Hoare, the head of a special intelligence mission, General Sir John Hanbury-Williams, and Admiral Sir Richard Phillimore, the two British representatives attached to the Tsar's military headquarters, and the various officers attached to the different armies on the Russian front. Of these officers, Colonel Knox, who had spent many years in Russia, was by far the best informed on military matters. Very early in the war he had seen the cracks in the Russian wall, and, if the Allies formed an exaggerated idea of the Russian strength, it was certainly not the fault of the English military attaché. Up to the revolution no man took a saner view of the military situation on the Eastern front and no foreign observer supplied his Government with more reliable information.

Of the others Sir John Hanbury-Williams was a charmer, who was popular with everyone. Admiral Phillimore maintained the highest traditions of the British Navy by persisting in rising daily at seven o'clock – or was it six? – in a country where nobody stirred before nine or ten. The impression on the Russians was immense and wholly beneficial. Sir Samuel Hoare triumphed over a whole field of obstacles by the same industry and persistence which today have elevated him to Cabinet rank. His appointment to St Petersburg was not popular with the regular soldiers. It was hard to understand in what respect his mission could supplement the work which was being done by the other British organisations. He himself had no special qualifications for the task, and, when he arrived, I anticipated friction and failure. With a less tactful man the forebodings would have been justified. Sir Samuel, however, beset himself to his task with unflagging and unobtrusive enthusiasm. He learnt Russian. He worked indefatigably. He made it his business to meet every class of Russian. He gathered in his information from many fields, and, unlike most intelligence officers, he showed a fine discrimination in sifting the truth from the chaff of rumour. In short, he made good. If, at the time, anyone had asked me to lay the odds against Sir Samuel as a future leader of the Conservative Party or as a possible Prime Minister of England, I confess that I should have had no hesitation in going the limit. Now, however, I realise that the same qualities which he showed in Russia in circumstances of great difficulty have stood him in good stead in his subsequent political career. Behind Sir Samuel's small frame there is, combined with considerable ability, courage, and capacity for mastering his subject, a strong and very persistent will-power. Where eighteen years ago I should have laid a thousand to one against, today I should not give more than two to one.

These, as I have said, were our regular visitors. Now they were to be supplemented by the various side-shows. The first of these to visit Moscow was the French political mission to Romania. Its object was to counteract German influences in Bucharest and to bring Romania into the war. It was composed of Charles Richet, the eminent scientist, Georges Lacour-Gayet, the historian, and M. Gavoty, the former proprietor of the *Revue Hebdomadaire*. I saw much of all three men during their long stay in Moscow for, strangely enough, the mission was held up for weeks before it reached its destination. It was combated – and, for a long time, successfully – by the French Minister in Romania.

This visit is very memorable to me for three reasons: the first, entirely creditable, the second purely vain, and the third slightly discreditable, for which, however, my wife must share the blame. The creditable reason is that in Richet I met the greatest genius and most attractive personality I have ever known. Few men who have seen anything of the politico-military administration of the war can have any faith left in the 'great man' theory. Most of our geniuses die unrewarded, but it is quite certain that they are rarely, if ever, found in the unfertile field of politics or modern warfare. Richet, however, is a genius who has found honour in his own time. Absolutely unaffected and simple as a child, he is wholly charming in character. The first constructor of a modern aeroplane and a poet and a prose writer of distinction, he received the Nobel prize for medicine. The war took six of his seven sons, but it left no rancour in Richet's heart – no hate except of war itself. He is still living; still at the age of eighty almost alone among his countrymen in throwing his weight into the scale of international understanding against the balance of malicious self-interest and ignorant nationalism.

At that time Richet was of course a patriot – that is, he believed in an Allied victory as an essential condition to the defeat of militarism. How well, too, he pleaded the Allied case before the Russians. How quickly he understood the Russian character. After his first speech in Moscow – a wonderful performance with all the University professors on the platform – he took me aside.

'This is our war,' he said, 'your country's and mine. We must be strong in ourselves and count only on ourselves.'

The second reason why this visit remains very vividly in my memory is that it was to have furnished the occasion for my first big public speech. It is true that a few weeks before I had made my first public speech in Russian at the opening of a hospital. It had been, however, very short. At the luncheon given by the British Club to the distinguished Frenchmen I was to have made my first attempt at war propaganda on a public platform. On the eve of the luncheon I was stricken with tonsillitis and influenza. I fainted at the telephone and cut my head on the receiver as I was in the act of summoning the doctor. It was perhaps a fortunate escape. The three Frenchmen were brilliant professional orators. It was better for me to make my début among my own countrymen who, in Parliament and outside it, are in my experience (and I have visited nearly every Parliament in Europe and have heard most of the great foreign orators) the worst speakers in the world.

The third and slightly discreditable reason was the procuring by my wife of a document of considerable importance. I have said that the French mission had not been allowed to proceed to Romania owing to the protestations of M. Blondel, the French Minister of Bucharest. The three Frenchmen were very indignant and made little attempt to conceal their anger or their intention of demanding explanations when they returned to Paris. Their hands had been strengthened against their own diplomatic representative in Romania by a report by Marshal Pau, the one-armed French general, who had just completed an extensive study of the whole situation in that country. Pau's report was known to be extraordinarily frank in its criticisms, and we were very desirous of seeing the original document. During the visit one of the Frenchmen (as all three are still living, it would be unfair to say which) stayed with us in our flat.

Like most Frenchmen he was a courtier. In Paris the most severe and respected of professors, he thawed in the warm and rather licentious atmosphere of Moscow. He made my wife his confidante. He became indiscreet. One afternoon, to relieve her of a headache, he gave her the famous Pau report to read. With great presence of mind she committed it to writing, and in this manner I was able to send a complete copy to Sir George Buchanan. Soldiers have a reputation for bluntness, but the marshal's report would have shocked even the bluntest fire-eater in our own War Office. In language more effective because it was unadorned by any extravagances of style, it gave a devastating picture of conditions at the Romanian court in 1915. The marshal had spared no one. There was a thumbnail sketch of the King with chapter and verse for the numerous weaknesses of a character in which there was little to admire. There was a complete dossier of romantic adventure in high places with a 'who's who' of the personalities involved and a record of their influence and political sympathies. There was an unflattering picture of the French, British and Russian Ministers, who were accused of setting a bad example in wartime to Romanian society and of wasting their diplomatic effort by unseemly dissensions among themselves. The marshal was frankly pessimistic. Romania's subsequent entry into the war was to justify his gloominess. He thought nothing of the Romanian army. He thought still less of Allied diplomacy in Romania. The full force of his indignation was reserved for the French and Russian Ministers, whose antipathy to each other enabled the pro-German party to drive a wedge between two influences which should have been paramount. England, said the old soldier, had no historical role to play in Romania. The only influence she could usefully exert would be through the good looks of her men. She should send her best-looking military attaché to the Romanian Court. As a result of the Pau report there were changes in Romania. As her new military attaché, England sent Colonel C. B. Thomson, who was subsequently to become the personal friend of Mr Ramsay MacDonald, to be made a Labour peer and a Cabinet Minister, and to perish in the ill-fated initial voyage of the dirigible R.101.

I remember little about that second Christmas of the war except that it was gay. Russians, rightly or wrongly, never allowed depression to interfere with their festivals, nor did they try studiously to cultivate a war attitude. They were undisciplined and amoral.

Their whole effort was individual and not co-operative.

On January 1st, 1916, my wife and I spent the whole day paying official visits – one of the few really irksome duties of officialdom in Russia. The beginning of the year must have inspired more people than myself with good resolutions, for as a result of my visits my diary notes for January are remarkably optimistic. Two factors were responsible for this healthier atmosphere. Our Russo-Greek friend, Lykiardopoulos, had just returned from an adventurous journey into Austria and Germany. He had gone to obtain information for the Allies, and, disguised as a Greek tobacco merchant, had visited the leading cities of both countries. 'Lyki' had left Moscow as a profound pessimist who was convinced of the invincibility of the German arms. He returned full of optimism, quite certain that Germany was feeling the pinch more than Russia and that Russia could hold out far longer. As far as supplies were concerned he was, doubtless, right. What he had miscalculated was the difference in the resisting power of the two peoples.

His news, however, made Moscow cheerful, and for a few weeks he was a national hero. Still more encouraging was the reception of Prince Lvov and Chelnokov by the Emperor at his military headquarters in Mogiliev. The visit had been arranged by General Alexeyev, the Chief of the General Staff and a sturdy patriot, who had a soldier's contempt for the average Russian politician. When the Grand Duke Nicholas was Commander-in-Chief, the Cities and Zemstvos Unions had always addressed their petitions to him personally. Their relations with the Emperor had been less happy. Disliking the various political resolutions which they had passed, he had hitherto refused to see them. On this occasion, therefore, they came to Mogiliev to see General Alexeyev and not the Emperor. As Mayor of Moscow Chelnokov brought with him the greetings of the 'heart of Russia' to the Army and an official resolution of the City Duma affirming that no peace must be made until complete victory had been attained. General Alexeyev, knowing the immense work these great public organisations were doing in equipping the Army with every kind of supply, was determined to restore good relations between the Emperor and the two unions.

'The Emperor's all right,' he informed the two Muscovites bluntly. 'The only trouble is the band of b—— who surround him. You wait here, and I'll take the resolution to him.'

Presently he returned with the order that Chelnokov was to enter the Imperial presence. When the broad-shouldered Mayor limped into the room, the resolution was lying on the Emperor's table.

'Why was this excellent resolution not sent to me direct?' asked the Tsar.

Chelnokov stammered out some clumsy excuse about etiquette and said that, if His Imperial Majesty would allow him, he would offer him the greeting there and then. He then stood up and in his best official manner conveyed Moscow's loyal greetings to the Emperor and read the resolution. The Tsar was greatly pleased.

'I agree with everything in this resolution,' he said. 'Peace will not be made until complete victory is attained. You are right, too, in expressing your gratitude to the Army. We should go down on our knees before it.'

The Tsar then questioned Chelnokov about the situation in Moscow. The Mayor replied that there was no fuel, and not enough to eat because the railways were being run so badly and that, in these circumstances, rioting during the winter months was a possibility that could not be excluded. The Emperor replied that, if people were cold and had not enough to eat, one could not be too severe on them if they complained with violence. He asked rather suspiciously if the Mayor were not exaggerating.

Chelnokov replied: 'No.'

The Tsar then said: 'Everything I can do to alleviate this situation will be done.'

I received a full account of this visit from Chelnokov as soon as he returned to Moscow. Both Prince Lvov and he – grave, bearded men with no frivolities in their lives – were as pleased as schoolboys. They had returned from the Stavka* with a whole heartful of optimism. The Emperor had been splendid. Their own work was now to go forward unimpeded. The Army was on their side. What, then, did St Petersburg matter? The Army was more important, more powerful, than any Government.

Alas! the high hopes raised by this visit were to be rudely shattered. Impending tragedy would not allow the Emperor to deviate from the fate which had been marked out for him. A little common sense, a few words of praise, on the Emperor's part, would have been sufficient to strengthen the ties of personal loyalty, to chain to his

* The Imperial Russian headquarters.

throne the patriotic fervour of the vast bulk of the people of Russia. How small was the effort required I had seen in the enthusiasm of these two public leaders, who, considerably less revolutionary in temperament than Mr Lloyd George, were to be driven unwillingly into revolution and to become its first victims. The effort, however, was beyond the Emperor's capacity of vision. The old system continued. The national effort was cramped in every way. Every Minister who sympathised with it was sooner or later certain to be dismissed. And as, one by one, the patriots and the men of confidence disappeared, the allegiances of three hundred years were undermined by despair. In my own mind the feeling of inevitable disaster became stronger and stronger. Yet in public I had always to appear ultra-optimistic, calm and resolute, and unshakeably convinced of the ultimate victory of the Allies. If my real optimism was confined to the west, I had to simulate increasing confidence in the east. And after a time a smile which has no heart behind it becomes visibly artificial.

In February, 1916, I was summoned several times to St Petersburg. We had a new scheme on foot: an official British propaganda office in St Petersburg to be run by British journalists. Hugh Walpole and Harold Williams (greatest and most modest of all British experts on Russia) were its chief sponsors. There was to be a sub-office in Moscow. This was to be under my charge, and as my propaganda officer I engaged the versatile Lykiardopoulos. In St Petersburg the propaganda bureau was a very official organisation with special offices and a proper staff. I ran my organisation in Moscow from the Consulate-General without any flourish of trumpets and without the knowledge of the outside world. In this way I was able to bring considerable influence to bear on the local newspapers without their feeling that they were being inundated with official propaganda. This part of my work I enjoyed, although here, too, great tact was necessary, especially when it came to the selection of Moscow journalists for the literary mission, which as part of the new policy we were sending to England. The bright idea was that, when these scribes had seen the tremendous efforts being made by England, they would write them up in the Russian Press, and we should then hear less about Britain keeping her Navy in a glass case and about our willingness to fight to the last drop of Russian blood. One writer, whom I invited or was instructed to invite, was Count

A. N. Tolstoy,* a sleek, fat Bohemian with a great literary talent but a strong predilection for the creature comforts of life. Today, in order to retain these comforts, Count Tolstoy has made his peace with the Bolsheviks and, at the expense of a play or two against the Romanovs, has succeeded in remaining a bourgeois individualist in a country where even literature has been communised.

It was at this moment that I received a telegram from Sir George Buchanan requesting me to make arrangements for the reception of a British naval mission which, as part and parcel of the new propaganda policy, was being sent to Moscow. I received exactly two days' notice of this visit. No information was vouchsafed me regarding the source from which I was to draw the financial sinews for the entertainment of His Britannic Majesty's Senior Service. This conundrum is one of the rare problems which the British Government leaves invariably to the initiative and to the pocket of the man on the spot. All I knew was that the seven leading officers of our submarine flotilla in the Baltic – all very gallant gentlemen, who had sunk several German cruisers and innumerable smaller craft – would arrive on February 15th and would spend four days in Moscow. They had received instructions to put themselves unreservedly in my hands.

Both the British colony and my Russian friends rallied to my support with remarkable spontaneity and generosity. In one afternoon I completed my programme. My old friend Chelnokov promised a 'rout' at the Town Duma. Madame Nossova, the sister of the Riabushinsky brothers, the richest millionaires in Moscow, undertook to provide a whole evening's entertainment at her house, with dinner for a hundred people and dancing afterwards. Princess Gagarina arranged a reception. The Intendant of the Imperial Theatre provided at the shortest notice a special gala performance at the opera. Baliev, the owner of the 'Bat', and the Moscow Artists' Club undertook to amuse the guests in their own exhilarating and invincible manner. The British Club, without whose aid my own efforts to entertain distinguished British visitors would have been unavailing, arranged the first of those sumptuous Anglo-Russian banquets which right up to the revolution provided the flesh and bones – not

* Count Alexei Nikolayevich Tolstoy (1882–1945). Under Stalin he was elected Chairman of the Writers' Union in 1936, and a deputy to the Supreme Soviet in 1937. Not to be confused with the famous author Count Lev Nikolayevich Tolstoy.

to mention the caviare and vodka – of Anglo-Russian friendship in Moscow.

The visit was a complete success. The Navy may now have fallen on evil days, but my own experience of British naval officers abroad has been of the happiest. Far better than Army officers do they understand the gentle art of placating and impressing the foreigner. They can relax without loss of dignity. There are few brass hats and few brass heads among them.

My seven submarine officers adapted themselves to their new role of public performers with remarkable skill. They had come to be 'lionised', but they were tame and friendly lions. They allowed themselves to be stroked. They fraternised with the ballerinas and with the officials. And Cromie, their leader and an officer grave beyond his years, roared on one occasion with splendid effect. The occasion was the supper given by the Alatr – an artists' and actors' club – in honour of our youthful guests. The supper was accompanied by an impromptu entertainment during which the best dancers and singers Moscow could provide had danced and sung for the good of our digestion. When the evening was well advanced, nothing would satisfy the Russians but that Cromie should make a speech. He was taken up on to the small stage. A tall, dark Byronesque figure with heavy eyebrows and side-whiskers, he faced his audience without a tremor.

'Ladies and gentlemen,' he said. 'You are all artists – musicians, poets, novelists, painters, composers. You are creators. What you create will live long after you. We are only simple sailors. We destroy. But we can say truthfully that in this war we destroy in order that your works may live.'

It was the shortest and in the effect it produced the most impressive speech I ever heard in Russia.

The Russians were delighted. The visit of the submarine officers coincided with the capture of Erzerum by the Russian army in the Caucasus, and for four days we lived in an atmosphere of jubilant optimism. As far as I was concerned, there was only one flaw in a programme which was carried out with harmonious smoothness. At the British Club dinner I made my first big speech. For two days I had rehearsed it before my wife and the faithful 'Lyki', who as secretary of the Moscow Art Theatre was an expert in elocution. I delivered it with emotion and modesty. There was a touching reference to those who in the literal sense of the words go down to the sea in ships. My oratory drew tears from my audience and from myself. But to my chagrin my speech was not reported. The Russian naval staff, fearful of what might happen to the Baltic fleet if the Germans were to know that the British submarine commanders were absent from their ships, had imposed the strictest censorship on the whole visit.

With the departure of the naval mission Moscow returned to its primordial pessimism – a depression distinct from the pessimism of St Petersburg in that it was free from malevolent pacifism. Moscow was prepared to fight to the end. It could not help feeling that the end was likely to be disastrous.

At this particular moment these forebodings were aggravated by the German offensive against Verdun and by the influx of aristocratic Polish refugees into Moscow. These Poles were an unhealthy influence. Superficially, they were attractive. They added to the amenities of Moscow social life. Their passion for political discussion provided fresh material for my reports. But, much as I was inclined to sympathise with their sufferings, closer acquaintance changed my sympathy into mistrust and even dislike. I found it natural that they should hate Russia. I could not tolerate the manner in which they accepted the warm hospitality that was offered to them everywhere and which they repaid by sneering at their hosts and hostesses and by affecting to despise the good Moscow bourgeois. Still less could I stomach their self-centred vanity and their pessimism. The climax came when, one evening, during the most critical period of the Verdun offensive, a frivolous but vain princeling remarked in the presence of the head of the French military mission: 'If Verdun is taken, Paris, too, will fall. What a terrible thing that will be for the Polish question.' This is only one of many examples of Polish tactlessness. Yet these people, who have never been able to help themselves and who certainly contributed little to the Allied cause in the war, have been rewarded with the largest slice of territory granted to any nation under the Treaty of Versailles.

In that spring of 1916 I had throat trouble again. This time it was accompanied by a bad attack of depression. Everything seemed to be going wrong. Even Chelnokov had complained to me about the failure of English firms to fulfil their war contracts, and for the first time I began to question the ability of the Allies to win through. My gloom was only partly relieved by a surprise visit from Hugh Walpole, resplendent in a Red Cross uniform and as tremendously enthusiastic and as refreshingly sentimental as ever. He had just returned from England, where the first of his Russian books, *The Dark Forest*, had had a great success. He brought me sugar and spice in the form of complimentary appreciation of my work from Lord Robert Cecil and other members of the Foreign Office. When he left, my depression returned, and with the arrival of Easter my wife induced me to take a few days' rest.

In order that I might have a change from Moscow, we went down to Sergievo, to the famous monastery. The indispensable Alexander had made the most elaborate preparations for our reception. Actually there was not much rest about our visit. We arrived on Thursday evening in Holy Week and were met at the station by a monk. By another monk we were driven straight from the station to a long service. The monastery itself, the most famous in Russia, was a miniature Kremlin, surrounded by a wall which was broad enough to allow two carriages to drive abreast along its cobbled stones. The place had stood a hundred sieges in the course of its history, and but for the presence of the monks was much more like a fortress than a place of worship.

After the service we had tea with the abbot – a fine, simple old gentleman with a flaxen beard and soft, spongy hands which he washed incessantly. It was nearly seven o'clock before we were allowed to seek our quarters – a little monastery hotel attached to the Church of the Chernigov Madonna about a mile from the monastery. Fortunately, it was very clean and comfortable.

On Good Friday the rain came down in torrents, and I stayed indoors all day and read the Sir Roger de Coverley papers* from the

* A series of articles by Joseph Addison and Richard Steele which recounts the adventures of the fictional Sir Roger de Coverley, 'a gentleman that is very singular in his behaviour'.

Spectator. On the Saturday, however, we were plunged again into a round of sightseeing and religious services. Early in the morning a monk waited on us to drive us to the Bethlehem monastery – a beautiful little place beside a lake about three miles away. Then in the evening we drove through the birch woods to attend the midnight service at the Lavra itself. The whole monastery was illuminated by electric light, and against the deep purple background of the sky the huge belfry stood out like a giant skyscraper. The service was impressive. For over an hour we stood in an evil-smelling crowd of soldiers and peasants all holding candles and tapers and sprinkling themselves and us liberally with candle-grease. So ineffable, however, was the singing that we never felt the fatigue.

The next two days were sheer joy. There was a warmth in the sun which banished all my fears and all my pessimism. The whole countryside was a mass of primroses and cowslips. White churches nestled peacefully in a background of birch trees. Above all, there were lakes with perch and carp as old as time itself. After Moscow the peacefulness of it all was wonderful.

On Easter Monday we attended another service and took part in a procession round the great wall of the Lavra, walking in the place of honour just behind the Archimandrites. We had, too, a stupendous luncheon, consisting of some six or seven courses of different fish, with the abbot, and while we ate, he spoke good words to us. In his conversation there was nothing martial, no 'God with us' boastfulness. He spoke of miracles, in which he was a firm believer – and, indeed, if Russia was to win the war, a belief in miracles was necessary – and of the virtues of Christian submission and of a contrite and holy spirit.

For the most part, however, we made long trips into the country, extracting the maximum of enjoyment from our stolen leisure and reaping the full benefit from the glorious sunshine. One drive, in particular, I remember very vividly – a long, rambling adventure along a narrow, disused track to a lake beyond the St Paraclete monastery. Our way ran through a narrow gorge covered with gorse and brambles, and neither coming nor going did we pass a living soul. It was almost the most perfect hour of complete contentment that I can remember.

I returned to Moscow full of energy and fresh hope and better able to battle with the irritations of my daily life. For, much as I loved my Russian friends, they *were* irritating. They were a charming people to know, a hopeless people to work with, and, fatalistic as I became, I never quite mastered the nuances of a language in which 'at once' means 'tomorrow', and 'tomorrow', 'never'.

I cannot illustrate better the difference between the Russian and the English attitudes towards life than by a reference to a Russian trial which took place at this time. In some of its aspects it bears a certain resemblance to the famous Malcolm trial in England. In Warsaw a Russian police officer called Zlatoustovsky had fallen in love with a certain Madame Marchevsky, the wife of an officer who was fighting for his country at the front. When Warsaw was evacuated, Zlatoustovsky (his name in Russian means golden-mouthed!) brought the woman to Moscow and took her to live with him in his own flat. Warned by a letter from the police officer's wife, Marchevsky came back from the front and tried to break into Zlatoustovsky's flat. Zlatoustovsky then emptied his revolver through the door and killed Marchevsky, who was unarmed. In spite of the bad conduct of the police officer in the whole case, he was acquitted. Public opinion made no protest against the verdict, nor did Zlatoustovsky lose his job.

Renewing my contact with Chelnokov and the other Moscow leaders, I found them more depressed than usual. The resignation of Polivanov, the War Minister, who had been dismissed for his too friendly co-operation with the public organisations, had made them downhearted. The fall of Kut, following on our failure in Gallipoli, and the Easter rising in Dublin had been a severe blow to British prestige. Chelnokov and I laid our heads together. What could we do to stimulate public confidence? How could we checkmate defeatism and lack of faith in the Western Allies? The Mayor, whose Anglophilism was proof against all shocks, suggested an official visit of the British Ambassador to Moscow. I said I was sure he would come if the visit would do good.

'We might give him the freedom of the city of Moscow,' said Chelnokov.

'Excellent,' I replied, 'it is in the best English tradition.'

There was, however, one drawback. Only one foreigner had ever been made a freeman of Moscow. The honour had never been conferred on an Englishman. It was a rare and precious gift, and it could be conferred only by a unanimous vote of the Town Council. Now the Town Duma was a replica of the State Duma. It was composed of representatives of all the political parties, including the extreme Right, which was not very pro-English and definitely opposed to the liberal parties. It was quite impossible for Chelnokov, even as Mayor, to obtain a unanimous decision. He stroked his long, patriarchal beard. Then, in his fine, deep voice, he gave me his considered opinion.

'I know my colleagues,' he said. 'They are like children. They will never accept a suggestion coming from me. But if you go to see the various leaders separately, tell them that Sir George Buchanan is coming to Moscow, and let them think that the suggestion of the freedom comes from them – well, if you do your work cleverly, they will jump at it.'

I carried out the plan exactly as he prescribed. I saw Nikolai Guchkov, Victor Briansky, and the other refractory leaders, and with the unanimous decision of the Duma in my pocket I went to see the Ambassador.

The visit, on my suggestion, took place on Empire Day. It was, I believe, the first occasion on which Empire Day was celebrated officially in Russia, and it was from first to last an immense success. The whole city showed a united front in welcoming the Ambassador. 'Black Hundred'* lions lay down with 'Cadet' lambs. Octobrists† and Social-Revolutionaries vied with one another in the vehemence of their protestations of friendship and of their determination to fight to a victorious end. The generals and officials fell over each other in their eagerness to contribute their share to the festivities. I wrote an Empire leader for the leading Moscow newspaper. Obviously, even at that moment, I was qualifying for my Empire Crusader's badge. I wrote an appreciation of Sir George Buchanan for the second most important Moscow newspaper. I persuaded the Ambassador to write his speech beforehand, enlisted the services of Lykiardopoulos to translate it, and had a beautifully printed Russian translation served with the caviare to our distinguished Russian guests. At the Empire banquet that evening I proposed the Ambassador's health in a speech, which a Moscow reporter described as a masterpiece of dignified eloquence and self-confidence. Alas! that was sixteen years ago.

* 'Black Hundreds' constituted the extreme right wing in Russian politics.
† Moderate reformists.

The Ambassador himself, as the main arch in this glorious edifice, was splendid. He was the most elegant figure that Moscow had seen for several generations, and his gentle manner and his obvious sincerity went straight to every Russian heart. The happiest omens were augured from his Christian name. Was not St George the patron saint of Moscow? In that hour the tide of Anglo-Russian friendship was at the flood.

There was, in fact, only one slight hitch to mar the perfection of the setting. On the next night the city fathers in solemn sitting, surrounded by all that was best and brightest in Moscow Society, formally conferred on his Super-Excellency Sir George Buchanan, Ambassador Extraordinary and Plenipotentiary of His Britannic Majesty to the Emperor of all the Russias, the title of honorary hereditary citizen of the city of Moscow. With the scroll of honour were conferred other more substantial gifts: a priceless icon and a loving cup. In the heart of Russia it was necessary for our man to say at least a word or two in Russian. Alas! Sir George was no Russian scholar. 'Benji' Bruce and I had reduced the formula to the least common denominator and we had carefully rehearsed the Ambassador to say, when he received the loving cup, 'spasibo', which is the shortest and most colloquial Russian term for 'thank you'. When the fateful moment came, the Comptroller of tongues intervened, and in a firm but low voice Sir George was heard to say: 'za pivo,' which, being interpreted, means 'for beer'!

No philological inexactitude, however, could mar the whirlwind success of those two triumphant days. Chelnokov was elated. I was elated. We felt we had scotched the German in our midst. Sir George himself was quietly emotional and grateful. As I said goodbye to him on the station platform, he took my hand in his.

'Lockhart,' he said, 'this is the happiest day in my life, and I owe it all to you.'

Sir George Buchanan's visit, as I see it now, was the turning point in my official career. It marked the zenith of my own influence with the Ambassador. It was the last occasion on which I was conscious of the youthful enthusiasm of hero-worship. True it is that it gave me a new confidence in my own ability. In the future I was to face the Foreign Office with the aggressiveness of a bumptious lion. But with increased confidence came a falling-away in my own character. I had become an oracle, and oracles are apt to be too cocksure. Perhaps at the time I was unconscious of my shortcomings. Perhaps I scarcely realised the wearing effect of months of excessive work on a highly strung temperament. Be this as it may, many of my ideals of 1914 had disappeared in the welter of inefficiency which surrounded me, and with their departure came a relaxation of my own self-discipline. The highest form of vanity is fame. I do not say that I have never had it, but it has never been able to compete with my passion for self-indulgence. The romance of the war had gone and with it all hope of a Russian victory. From now on there were to be no illuminating intervals to dispel the gloom which had settled like a pall over the prostrate body of Russia.

As far as my personal feelings were concerned, the first shock came within a few days of the Ambassador's departure. During his visit he had told me in strictest confidence – a confidence not to be broken even in the case of my wife – that Lord Kitchener was coming to Russia. The great man would visit Moscow. I was to hold myself in readiness to attend to all his desires. Even now I might begin discreetly to mark down in the antique shops any genuine examples of old china, in which Lord Kitchener was greatly interested.

Within the next few days half a dozen Russian journalists must have telephoned to ask me if the news were true. At my wife's weekly reception General Wogak, a charming, cultured soldier, who had at one time been military attaché in Peking and Washington, announced the visit, with its date and object, as if no secrecy were needed. Long before Kitchener had sailed from Scotland the news of his mission was common property in both St Petersburg and Moscow.

I quote these indiscretions merely as an instance of the leakages that were so frequent in the Russia of these war days. I do not suggest that they bore any relation to the sinking of the ill-starred *Hampshire*.*

I never met Lord Kitchener. I am, therefore, not in a position to say authoritatively what he might or might not have done in Russia. I venture, however, to doubt the opinion, so frequently expressed by English writers on Russia, that, if he had come face to face with the Tsar, the whole course of the war would have been

* Kitchener was drowned when HMS *Hampshire*, en route to Russia, struck a mine off Orkney in June, 1916.

94

changed. I have little faith in the great man theory – perhaps because I have the valet mind. The strength of nations is in their collective force. Strong nations produce strong men. Weak nations go to the wall. But, even admitting that Kitchener was a superman, I do not believe that his influence on the Tsar would have been more than ephemeral. Even strong men cannot compete with nature. In any case, his visit would have been too late. The inexorable hand of Fate was already stretched out over the ruling class of Russia.

Nevertheless, the tragedy of Kitchener was a disaster which aggravated the sickness of the Russian body and the faintness of the Russian heart.

It was followed by another shock which had even more serious repercussions on the Russian situation. Early in August, Sazonov, the pro-Ally Russian Minister of Foreign Affairs, resigned or, to be accurate, was forced to resign. The circumstances of his dismissal were similar to those in which other loyal and pro-war Ministers had been dismissed. For some time he had felt insecure. He had, therefore, been to the Stavka (Russian headquarters) to see the Emperor. He had been delighted with his reception. On his return to St Petersburg his train had crossed the train bearing M. Stürmer, the most unpopular of all the Tsar's Prime Ministers, to headquarters. Almost before M. Sazonov reached St Petersburg the Emperor had reversed his plans. M. Sazonov was requested to take a holiday in Finland. His dismissal followed soon afterwards. The forces of darkness had triumphed once again.

M. Sazonov was an honest, if not a great, man. He had been most loyal in his co-operation with Sir George Buchanan and M. Paléologue, the French Ambassador. He had sought to work with the Duma and was trusted by the public organisations. His name figured in every list of 'cabinets of public confidence' which were the favourite pastime of the liberals and the maxima of their demands at that time. A firm supporter of the monarchy, he was one of the few men whose advice, if it had been listened to, might have kept the last Romanov on his throne. His place in the Russian Foreign Office was taken by Stürmer himself, and even in the drawing-rooms of the Grand Dukes the new appointment was received with scowls and bitterness. Under the strain of so much madness the last props of Tsardom were falling away. Amongst the patriots depression assumed the proportions of hopelessness.

Sazonov has embellished the history of diplomacy with one imperishable anecdote. I did not hear him tell it. When I saw him again in Prague some years after the revolution, he neither admitted nor denied its authenticity. I am assured, however, that the story is true in substance, if not in detail. This is the generally accepted version:

There had been a dinner-party at the British Embassy at which both Sazonov and the French Ambassador were present. After dinner the three 'big shots' – Sazonov, Sir George Buchanan and M. Paléologue – had retired to the Ambassador's study to discuss the situation over their cigars. The conversation had turned to diplomacy. What nation supplied the finest diplomats? M. Paléologue, who was a Frenchman and therefore a flatterer, was loud in his praise of the Russians. Sir George, who was a Scot and, therefore, strictly honest, gave his vote to the Germans. They argued the point without being able to agree and finally appealed to Sazonov. The Russian smiled.

'Your Excellencies', he said, 'are both wrong. In my opinion there can be no question of dispute. The palm belongs surely to the English.'

M. Paléologue, already sufficiently jealous of Sir George, made a sour face. Sir George's eyes registered an innocent astonishment.

Again Sazonov smiled.

'You would like my explanation. When I have given it, you will admit that my argument is irresistible. We Russians – and I thank M. Paléologue for his compliment – are a talented race. We are admirable linguists. Our sources of knowledge are unlimited. Unfortunately, however, we cannot trust ourselves. There is no continuity about our work. We never know what our most trusted Ambassadors are going to do next. They may fall a hopeless victim to the first unscrupulous woman, and in that condition they are capable of selling the ciphers to the enemy.

'Now the Germans are just the reverse. They are admirable workers. They are all continuity. But they begin laying their plans so many years beforehand that, long before the plot is hatched, the whole world knows what they intend to do.

'The whole art of diplomacy is to mask one's intentions. And that is where the English excel. No one ever knows what *they* intend to do' – here the Russian stroked his beard and smiled affectionately at Sir George – 'because they never know themselves.'

Assuredly, the dismissal of a man who knew the Allies so well was a heavy loss to the Allied cause.

The story of the next few months leading up to the first revolution is a chronicle of almost unrelieved pessimism: failures on the front (the Brusilov offensive against Austria had flattered only to deceive), boredom and ennui in official circles in the rear, bewildering changes of Ministers, impotent protestations by the Duma, increasing discontent and murmurs not only in the villages, but also in the trenches.

In St Petersburg and even in Moscow the war had become of secondary importance. The approaching cataclysm was already in every mind, and on everybody's lips. The ruling class, awakened at last to the impending disaster, sought to warn the Emperor. Political resolutions, passed now, not only by the liberals, but by the nobility, were showered like autumn leaves upon the Emperor. There was no disloyalty in these addresses. They merely begged the Tsar to change his counsellors, to replace them with men enjoying the confidence of the country. The Emperor made changes with the rapidity of a card-trick expert, but very rarely did they satisfy public opinion. On no occasion were they ever made in response to the demand, however discreetly made, of a public body. For this man of all the domestic virtues, this man of no vices and no will-power, was an autocrat by divine right. He could change his mind four times in as many minutes, but he could never forget his inheritance.

'What is all this talk about the people's confidence?' he said. 'Let the people merit *my* confidence.'

During these last six months of the monarchy my Consulate-General became a kind of post-box for complaints. My time was occupied in translating resolutions – today I still have scores of them among my private papers – and lampoons. At this time there was a salon poet called Miatliev, a cavalry officer with a knack for versification, which he employed to attack the more unpopular members of the Government. I translated the resolutions into prose. I paraphrased Miatliev into English doggerel. I sent both prose and verse to the Embassy. In the end it must have been wearied by my wasted energy.

The tragedy was that both the resolutions and the lampoons were written by men who had no thought of revolution in their hearts, who earnestly desired a more efficient prosecution of the war, and who today, if they were alive, would give their right hand to replace the Emperor or, at least, *an* Emperor on the throne of Russia.

As far as Moscow is concerned, I do not exaggerate. I was in almost daily contact with the men who, sorely against their wish, formed the first Provisional Government after the abdication of the Tsar:* Prince Lvov, Chelnokov, Manuilov, Avinov, Maklakov, Novikov, Kokoshkin. From intimate personal intercourse I knew that they were appalled by the problem which confronted them as Russian patriots. The problem itself was very succinctly put by Maklakov, the famous Russian orator and subsequent Ambassador of the Provisional Government in Paris, in one of those parables in which, owing to the censor, Russians were experts. A motor car is going down a steep hill. At the bottom there is a yawning precipice. Your mother is seated in the front seat next to the driver. You yourself are in the back seat. Suddenly you realise that the driver has lost control. What are you to do?

As one of those quandaries set as a competition in the popular Press, it would have been an interesting conundrum, which would have evoked entirely satisfactory answers from Mr Lansbury, Sir Malcolm Campbell, Miss Ethel Mannin, Lord Castlerosse, and Lady Inverclyde;† in the life of a nation, plunged in the vortex of a world war, it was a matter of life or death. In this case there was no attempt at a solution. The driver was left to run his car over the precipice.

During that torrid summer visitors came to Moscow and went – English generals, Locker-Lampson's armoured car unit,‡ English journalists, the Grand Duke Michael, the brother of the Tsar. I entertained the English visitors and listened to their views. I had a long and rather futile conversation with the Grand Duke Michael when he came to a private show of some French war films. In his Cossack uniform he made a pleasant impression. A tall, handsome figure of a man with charming manners and an easy-going disposition, he

* Tsar Nicholas II abdicated on March 15th, 1917.
† George Lansbury (1859–1940), leader of the Labour Party 1931–5; Sir Malcolm Campbell (1885–1949), holder of land and water speed records from 1927 onwards; Ethel Mannin (1900–84), author; Lord Castlerosse (1891–1943), Press magnate and popular columnist; Lady Inverclyde (*c.*1900–85), actress.
‡ Under the leadership of Commander Oliver Locker-Lampson, the Royal Navy's Russian Armoured Car Division fought alongside the White Army from 1916 until 1918.

struck me as a prince who might have made an excellent constitutional monarch. He talked quite freely about the war, about the lack of munitions and the need for an improved transport system, but he made only one remark which could be interpreted as political. 'Thank God,' he said, 'the atmosphere at the front is far better than the atmosphere of St Petersburg.' He was the quietest and perhaps the least confident of all the Grand Dukes.

When summer passed into winter there were more visits to the Embassy. There was one gala dinner given by Sir George Buchanan to Chelnokov and a small deputation of the Moscow Duma – a return for the hospitality lavished on the Ambassador during his Moscow visit. Chelnokov and I travelled to St Petersburg together. At the dinner he singled me out for special praise, greeting me in his speech as a true friend of Russia.

I was invited to luncheon by the French Ambassador. I had a one-sided conversation with Sazonov, who asked many questions and vouchsafed no information. The young man from Moscow was an object of interest.

But – and it was a big but – I found the atmosphere of St Petersburg more depressing than ever. Champagne flowed like water. The Astoria and the Europe – the two best hotels in the capital – were thronged with officers who should have been at the front. There was no disgrace in being a 'shirker' or in finding a sinecure in the rear. I had an impression of senseless ennui and *fin de siècle*. And in the streets were the long queues of ill-clad men and garrulous women, waiting for the bread that never came. Even in the Embassy hope had sunk to a low ebb. Sir George himself looked tired and ill. He still wore his hat at the same rakish angle. Never for one moment did he relax his optimism in the presence of the Russians. But, when he walked, his shoulders drooped as though his burdens were more than he could bear. In the Chancery there were signs of frayed nerves – the inevitable result of long months of monotonous and profitless work. My own conduct was puerile and reprehensible. I protracted my visits longer than was necessary, making bogus excuses of work in order to go to Russian parties and to be entertained by those whom I had entertained in Moscow. I drank the champagne – more than was good for me – of those I criticised, and I returned to Moscow ashamed and unhappy. My life at this moment gave me no satisfaction.

With the advent of December the tone of the various anti-Government resolutions became bolder. In the factories the Social-Democrats and the Social-Revolutionaries were now conducting an active revolutionary propaganda. Goaded to fury by the inanities of Protopopov – a former liberal member of the Duma, who as Minister of the Interior revealed himself as more reactionary than any member of the Black Hundred – the Zemstvos and Cities Unions defied his action in forbidding their Congress by passing a secret resolution which in the violence of its language exceeded all their previous political demands. There was, it is true, no word against the Emperor, but after a long preamble, in which full emphasis was laid on the ills from which Russia was suffering, the resolution declared that 'the Government, now become an instrument of the dark forces, is driving Russia to her ruin and is shattering the Imperial throne. In this grave hour in its history the country requires a Government worthy of a great people. Let the Duma, in the decisive struggle which it is waging, justify the expectations of the people. There is not a day to lose!'

This document was only secret in so far as it was forbidden to be published. It was circulated in roneoscript in thousands of copies, both at the front and in the rear.

This resolution was passed just before Christmas. Two days before the end of the year Rasputin was assassinated. The story has been told too often to bear retelling. Of the three participants in this perhaps mistaken act of patriotism only the Grand Duke Dmitri was known to me personally at the time. All three – the two others were Prince Felix Yusupov and M. Purishkevich – were supporters of the old régime. Their act was intended to save the old régime. Although for a moment it raised the hopes of the patriots, its only effect, viewed today in the light of history, was to assist the anti-war elements and to hasten the revolution, which unbiased observers had long realised was sooner or later inevitable.

The only person to benefit from this assassination was the Grand Duke Dmitri – the best-intentioned and most pro-English of the Grand Dukes. The banishment to the Caucasus which his complicity in the murder brought down upon his head enabled him to escape through Persia, when the revolution broke out, and to avoid the terrible fate which was meted out by the Bolsheviks to so many of his relations.

Before the lamp of Tsardom was finally extinguished, it was to flicker up in one last feeble flame of hope. Towards the end of January, 1917, an inter-Allied delegation arrived in St Petersburg. The object of this visit was to secure a more efficient co-operation between the Allies to put the final dots on the 'i's' of the peace terms, and to consecrate the victory which was always on the lips of the French and English and in which so few Russians now believed. Rarely in the history of great wars can so many important Ministers and generals have left their respective countries on so useless an errand. The British mission was the largest. It was headed by Lord Milner, who had with him as his political advisers Lord Revelstoke and George Clerk,* and as his military advisers Sir Henry Wilson and five other generals. The French were more economical. They sent only one politician – M. Doumergue – and two generals, one of whom, however, was the gallant Castelnau.† The Italian mission was headed by Signor Scialoja, who was supported by General Ruggieri.

In the presence of so much magnificence my own little star sank into insignificance. Nevertheless, I had my part in the proceedings. The mission was to visit Moscow, and I was summoned to St Petersburg to discuss the situation and arrange the programme with Lord Milner. Moscow, as usual, had set high store by the arrival of the delegation, hoping for some last-minute action by the Allies, which would restore the fallen fortunes of Russia. Such hopes as may have been raised in my own breast were shattered as soon as I arrived in St Petersburg. I lunched with Lord Milner at the British Embassy. I had a long talk with him in the afternoon, and in the evening I dined alone with him in his rooms at the Europe. I think he was glad to escape at least for one night from the interminable round of festivity to which he and the other delegates were being subjected. Of all the great figures in public life with whom I have come into contact I found him the most understanding and sympathetic. He was, too, extraordinarily well informed about facts and figures, which he seemed to carry in his head without effort. I doubt if his intuition was as remarkable as his knowledge. But from the first day of his arrival he had realised the inefficiency of the Russians, and he made

* Later Sir George Clerk, HM Ambassador to Turkey.
† General N. M. J. E. de Curières de Castelnau (1851–1944), commander of the Second Army in 1914, and of the Central Army Group in 1915.

no attempt to conceal his opinion that he was wasting his time. He looked tired and overworked, but he listened to me with infinite patience. He was, I believe, at his best with young men, and I, like most other young men, fell at once before his charm. He asked me several questions, and I gave him my opinion candidly: that if some concession was not made to public opinion trouble was inevitable. He sighed.

'I do not say you are wrong,' he said gently. 'But I am bound to tell you two things. First, the general consensus of informed opinion, both Allied and Russian, in St Petersburg, so far as I can gather, is that there will be no revolution until after the war. And, secondly, I see no means of enforcing the concessions to which you refer.'

The next day I returned to Moscow, and Lord Milner resumed his place at the conference table. And, while the delegates were discussing Constantinople, Alsace-Lorraine, and the spoils of war, there were riots round the bread-shops, workmen were being arrested by the Okhrana, and in the entourage of the Imperial family frightened women were repeating the prophecy of Rasputin: 'If I die or you abandon me, you will lose your son and your throne within six months.'

A week later Lord Milner, accompanied by Lord Revelstoke and George Clerk, came to Moscow. (Sir Henry Wilson and the other British generals had gone to the front. Their visit was to come later.) To the end of his life Lord Milner never forgot those two days in Moscow. They were the last nail in the coffin of his discomfort. There was a reception at the Town Duma at which he had to make a speech and to present Chelnokov with the KCMG, which the King had conferred upon him as a reward for his services to the Anglo-Russian entente. (Poor Chelnokov. This was the final hour of his reign as Mayor. When the revolution came, he had to flee the country, leaving his precious KCMG behind. Today, he is dying of cancer in the Belgrade Russian hospital. When I saw him there a few years ago, he expressed the wish that fresh insignia might be given to him. I tried to obtain a new Order for him through the Foreign Office and was informed that he would have to purchase it himself!) There was an Anglo-Russian luncheon, which lasted five hours, and at which various members of the Imperial Duma were determined to deliver their set speeches even at the risk of prolonging luncheon into dinner. The unfortunate Englishman, who understood no Russian and who, doubtless, would have liked to see something of the Kremlin and the ancient city, was chained to his duty from early morning to late night. I cannot congratulate myself on my staff work on this occasion.

And yet the visit was the occasion of one historical meeting. I arranged a private interview between Prince Lvov and Chelnokov on the one side and Lord Milner and George Clerk on the other. I acted as interpreter. Prince Lvov, a quiet, grey-bearded man, tired out with overwork, spoke with great moderation. But lest there should be any doubt as to his views he brought a written memorandum with him. It was a long document, but the gist of it was that, if there was no change in the attitude of the Emperor, there would be a revolution within three weeks.

My duties were not ended when I had put Lord Milner to bed. I had my report to send to the Embassy. There was George Clerk, determined to see something of Moscow by night, and still young enough to sacrifice his sleep to his determination. Enlisting the services of a young Russian millionaire, we took him to a gypsy party – doubtless one of the last of the great gypsy parties celebrated under the monarchy. Goodness knows what it cost. I could not have paid. There were eight of us: four English and four Russians, and as the guest of honour George Clerk had to bear the brunt of the champagne bombardment. My young Russian millionaire did his best. Maria Nikolayevna sang countless 'charochki', and with her own hands offered countless bumpers to George Clerk. As a diplomat he has had many triumphs, but never has he borne himself more bravely than on that last evening in Moscow. He never refused a toast. He drank each one down in the approved Russian manner, and his monocle never moved. Not a hair of his head was ruffled. There was neither flush nor pallor on his cheeks.

In the early hours of the morning Prokhorov, my young millionaire officer, signed the bill and distributed the necessary largesse, and we set off home; my wife, George Clerk, 'Jimmie' Valentine and I in one car; Prokhorov and his Russian friends showing the way in another. A quarter of a mile down the road we passed him. He had pulled up beside a policeman and was standing in the road. For George Clerk's edification we stopped to watch. Prokhorov was fumbling in his pockets. He pulled out his purse and handed a rouble to the policeman, who clicked his heels together and saluted. His hand on his sword, Prokhorov drew himself up to his full height. There was a sparkle in his eye, and he looked as though he were about to lead a charge.

'Boje Tsaria Khranee!' he thundered. 'God save the Tsar,' repeated the policeman. And 'bey Jidoff!' (beat the Jews).

We drove on. Prokhorov did not hate the Jews. In so far as he had any political views he was a liberal. But he would go on with his 'God save the Tsar and beat the Jews' refrain all the way home. It was the prescribed ritual. It was the pre-revolutionary tradition.

Lord Milner and George Clerk having returned to St Petersburg, we were promptly inflicted with the military invasion of Sir Henry Wilson and his brother officers. There was no political significance attached to this visit. Yet it nearly ruined my relations with my Russian friends and involved me in one of the most uncomfortable incidents in my official life.

The generals had come to Moscow, not for business but for relaxation. They had had their bellyful of official entertaining. In any case they were not interested in the political views of Moscow malcontents or, for that matter, of a beardless Consular officer. What could I do to amuse them? Could I arrange a small dinner and a dance for them? And, as they were fifteen strong, need I invite the husbands? This was the burden of my conversation with Sir Henry Wilson on his arrival, and, anxious to please so great a soldier, I rushed away to fulfil his commands.

I sought the assistance of my wife. She rang up the wives of the Russians who throughout the war had done most to help us to entertain the various English missions which had visited Moscow. With delicious zest they entered into the spirit of the adventure, and before luncheon time we had arranged an almost perfect party. Need I say that our invitations had been extended only to the young and pretty wives and that their husbands had not been taken into their confidence. Oh, egregious, over-zealous youth!

The party was held in a private room in the Hermitage restaurant. The food, the wines, were the best that Moscow could provide. The orchestra was Korsch, and in honour of the English guests Krysh played 'Love Me and the World is Mine' with even more than his usual feeling. The party was a complete success. It was friendly. It was decorous. In the presence of such pillars of respectability as General Clive, Lord Duncannon (today Lord Bessborough), and Sir

Henry Wilson himself how could it have been otherwise? And yet in this fold of innocents there was one black sheep. Lord Brooke asked if he might bring a friend to the dinner. She was unknown to my Moscow friends. She was an aristocrat. She had been divorced. Worst of all, she came from St Petersburg.

Let me hasten to say that both she and Lord Brooke behaved even more decorously than the most decorous member of this decorous gathering. But the mischief was done. And at an early hour next morning my telephone buzzed incessantly with calls from irate husbands demanding apologies for my conduct. The final blow came when my richest, most influential Russian friend called at the Consulate-General and asked to speak to me. He was shown into my room. He walked up to my desk and clicked his heels. There was a look of steel in his eyes.

'Roman Romanovich,' he said, 'You were my friend. I consider it my duty to inform you that your conduct in inviting my wife without me last night was ungentlemanly. Goodbye.'

And, righteously indignant, he strode out of the room.

It took me weeks of arduous attention to gather up the fragments of my broken friendships.

A few days later the assembled delegations left for England, France and Italy. There were no bands to play them off, no official farewells. They travelled via Murmansk, where the *Kildonan Castle* was waiting to pick them up, and, mindful of the fate of Kitchener, they kept the day and the hour of their departure secret. And, in order that the secret might be better guarded, they sacrificed their shoes, which, at the request of those responsible for their safety, were left outside their bedroom doors long after the occupants had stolen away.

There is a story current that on his return to England Lord Milner wrote a Cabinet report in which he expressed his firm conviction that there would be no revolution, and that before the ink on it was dry the revolution had already started.

I have been unable to verify the authenticity of this account, which was given to me by a Cabinet Minister. But for the respect in which I hold Lord Milner's memory I should like to believe that it were true. It is an ending which flatters my complacency as much as it appeals to my sense of the dramatic. After all, I had given an accurate forecast, and it had been disregarded.

Truth, however, compels me to doubt if Lord Milner ever wrote such a report or made such a categorical expression of his opinion. The Foreign Office, it is true, was furnished with a report which began: 'It may seem presumptuous in one who has spent only a fortnight in Russia,' and which ended with a bold prophecy that there would be no revolution. But that report was not signed by Lord Milner.

Nor was there anything in Lord Milner's attitude during his Russian visit, or in the numerous conversations which I had with him, to give the impression that he had any confidence in the permanence of the Tsarist régime. What advice he gave to Mr Lloyd George I do not know, but I cannot believe that it was optimistic. Sir Samuel Hoare, who accompanied the Milner mission on its return journey to England and whose evidence cannot be lightly disregarded, is emphatic in his statement that all the members of the mission were mistaken in almost all their conclusions and that their reports, written on the *Kildonan Castle*, were absurdly over-confident.

In spite of Sir Samuel's evidence I still maintain that Lord Milner's optimism must have been qualified. His Russian visit cast a gloom over him which could not have been dispelled by the exuberance of his subordinates. Certainly, there was no evidence of optimism in his subsequent letters to those British officials who remained in Russia. One quotation will suffice – an extract from a letter written to 'Benji' Bruce, the head of the Embassy Chancery, a few weeks after Lord Milner had returned to London. It runs as follows: 'Alas! alas! I fear all the missions of British Labour leaders and all the compliments we have showered on the Russian revolution – "triumph of democracy", "the union of free peoples against the tyrants", etc., etc., are perfectly futile. It is evident to me that, intentionally or not, Russia is going out of the war. It must be heartbreaking for your Chief, who has done so much in the past to cement the friendship between Russia and England, and who would have averted the catastrophe which has actually occurred if his advice had been listened to. Even now he seems to be managing wonderfully in a very difficult situation, but I fear no steering is of much avail in the teeth of such a typhoon.'

This does not read much like optimism. One thing is certain. If this mission did not open the eyes of its members to the state of Russia, it was useless even as an object-lesson to the Western Allies. As far as Russia was concerned, it might just as well have remained in London, Rome and Paris.

On March 12th, less than three weeks after the departure of the Allied delegates, the storm broke, and in a night a bread-riot, similar to hundreds which had taken place during the previous twelve months, had become a revolution. In Moscow there was no bloodshed. There was no one left to defend the old régime. It was a bitterly cold day. Our house, which was central-heated, had been short of fuel for nearly a week, and I went out into the crowds in the street. My most vivid memory of that afternoon was the warmth of the surging mob before the Town Duma. There was no hooliganism. The crowd was willing enough to let me through, but before I reached the door I was roasting with heat and glad to take off my fur cap. I was the first foreigner to enter the Moscow headquarters of the revolution. Inside, the rooms and passages of the huge Town Hall were thronged with bands of students and soldiers – the soldiers hot, greasy and officious; the students raucous and exultant. Nor was only youth in the ascendant. There were grey-bearded men, bent with years – men who had suffered exile, who had lived in mouse-holes, and who, with trembling knees and a strange light in their eyes, were now rejoicing over the hour of their triumph. The enthusiasm was compelling, almost infectious, but it was more impressive in the masses outside than in the delegates inside the building. I sought out Chelnokov. He came out of the Council room to see me. Beads of sweat were standing on his brow. His limp was more pronounced than ever. His voice had gone.

'I'm fighting for my life, Roman Romanovich,' he said. 'The Social-Revolutionaries and the Social-Democrats don't want me as Mayor. But, never fear, I'll master them yet. But it's a bad business – and not good for the war.'

And with that he left me and returned to the battle of tongues which had now been unloosed. The man who yesterday had been too revolutionary for the Emperor was already too reactionary for the revolution.

On my way out I met Gruzinov, the President of the Moscow Provincial Zemstvo. He had just been appointed to the command of the revolutionary troops. He, too, seemed embarrassed by the enthusiasm and hero-worship of the band of women students and high-school girls who surrounded him. The fire was travelling fast.

One other scene in that first day of good-tempered confusion remains clear-cut before my eyes. On my way home I met Harry Charnock in the street. For months he had been negotiating for the sale of the great Vicoul Morozov textile works to a rich American group. As far as the Americans were concerned the contract would have been signed months before and the purchase money paid over. Charnock himself, who was general manager and stood to make a small fortune by the deal, had been in favour of signing, but the Morozovs with peasant obstinacy had haggled and haggled until now it was too late. Laconically Charnock handed me a paper. It was a telegram from the Americans saying the deal was off. Big capital had taken fright.

As I passed through the Theatre Square Socialist agitators, mostly students and schoolgirls, were distributing anti-war pamphlets to the troops. Opposite the National Hotel someone in the crowd recognised me. 'Long live England,' cried a student voice. 'Long live England and the revolution,' answered the greasy mob. It was a disturbing and confusing day.

The story of the revolution has been told by many pens. It will be a theme for historians for all time. I do not propose to discuss it in detail except in so far as I myself was concerned in it. Nor do I intend to analyse its causes or speculate on what might have happened if Kerensky had done this on this date, and General Ivanov that on that date. My own views on the revolution can be given in a single paragraph.

The revolution took place because the patience of the Russian people broke down under a system of unparalleled inefficiency and corruption. No other nation would have stood the privations which Russia stood, for anything like the same length of time. As instances of the inefficiency, I give the disgraceful mishandling of food-supplies, the complete breakdown of transport, and the senseless mobilisation of millions of unwanted and unemployable troops. As an example of the corruption, I quote the shameless profiteering of nearly everyone engaged in the giving and taking of war contracts. Obviously, the Emperor himself, as a supreme autocrat, must bear the responsibility for a system which failed mainly because of the men (Stürmer, Protopopov, Rasputin) whom he appointed to control it. If he had acted differently, if he had been a different man ... These arguments are childish.

What it is important to realise is that from the first the revolution was a revolution of the people. From the first moment neither the Duma nor the intelligentsia had any control of the situation. Secondly, the revolution was a revolution for land, bread and peace – but, above all, for peace. There was only one way to save Russia from going Bolshevik. That was to allow her to make peace. It was because he would not make peace that Kerensky went under. It was solely because he promised to stop the war that Lenin came to the top. It will be objected that Kerensky ought to have shot both Lenin and Trotsky. The soldiers, who argue in this way, always ignore the psychological premises. The old régime having broken down, the type of leader (i.e. a Kerensky) whom the first revolution threw up was bound to be a man who would not shoot his opponents. It was the first state of a natural process. Secondly, even if Kerensky had shot Lenin and Trotsky, some other anti-war leader would have taken their place and would have won through on his anti-war programme.

This was so fundamentally true of the Russian situation that only the gravity of our own situation in the West can excuse us for the folly of the various schemes (from the futile feebleness of the

Archangel expedition* to the greater, but, fortunately, unfulfilled stupidity of Japanese intervention) which we advocated for the reconstruction of the Eastern front. Among the foolish and the egregious I include myself. And among the soldiers General Macready† stood alone in his sane common sense.

My own contact with the first revolution lasted for eight months. It was a period of depression and disintegration, of a new activity from which all hope and faith had gone. I had been no admirer of the old régime, but I had little difficulty in realising what the effect of the new must be on the war. Three days after the outbreak of the first rioting I sent off a long analysis of the revolutionary movement to the Embassy. The précis of this despatch entered in my diary at the time runs as follows: 'The position is so unclear and so uncertain that any attempt at prophecy is difficult. It seems impossible that the struggle between the bourgeoisie and the proletariat can be liquidated without further bloodshed. When this will come no one knows, but the outlook for the war is full of foreboding.'

The revolution had begun on a Monday. On the Saturday I took part in my official capacity in a grand review of the revolutionary troops on the Red Square. It was an inspiring sight – 40,000 troops celebrating a newly-won freedom by a march-past executed with perfect precision and order. And yet in spite of the cloudless sky and sparkling air I had a feeling as though I were in a prison. That vast Red Square, which has witnessed so much repression of freedom from the time of the executions of Ivan the Terrible to the May Day parades of the Bolsheviks, that grim background of high red wall furnished by the Kremlin – these are no symbols of liberty. Russians, as I was to learn later in even more disturbed times, have a genius for pageantry and processions. And if there was any tendency to over-enthuse on my part (and I am a romanticist who hates all Governments by instinct), there were the generals – liberal patriots like Oboleshev, who had just returned from the front – to supply the necessary correction. Discipline had disappeared. Men no

* After the Bolsheviks made a separate peace with Germany at Brest-Litovsk in February, 1918, a force comprising British, French and American units occupied Murmansk and Archangel, initially to protect munitions supplies.
† General Sir Nevil Macready (1862–1946), Adjutant-General to the Forces 1916–18.

longer saluted their officers. Deserters were seeking the villages in their thousands. The floodgates of three hundred years had been swept away. The tide was not to be stemmed by any individual effort until it had spent itself. Guided skilfully into less dangerous channels it might have been. But that was not the method of the Allies, who had greeted the revolution first with feigned enthusiasm and then with increasing alarm. They wanted – and on the part of the military advisers the wish was natural – things to be put back where they were before. And, unfortunately, there is no 'as you were' either in time or in revolution.

A fortnight after the revolution I went to St Petersburg to see the members of the new Provisional Government. Prince Lvov, the Prime Minister, was my intimate friend. With most of the others I had been in close contact for the past two years. Men like Shingariev, a St Petersburg doctor, Kokoshkin, the great Moscow expert on international law, and Manuilov, the rector of Moscow University, were men of the highest integrity and ability. To the English Liberal Cabinet of 1906 they would have been an addition of strength and an ornament of distinction. They were too gentle to deal with the turbulent elements in the Soviets, which had made the revolution and which now virtually controlled the Duma.

Before catching my train, I dined with Chelnokov, who had been appointed Commissar for Moscow. He gave me a forecast of what I might expect to find. His own position was becoming unbearable. He confessed that he had no chance of surviving the new elections, which now of course had been proscribed on a basis of universal suffrage for every municipality and every Zemstvo in Russia. Lvov's reign, he said, would be no longer than his own.

The most phlegmatic of men, he spoke without anger or prejudice. I felt that he was right. Already 'a free and unfettered democracy' (how later the Bolsheviks were to sneer at these slogans of the first revolution!) had no use for the liberal leaders whose cry for years had been 'trust the people'.

I found Prince Lvov at the Taurid Palace amid a scene of indescribable confusion. He had been presiding at a Cabinet meeting. Secretaries kept rushing into his room with papers to sign, decisions to be taken. He would start to talk to me, and then the telephone would ring. In the corridor outside, deputations from the front, from the villages, from goodness knows where, were waiting to see him.

And in this restless, bustling turmoil there was not one man or woman who seemed capable of protecting the Prime Minister or relieving the burden on his shoulders. Everyone seemed to be playing a game of general post to escape from responsibility. I longed for a Miss Stevenson* to send the whole pack of delegations about their business and to put some order into this warren of chaos.

Our conversation was conducted in snatches. Finally he gave it up.

'You see how it is,' he said. 'We are doing our best, but there is so much to do. Come and see me tonight at my flat at twelve o'clock.'

He ran his hand through his grey beard and looked at me with a flickering smile. He looked tired and wan, and his eyes, small at all times, had almost vanished behind his eyelids. In two weeks he had aged ten years. A man of great charm, he would have made an excellent chairman of the London County Council. He was an ideal President of the Zemstvos Union, but he was not the stuff of which revolutionary Prime Ministers are made. And yet I doubt if at this period any member of his class could have 'held down' his post. Nature brooks no interference with her processes, and the time for dictators had not yet come or had already passed.

I went to see Lvov at his flat – a modest two-roomed affair, where he had remained ever since the night he had arrived from Moscow to take over the reins of the Government. He was still in the same suit. The carpet bag, in which he had packed his clothes for the night, still stood in the hall. My heart went out to him. He seemed so forlorn and alone. As always, he spoke in his rather jerky little monotones. He was a shy man and, although he bore an aristocratic name, more like a country doctor than an aristocrat. To those who knew him slightly he gave an impression of cunning – due actually to his timidity. To those whom he trusted he was open and without restraint. He made no concealment of his fears and anxieties. Russia would come through, but . . . Russia would carry on with the war, but . . . His whole conversation was a confession of the weakness of his own position.

When I went to see my other Moscow friends in the Government I found the same helplessness, the same apprehensions. There was only one man in the Cabinet who had any power. That was the nominee of the Soviets – Kerensky, the Minister of Justice. The revolution had destroyed my old liberal friends. Now I had to seek new gods.

* Most probably an allusion to Frances Stevenson (1888–1972), secretary, mistress and eventually wife of David Lloyd George.

It was Prince Lvov who arranged my first meeting with Kerensky. I could not have had a better introduction. Like most Socialists Kerensky admired and respected Lvov as much for the integrity of his character as for the work he had done for the Russian people. I received an invitation to luncheon.

At the appointed hour my sleigh drew up before the Ministry of Justice, and I climbed up the long steps of the official staircase, where only three weeks before had reigned all the rigid ceremonial of the ancient régime, into an antechamber filled with a crowd of soldiers, sailors, legal functionaries, students, schoolgirls, workmen and peasants, all waiting patiently like one of the bread queues in the Liteinaya or the Nevsky. I pushed my way through the throng to a tired and much-harassed secretary.

'You wish to see Alexander Feodorovich Kerensky? Quite impossible. You must come tomorrow.'

I explain patiently that I am invited to luncheon. Again the machine-like voice breaks in: 'Alexander Feodorovich has gone to the Duma. I have no idea when he will be back. In these days you know . . .'

He shrugs his shoulders. Then, almost before I have time to allow the disappointment to show on my face, the crowd surges forward. 'Stand back, stand back,' shout the soldiers. Two nervous and very young adjutants clear a passage, and in half a dozen energetic strides Kerensky is beside me. His face has a sallow and almost deathly pallor. His eyes, narrow and Mongolian, are tired. He looks as if he were in pain, but the mouth is firm, and the hair, cropped close and worn *en brosse*, gives a general impression of energy. He speaks in quick, jerky sentences with little sharp nods of the head by way of emphasis. He wears a dark suit, not unlike skiing kit, over a black Russian workman's blouse. He takes me by the arm and leads me into his private apartments, and we sit down to luncheon at a long table with almost thirty places. Madame Kerensky is already lunching. By her side are Breshkovskaya, the grandmother of the Russian revolution, and a great brawny-armed sailor from the Baltic fleet. People drift in and out at will. Luncheon is a floating meal and it seems to be free to all. And all the while Kerensky talks. In spite of the Government prohibition order there is wine on the table, but the host himself is on a strict diet and drinks nothing but milk. Only a few months previously he has had a tubercular kidney removed. But his energy is undiminished. He is tasting the first fruits of power. Already he resents a little the pressure that is being put on him by the Allies. 'How would Lloyd George like it if a Russian were to come to him to tell him how to manage the English people?' He is, however, good-natured. His enthusiasm is infectious, his pride in the revolution unbounded. 'We are only doing what you have done centuries ago, but we are trying to do it better – without the Napoleon and without the Cromwell. People call me a mad idealist, but thank God for the idealists in this world.' And at the moment I was prepared to thank God with him.

Since that first luncheon I have had many meetings with Alexander Feodorovich. In Russia I suppose I knew him better – far better indeed – than any other British official. I interpreted for him on several occasions in his negotiations with Sir George Buchanan. I saw him frequently alone. It was to me that he came when he was in hiding from the Bolsheviks. It was I who was instrumental in getting him out of Russia. And today, when thousands of anti-Bolshevik Russians – and English, too – revile him; when the men and women who once sought his favour and leant upon his words curse his name; I have remained his friend.

Kerensky was the victim of the bourgeois hopes which his short-lived success aroused. He was an honest, if not a great, man – sincere in spite of his oratorical talents, and, for a man who for four months was worshipped as a god, comparatively modest. From the start he was fighting a hopeless battle, trying to drive back into the trenches a nation which had already finished with the war. Caught between the cross-fires of the Bolshevik Left, which was screaming peace at every street-corner and in every trench, and of the Right and of the Allies, who were demanding the restoration of discipline by Tsarist methods, he had no chance. And he fell, because whoever had tried to do what he did was bound to fall.

Yet for a few weeks it seemed that his oratory might work a miracle and that his ridiculous belief (shared by all the Social-Revolutionaries and most of the liberals) in the common sense of the Russian people might justify itself. For, in his own peculiar way, Kerensky must be regarded as one of the great orators of history. There was nothing attractive about his delivery. His voice was raucous from much shouting. He had few gestures – for a Slav amazingly few. But he had words at his command and he spoke with a conviction that was all-compelling. How well I remember his first visit to Moscow. It was, I think, soon after he had been made Minister for War. He had just returned from a visit to the front. He spoke in the Big Theatre – the platform on which, later, the Bolsheviks ratified the Peace of Brest-Litovsk. Kerensky, however, was the first politician to speak from that famous stage, which has given to the world Chaliapin, Sobinov, Geltzer, Mordkin,* and scores of other famous dancers and singers. On this occasion the huge amphitheatre was packed from top to bottom. In Moscow the embers of Russian patriotism were still warm, and Kerensky had come to stir them into flame again. Generals, high officials, bankers, great industrialists, merchants, accompanied by their wives, occupied the parterre and first balcony boxes. On the stage were the representatives of the Soldiers' Councils. A small pulpit had been erected in the foreground of the stage just above the prompter's trapdoor. There was the usual ten minutes' delay, the customary rumours among the audience. Alexander Feodorovich was ill. A new crisis had recalled him to St Petersburg. Then the buzz of conversation gave place to a burst of clapping, and from the wings the pale figure of the War Minister made its way to the central dais. The audience rose to him. Kerensky held up his hand and plunged straight into his speech. He looked ill and tired. He drew himself up to his full height, as if calling up his last reserves of energy. Then, with an ever-increasing flow of words, he began to expound his gospel of suffering. Nothing that was worth having could be achieved without suffering. Man himself was born into this world in suffering. The greatest of all revolutions in history had begun on the Cross of Calvary. Was it to be supposed that their own revolution was to be consolidated without suffering? They had a legacy of appalling difficulties left to them by the Tsarist régime: disorganised transport, lack of bread, lack of fuel. Yet the Russian people knew how to suffer. He had just returned from the trenches. He had seen men who had been living for months on end with mud and water up to their knees. Lice crawled over them. For days they had had noth-

* Chaliapin, see p. 49n; Leonid Sobinov (1872–1934), tenor singer; Ekaterina Geltzer (1876–1962), ballerina; Mikhail Mordkin (1880–1944), ballet dancer.

ing but a crust of black bread for sustenance. They were without the proper equipment for their self-defence. They had not seen their womenfolk for months. Yet they made no complaint. They had promised to do their duty to the end. It was only in St Petersburg and in Moscow that he heard grumbling. And from whom? From the rich, from those who, in their silks and ornaments of gold, came here today to listen to him in comfort. He raised his eyes to the balcony boxes, while with fierce staccato sentences he lashed himself into a passion. Were they to bring Russia down in ruins, to be guilty of the most shameful betrayal in history, while the poor and the humble, who had every reason to complain, were still holding out? He was ashamed at the apathy of the big cities. What had they done to be tired! Could they not watch a little longer? He had come to Moscow for a message for the men in the trenches. Was he to go back and say that their effort was in vain because 'the heart of Russia' was now peopled by men of little faith?

As he finished his peroration, he sank back exhausted into the arms of his aide-de-camp. In the limelight his face had the pallor of death. Soldiers assisted him off the stage, while in a frenzy of hysteria the whole audience rose and cheered itself hoarse. The man with one kidney – the man who had only six weeks to live – would save Russia yet. A millionaire's wife threw her pearl necklace on to the stage. Every woman present followed her example, and a hail of jewellery descended from every tier of the huge house. In the box next to me, General Wogak, a man who had served the Tsar all his life and who hated the revolution as the pest, wept like a child. It was an epic performance – more impressive in its emotional reactions than any speech of Hitler or of any orator I have ever heard. The speech had lasted for two hours. Its effect on Moscow and on the rest of Russia lasted exactly two days.

Today the reactionaries and Imperialists, who once fawned on him, have no good word to say of Kerensky. More even than the Bolsheviks, he is made the scapegoat of their shortcomings.

In 1923 two young scions of the Russian nobility came to see me in Prague. They were in high spirits. They informed me that they had spent the afternoon reviling Kerensky. They had discovered that he was living in the Hotel Paris in Prague. They had hired the room next to his and had spent the afternoon shouting 'dirty dog' and other abuse through the thin partitions. That is typical of the attitude of most Russians towards the man whose chief sin was that he had disappointed impossible hopes.

Kerensky was the symbol of a necessary interlude between the Tsarist war and the Bolshevik peace. His failure was inevitable. In the eyes of the Russia which supported him, it would have been a greater failure if he had died at his post.

In June, 1931, he was lunching with me in the Carlton Grill Room in London, when Lord Beaverbrook came over and joined our table. With his keen interest in human psychology he began at once to ply Kerensky with questions.

'What was the reason of your collapse?'

Kerensky's reply was that the Germans forced on the Bolshevik rising because Austria, Bulgaria and Turkey were on the verge of making a separate peace with Russia. The Austrians had decided to ask for a separate peace less than a fortnight before the October revolution.

'Would you have mastered the Bolsheviks if you had made a separate peace?' asked Lord Beaverbrook.

'Of course,' said Kerensky, 'we should be in Moscow now.'

'Then why', said Lord Beaverbrook, 'didn't you do it?'

'We were too naïve,' was the reply.

Naïvety is Kerensky's proper epitaph.

Today, he is fifty. He looks marvellously well. Since the removal of his tubercular kidney he has never had a day's illness. He lives in Paris and still dreams of the day when Russia will come back to him. He is still an idealist. He lacks, as he has always lacked, the ruthlessness of the successful revolutionary. He has two sons. Both are engineers and both are working in England.

By a strange coincidence Kerensky, Lenin, and Protopopov (craziest of all the Tsarist Ministers) all came from the same Volga town of Simbirsk. Kerensky comes of a family of Orthodox priests. His father was a state official and was Lenin's trustee. In spite of this connection Kerensky never met Lenin and only saw him once or twice from a distance.

Other new revolutionary acquaintances with whom I came into contact during this period were Boris Savinkov, Filonenko, Chernov, Zenzinov, Rudniev, the new Moscow Mayor, Urnov, the President of the Soldiers' Soviet, Minor, the venerable Social-Revolutionary editor, Prokopovich and his wife Ekaterina Kuskova, a remarkable couple, who both in their personal appearance and in their work may be aptly described as the Russian counterpart of Mr and Mrs Sidney Webb. Some day, when the story of the Russian revolution fades into the same background of time as the French revolution, their names will figure in the Russian history books. To the foreign reader they are, with the exception of Savinkov, of no significance.

For some reason, which I have never been able to understand, Boris Savinkov has always been regarded by Englishmen as a man of action and therefore as a hero. More even than most Russians, Savinkov was a schemer – a man who could sit up all night drinking brandy and discussing what he was going to do the next day. And, when the morrow came, he left the action to others. His talents cannot be denied. He wrote several excellent novels. He understood the revolutionary temperament better almost than anyone, and knew how to play on it for his own ends. He had mingled so much with spies and *agents provocateurs* that, like the hero in his own novel, he hardly knew whether he was deceiving himself or those whom he meant to deceive. Like most Russians, too, he was a forcible speaker who could impress his personality on his listeners. At one time he entirely captivated Mr Churchill, who saw in him a Russian Bonaparte. There were, however, fatal defects in his character. He liked luxury, and, although he was ambitious, was not prepared to sacrifice his self-indulgence to his ambition. His chief weakness was my own – a fatal capacity for short spells of frenzied work followed by long periods of indolence. Him, too, I saw frequently after the collapse of the Kerensky régime. He came to see me in Moscow in 1918 at a moment when a price was on his head. The danger to himself – and, incidentally, to me – was considerable. His only disguise was a pair of huge horn-rimmed spectacles with darkened glasses. His conversation was mostly recriminations against the Allies and against the Russian counter-revolutionaries, with whom he was supposed to be co-operating. The last time I saw him was in a night-haunt in Prague in 1923. He was a pathetic figure for whom one could not help feeling the deepest sympathy. He had exhausted all his friends, and, when later he returned to Moscow and offered his services to the Bolsheviks, I was not surprised. Doubtless behind that tortured brain there was some grandiose scheme of striking a last blow for Russia and of carrying out a spectacular coup d'état. It was a gambler's throw (all his life he had played a lone hand), and, although anti-Bolsheviks maintain that he was murdered – poisoned and thrown out of a window – I have little doubt that he went to his own end.

The period of the Kerensky régime was the most unhappy in my official career. I had lost hope and with it my own balance. I sought relaxations from the stress of overwork in material pleasures. I was restless and uncontrolled. The war, which has branded so many of my generation, had destroyed all the former zest of my life. I longed for the peace of the country and the calm of the cooling fields, and, unable to obtain them, I abandoned myself to the temptations of the town. I was definitely on the downgrade.

As the dangers of the Russian revolution came home to the British Ministers at home, strenuous efforts were made to bring the Russians to their senses and to recall them sternly to the obligations of their alliance. Some genius hit on the idea of sending out a Franco-British Socialist delegation to persuade the Russian comrades to continue fighting. And in the middle of April, MM. Moutet, Cachin, and Lafont, representing French Socialism, and Messrs Jim O'Grady, Will Thorne, and W. W. Sanders, as stalwarts of British Labour, arrived in St Petersburg to preach wisdom and patriotism to the Soviets. The three Frenchmen were intellectuals. Moutet was a lawyer. Cachin and Lafont were professors of philosophy. On the British side Sanders was then secretary of the Fabian Society. To the British public O'Grady and Thorne require no introduction.

From the first the visit was a farce. The delegates fulfilled their task honourably. But, as anyone might have foreseen, they were completely lost in the wilderness of Russian revolutionary phraseology. They were bewildered by the endless discussions on peace terms. They understood the jargon of the Russian Socialists far less than I did. They were handicapped by their ignorance of the language. Worst of all, they never succeeded in winning the confidence even of the moderate Socialists, who from the first regarded them as lackeys of their respective Governments.

If the effect on the Russians was less than nothing, the reaction of the delegates themselves to the revolution was amusing. O'Grady and Thorne – especially Thorne – were splendid. Never shall I forget that luncheon at the Embassy, when this honest giant regaled us with stories of his adventures. He had all the Englishman's contempt for verbiage, and the babel of foreign tongues had disgusted him. He longed to use his strong arms and to knock the heads of the garrulous comrades together.

The Allied delegates came to Moscow. They visited the front. They delivered – through the aid of their interpreter – innumerable patriotic speeches, and in the end they went away, sadder and wiser men. The sequel to this visit is amusing. O'Grady has become Sir James O'Grady and a Colonial Governor. Will Thorne is today the Labour doyen of the House of Commons and remains what he has always been – a Trades Union leader. Mr Sanders was a member of the 1929 Labour administration. He, too, is the mildest of pinks. Of the Frenchmen Lafont has passed through and out of Communism. Moutet is still a moderate Socialist. And Cachin – the most perfervid patriot of the six, the man, who, with tears of emotion in his eyes, implored the Soviets not to go out of the war until the triumph of the Allies was complete – has given himself body and soul to Moscow and today holds the fort of Bolshevism in France.

Events now began to move rapidly. A few days after the arrival of the Franco-British Labour delegation, and almost simultaneously with the return to Russia of Lenin, came M. Albert Thomas, the French Socialist Minister of Munitions. He, too, had been sent out by a French Government, claiming by its traditions to possess a special knowledge of revolutions and anxious to secure the co-operation of revolutionary Russia with the Allied cause. Thomas, whose Socialism was a shade less pink than the Conservatism of Mr Baldwin, was accompanied by a host of secretaries and officers. Moreover, he carried in his pocket the recall of M. Paléologue, the French Ambassador and a cynic who never struck me as really serious, but who understood Russia much better than most people suspected. The recall was part of the new policy.

I saw a certain amount of Thomas – a jovial, bearded man with a sense of humour and a healthy, bourgeois appetite. He made friends with Sir George Buchanan. He stimulated the war loyalty of Kerensky. He visited the front and harangued the troops with patriotic speeches well larded with revolutionary sentiment. And he argued with the Soviet. One service, which seemed important at the time, he rendered to the Allies. The Soviets, at this moment, were engaged in abstract discussions about peace terms. They had invented the formula of 'peace without annexations and contributions', and this phrase, adopted at thousands of meetings in the trenches and in the villages, had spread like wildfire throughout the country. It was a formula which caused considerable annoyance and even anxiety to the English and French Governments, which had already divided up the spoils of a victory not yet won, in the form of both annexations and contributions. And both the French Ambassador and Sir George Buchanan had been requested to circumvent this new and highly dangerous form of pacifism. Their task was delicate and difficult. There seemed no way out of the impasse, and in despair they sought the advice of Thomas. The genial Socialist laughed.

'I know my Socialists,' he said. 'They will shed their blood for a formula. You must accept it and alter its interpretation.'

So annexations became restitution and contributions reparations. It was, I imagine, the first time the word reparations was used officially, and Thomas certainly succeeded in persuading the Soviets to accept a clause in their formula for the restitution of Alsace-Lorraine.* At the time it seemed an important achievement. Actually, as the Mensheviks and Social-Revolutionaries, who had yielded to the Thomas subtlety, were so soon to be swept away, it made no difference whatsoever.

M. Thomas was the most entertaining of the French and English Socialists who visited Russia during this period of the first revolution. He spoke well. He was adaptable. And he had courage. But the results were insignificant. His speeches were no more effective than those of our military attachés, Colonel Knox and Colonel Thornhill, who with more sincerity besought the Russian soldier not to abandon his Allies, who were fighting his battle on the other side of Europe. To the Bolsheviks he was of course a renegade, a Socialist traitor, who had sold himself to the bourgeoisie, and as such he was denounced in all the highways and byways of the revolution.

The position of the Allied missions in Russia was, in fact, rapidly becoming impossible. Everyone was engaged in trying to persuade the Russian to continue fighting when he had just overthrown a régime because it refused to give him peace. A little plain thinking should have made anyone see that in these circumstances the success of the Bolsheviks was merely a question of time.

Hot on the heels of M. Thomas came Mr Arthur Henderson,

* Alsace and eastern Lorraine had been ceded to Germany in 1871 after the Franco-Prussian War. Alsace-Lorraine was restored to France by the Treaty of Versailles in 1919.

despatched on a similar mission of fraternal goodwill by Mr Lloyd George. Mr Henderson, too, carried a letter of recall in his pocket. To be strictly accurate, the letter of recall was not actually included in the Henderson baggage-train. What had happened was this: when the British Labour Minister – and Mr Henderson was the first Labour representative in the history of England to achieve Cabinet rank – was actually on his way to St Petersburg, the Foreign Office sent a telegram to Sir George Buchanan extolling his work and suggesting that he should take a rest. In other words, he was to be recalled and his post given to Mr Henderson.

On deciphering the telegram and without consulting the Ambassador, 'Benji' Bruce, head of the Chancery, rushed off to see Sazonov, ascertained from him that Tereschenko, the Finance Minister of the Provisional Government, would be very sorry to see Sir George Buchanan replaced, and then went back to the Embassy and sent off a long private telegram in cipher to George Clerk at the Foreign Office, saying that Henderson's appointment would be a disaster.

As it turned out, this bold initiative on the part of a subordinate proved to be unnecessary. Mr Henderson has been described by one of his Labour colleagues as the greatest Foreign Secretary England has ever had. True it is that Dr Dalton, the colleague who made this remarkable statement, was Mr Henderson's trusted lieutenant and assistant during his conduct of the foreign affairs of Great Britain and that, in praising his chief, he is casting reflected glory on himself. Nevertheless, on the occasion of his Russian visit, Mr Henderson certainly showed an admirable discretion. Accompanied by George Young,* he took up his quarters at the Europe – the same hotel which had provided such luxurious shelter for Lord Milner, George Clerk, Sir Henry Wilson, and numerous other distinguished visitors to Russia. There, at the Ambassador's request, I came to see him. I dined with him in his private room. Throughout one long summer evening I walked with him down the Nevsky, across the Winter Square, past the Palace Quay. Beneath the gold reflection of the Admiralty Arch I heard the whole legend of the Hendersonian career. I accompanied him to Moscow. I took him to a full-dress meeting of the Moscow Soviet. And in the inner chamber of his Moscow hotel I arranged for him a private conversation (with myself as interpreter) with Urnov, the then all-powerful President of the Soldiers' Soviet.

* George (G. M.) Young (1882–1959), later a distinguished historian.

Mr Henderson has the reputation – doubtless well deserved – of being a first-class organiser. He is a great man at party meetings, which he succeeds in dominating by concealing his own intentions to the last moment. He is a man who is slow to commit himself. He does not give himself away.

On this occasion, however, I looked into Mr Henderson's soul. His geography was a little weak. He was not quite sure where he was, but he was speedily convinced that the locality was unhealthy. The comrades in the Soviets bewildered him. He did not understand their language. He did not like their manners. Doubtless he would have liked to be the first Labour Ambassador. But after all, a Cabinet Minister is a more powerful person than the greatest of modern Ambassadors. Moreover, Sir George Buchanan was not the failure he had been painted. Sir George, as Mr Henderson soon discovered, understood the wild men much better than did Mr Henderson himself. Further, Sir George had been kind, and Mr Henderson is susceptible to kindness and to flattery. The great sacrifice was therefore easily made. Mr Henderson explained that, while the Embassy was his for the asking, he had come to the conclusion that no good purpose would be served by the removal of a man who understood Russia far better than he did and who had shown himself remarkably free from all party bias. Sir George was not even opposed to the Stockholm Conference,* and Mr Henderson, whose undoubted patriotism was tempered by the common sense of internationalism, saw a glimmer of hope in the Stockholm meeting. So, shaking the dust of St Petersburg off his feet, he returned to London to make the great renunciation and to recommend that Sir George Buchanan be retained as His Britannic Majesty's Ambassador and Envoy Extraordinary to the Revolutionary Government of Russia. On his return he had his historic wait on Mr Lloyd George's doormat – a wait which ended with his resignation. In this manner he lost both his Embassy and his place in the Cabinet. It was a bitter reward for a mission which had been honestly if somewhat timorously fulfilled, and which, whatever its effect on the Russians, had the advantage of curing Mr Henderson of any revolutionary tendencies for the rest of his life. As for the Stockholm Conference, the advocacy of which had

* A proposal that Socialist parties, including those of Britain, Germany and Russia, should convene in Stockholm to discuss the terms of ending the war.

caused Mr Henderson's downfall, the proposal had the support of several British diplomats, including Sir Esmé Howard,* and, in turning it down, Mr Lloyd George, who had blown hot and then cold on the idea, probably made a great mistake. At Stockholm we should have had everything to gain and almost nothing to risk.

During that disastrous summer of 1917 I had one novel experience which I must chronicle, if only for the serio-comic light it throws on the Russian character. As part of our propaganda baggage-train we had a travelling film mission, of which the able chief was Colonel Bromhead, the subsequent chairman of the British Gaumont. He, too, was enlisted to coax the Russians into fighting by showing them war films of the fighting on the Western front. The effect of these war pictures on the mind of the now undisciplined Russian army can be imagined. Not unnaturally, they served merely to increase the number of deserters.

It was not Bromhead's fault. He was a splendid fellow, who realised the futility of showing war pictures to men whose sole thought was peace. Still, he had his duty to do. Films were part of the Whitehall scheme for the regeneration of Russia, and shown they had to be.

To Moscow, then, came Bromhead for a monster demonstration of the British effort. Would I help to make his show a success? Could I enlist the services of patriotic speakers? Nothing seemed easier. Moscow, alas! had more orators than fighters.

We secured a theatre. We arranged a programme. And then the Soldiers' Soviet, infinitely more powerful than the Provisional Government, intervened. The show was for the Moscow troops. The soldiers might see the films. They were not to be exposed to the harangues of Imperialist jingoes. There must be no speeches.

In vain I went to see the Presidium of the Soldiers' Soviet. In vain I argued the merits of free speech. The utmost concession I could wring from them was that Lockhart himself – Lockhart who sympathised with the revolution and knew the views of revolutionary Russia regarding the peace terms – might speak. But there were to be no other orators. On these conditions the Presidium would guarantee the success of the show. They would be present in full force to see that the conditions were carried out.

Bromhead accepted the situation with unfeigned delight. My own

* Sir Esmé Howard (1863–1939), then British Ambassador to Sweden.

consent was given with reluctance. An after-dinner speech before an audience rendered innocuous by good food and champagne was one thing. I saw nothing attractive in addressing twelve hundred sceptical and severely critical revolutionaries in their own language.

I took pains over that speech. I wrote it out very carefully in English and had it translated into mellifluous Russian by a Russian poet. I learnt it off by heart. Indeed, I made myself something more than word perfect. I rehearsed my effects even down to the place where my voice was to break. Not in vain had I gone the rounds with Kerensky.

My appeal was frankly sentimental. There is no other reason I know that will compel large bodies of men to fight. But my sentiment was Russian. I made no reference to the crime of deserting their Western Allies. I discussed quite frankly Russia's desire and even need of a separate peace, and then I drew a picture of a better world created by the glorious revolution. But neither the better world nor the revolution itself could stand, if discipline was to be thrown to the winds and the road to Moscow opened to the enemy. Lenin would have demolished the argument with one sentence. But Lenin, fortunately, was still in hiding in St Petersburg.

On the day of the ordeal I made my way to the theatre, secretly hoping that I might have no audience to address. But the Soldiers' Council had kept its word. The house was packed. Moreover, seated beside the Presidium in the balcony were the Assistant Minister of Marine and Kishkin, the High Commissar for Moscow. Our films were of two kinds: naval and military. Very wisely we showed the naval films last. They were impressive and free from all horrors. My speech came at the end. There was no applause when I stood up on the narrow stage before the curtain, and I began nervously. The silence, however, was respectful. I was to be given a hearing. I forgot all the tricks I had practised. I almost forgot my words. I spoke with a quivering anguish in my voice which the Russians mistook for genuine emotion. For twenty minutes I strove to master my nervousness, my voice now raucous, now breaking queerly at the oddest moments. To the end I was listened to in deathly silence. When I had finished my peroration, my knees shook and the sweat streamed like tears down my face.

Then pandemonium broke loose. A soldier jumped on to the stage and kissed me on both cheeks. In the box of the Presidium Kishkin stood up, and in stentorian tones declared that Russia would never desert her Allies. That afternoon he had received official news that the Russian fleet had sailed out into the Baltic in full fighting trim. More cheers. More pandemonium. In every corner of the house soldiers were standing up and clamouring to be heard. The scene was almost like the opening of the war. I had unloosed the strings of Russian hysteria. It was a short-lived triumph. The next day the account of the meeting was severely censored. The Socialists had repented of their emotion.

This was my last public appearance as Acting Consul-General in Moscow. Just as the old Russia was advancing inevitably to her final tragedy, so, too, there was a minor tragedy in my own life. I relate it frankly and without excuses. Some months before I had formed an attachment to a Russian Jewess – whom I had met casually at the theatre. I had made myself talked about.

The matter came finally to the ears of the Ambassador. He sent for me, and we went for a walk together. No man could have been kinder. No man could have made a more successful appeal to my better nature. He told me the story of his own life. When he was young, he had undergone a similar temptation. Real happiness consisted in resisting temptations which one was bound to regret later. He referred to the good work I was doing. It was a pity to wreck what might be a wonderful career for what was merely a passing infatuation due to war strain. Convention might be the first cousin to hypocrisy, but in Government service it had to be observed. Besides, there was the question of duty and of the war. I should put my country before my self-indulgence.

I was deeply moved. We shook hands emotionally – my emotion being due to genuine affection for this splendid old man, who had treated me with so much understanding, and his, I believe, to an equally genuine regret for his lost youth – and I returned to Moscow, having pledged myself to make the grand renunciation. I made it, and it lasted exactly three weeks. Then one day the telephone rang, and I went back.

This was the end. I had broken my word, and this time the Ambassador sorrowfully but firmly decided that I was on the verge of a nervous breakdown and that I must go home to England for a rest. Perhaps he was right.

There was no scandal. I do not suppose that even the Private

Secretary at the Foreign Office was informed of the real reasons for my sudden return. It was said that I had broken down from overwork, and in this manner I received much sympathy. For the same reason I was able to avoid all the publicity of an official farewell. My friends in Moscow were kindness itself. They were told I was ill and not to be worried. They all expected me to be back within six weeks, and in any case the approaching collapse of Russia was now so apparent that everyone was fully occupied with the salvage of his own affairs. To such of the public as thought about me I was a martyr to duty. But, knowing that my enforced sick-leave was really a recall and that I should never come back, I felt my position keenly, and it was as a culprit rather than as a martyr that I slunk out of Moscow in those early days of September, 1917. I left St Petersburg just as the Kerensky–Kornilov duel* was starting. I arrived in London six weeks before the Bolshevik revolution.

* See Editorial Note, p. xvii.

PART THREE

HISTORY FROM THE INSIDE

History is generally only the register of the crimes, the follies, and the mistakes of mankind.

GIBBON

Of that voyage home to England I remember very little. I had to travel via Finland and Scandinavia and was seeing Stockholm for the first time. On this occasion it made no impression on me. I do not remember where we stayed. As far as I can recollect, I avoided our Legation. I kept no diary during this period. My mental anguish was extreme, and I wanted to forget.

All that remains in my mind is the memory of the railway journey from Christiania* to Bergen. The scenery, wilder, more picturesque than the Canadian Rockies, provided the proper background for my own melancholy. The wild stretches of moor, the lofty peaks and tortuous ravines, the lochs and turbulent trout-streams, above all, the firs and the birches, their leaves golden with the first tints of autumn, reminded me of Scotland. At Bergen I met Wardrop, who was to take my place in Moscow. He was an elderly, scholarly man, and the personification of caution. Obviously, the Foreign Office were taking no more chances with youth. Mechanically I gave him the information he required about Moscow. I cannot say I enjoyed the interview. I could not bear the thought of having to talk about Russia. All I wanted was to go to my own country and fish.

I assume that I made the dreary journey – exciting only because of the danger from submarines – from Bergen to Aberdeen and that I crossed in the *Vulture*. In a court of law I could not swear either to the name of the ship or to the port of landing. I know that I arrived in London on the morning of the day on which Kornilov's troops were marching on St Petersburg. I went straight to the Foreign Office to report myself. I was received with the greatest kindness. I was a man who had accomplished great things at the expense of his health. I was to take a long rest and not to think about the war or work or Russia until I had made a complete recovery. With disgust in my heart I accepted the rôle which had been forced on me, and that same day I made arrangements to go to the Highlands to stay with my uncle. Before I left I had one more ordeal to face. Within a few hours of my arrival in London the *Daily Mail* succeeded in tracking me down. They wanted information about the outcome of the Kerensky–Kornilov clash. Opinion in London favoured Kornilov's chances. I held definite views regarding the inevitability

* Former name of Oslo.

of Kornilov's failure. Would I write an article? It would have to be done at once. The *Mail* would pay handsomely for it.

There and then, with the sacrifice of my dinner, I scribbled out the article with the *Mail*'s representative looking over my shoulder. I threw in some new photographs of Kerensky and Savinkov and I received a cheque for twenty-five guineas. I showed my customary lack of business instinct. I sold my article for probably less than half the sum a more astute journalist might have received. On the other hand, the article had to be anonymous (as a Government servant I could not use my name), and the cheque paid for my return fare to Scotland. It was my first experience of frenzied journalism.

The ways of Providence are not only incalculable. They are on occasions highly diverting. Greatly refreshed in mind and body, I returned from Scotland to London fourteen days after the Bolshevik revolution. I was to start work again. I had been temporarily attached to Sir Arthur Steel-Maitland* as his Russian expert in the new Department of Overseas Trade. I owe much to Sir Arthur. He overwhelmed me with kindness and insisted on my staying with him at his house in Cadogan Square. What was more important, he plunged me again into the very heart of Russian affairs. The Bolshevik coup d'état had completely nullified the value of my services to the Department of Overseas Trade. Sir Arthur helped me or rather pushed me into finding a new outlet for my activities.

During a hectic period of three weeks I lunched and dined with the politicians. Russia, of course, was the one topic of conversation, and in the prevailing ignorance I regained my self-confidence. I had long foreseen the inevitability of the Bolshevik revolution. I could not share the general belief, stimulated by the opinion of nearly all the Russian experts in London, that the Lenin régime could not last more than a few weeks and that then Russia would revert to Tsarism or a military dictatorship. Still less could I believe that the Russian peasant would return to the trenches. Russia was out of the war. Bolshevism would last – certainly as long as the war lasted. I deprecated as sheer folly our militarist propaganda, because it took no account of the war-weariness which had raised the Bolsheviks to the supreme power. In my opinion, we had to take the Bolshevik peace proposals seriously. Our policy should

* Sir Arthur Steel-Maitland (1876–1935), then Under-Secretary for the Colonies.

now aim at achieving an anti-German peace in Russia.

Rather futilely I sought to combat the firmly rooted conviction that Lenin and Trotsky were German staff officers in disguise or at least servile agents of German policy. I was more successful when I argued that it was madness not to establish some contact with the men who at that moment were controlling Russia's destinies.

The reactions to my pleading were varied. At that moment the general atmosphere in political circles was pessimistic. I think that in their hearts the Cabinet realised that Russia was out of the war for good, but with an obstinate lack of logic they refused to accept the implications of their secret beliefs. Hate of the revolution and fear of its consequences in England were the dominant reactions of Conservatives, who at that moment had an unnatural and today inexplicable dread of the machinations of Mr Arthur Henderson. I found the same fears among the Labour patriots. At Cadogan Square I renewed my acquaintance with Jim O'Grady and Will Thorne. They, too, were critical of Mr Henderson, who, they said, had gone over to the Snowdenites* and was playing for revolution and the Labour premiership. I saw Mr Henderson himself at 1 Victoria Place. I found the same man as I had met in Russia seven months before. He was as God-fearing, as conventionally Methodist, as petit bourgeois, and as scared of revolution as he always has been and always will be. He talked to me very frankly about his own position. He was bitter about his treatment by Lloyd George which, he said, had only strengthened his own standing in Labour circles. His views on the Russian situation were not very different from my own. He was entirely in favour of establishing contact with the Bolsheviks. He went further. He was in favour of a Conference – a form of negotiation which would have been infinitely more dangerous than the original proposal of the Stockholm Conference. In those days, however, Mr Henderson, like Mr Lloyd George, was convinced that he had only to meet Lenin face to face in order to vanquish him in the ensuing battle of wits.

During these three weeks from November 27th to December

* Advocates of Philip Snowden (1864–1937), who was then an influential Labour MP. Snowden was vehemently opposed to British involvement in the war, and had urged the acceptance of Russian peace proposals.

18th, 1917, I must have met scores of politicians and experts. The endless conversations seemed to lead no further. One lesson that period should have taught me: that the man in London has a thousand advantages over the man on the spot. Then I was too young to profit by it. During the next year I was to acquire it by the bitter experience of being myself the man on the spot.

One exciting adventure I had at this time. On December 18th I was to dine at Cadogan Square to meet Bonar Law.* It was a night of fog, and to the inconvenience of the fog was added the unpleasantness of an air raid. I dressed to the accompaniment of gunfire and the crash of bombs. To the same discords I forced my way through the huddled crowds in the Piccadilly tube station, and after long delays and some trepidation I reached Sir Arthur Steel-Maitland's house an hour late. The table was set for eight people. Sir Arthur was in his day-clothes. There was no Bonar Law. I was the only guest who had succeeded in reaching his destination.

The next day, however, the weeks of talk were translated into action. Sir Arthur gave another dinner party. This time there were only two guests in addition to myself: H. W. C. Davis, the Oxford historian, and Lord Milner. We talked until late in the night, and I repeated all my arguments about the necessity of establishing contact. Lord Milner was very sympathetic. When he went away, he told me that I should hear from him very soon. The next morning I was summoned to Downing Street. I met Lord Carson† and Lord Curzon,‡ both of whom referred very flatteringly to my work, and we had a long discussion on Russia. That same afternoon we had another meeting at the War Cabinet offices in Whitehall Gardens. Several Russian experts were present, including Rex Leeper and Colonel Byrne. The Ministers who listened to our words of wisdom were General Smuts,§ Lord Carson, and Lord Milner. The discus-

---

* Andrew Bonar Law (1858–1923), then Chancellor of the Exchequer. He was later Prime Minister 1922–3.
† Edward, Lord Carson (1854–1935), Ulster Unionist and Conservative MP, First Lord of the Admiralty 1917–18.
‡ George, Lord Curzon (1859–1925), Conservative politician. He was a member of the War Cabinet from 1916.
§ General Jan Smuts (1870–1950), former Boer guerrilla, South African politician and soldier. As an independent military adviser, he was a member of the War Cabinet from 1917.

sions were rather futile. Lord Milner was the only Minister who seemed to have even an elementary knowledge of Russian geography, and Lord Carson nearly upset my unnatural solemnity by asking me seriously if I could explain to him the difference between a Maximalist* and a Bolshevik. At the end of the meeting Lord Milner told me that the Cabinet approved in principle the necessity of establishing contact with the Bol- sheviks, but that they were unable to find the right man for the task.

On the morning of December 21st I was again summoned to 10 Downing Street. I was kept waiting about ten minutes. Then I was ushered into a long, narrow room which seemed to me all table. A Cabinet meeting had just ended. Mr Lloyd George, his pince-nez in his hand, was standing by the window, talking and gesticulating to Lord Curzon. My sponsor, Lord Milner, was not present, and for what seemed an eternity I stood waiting. Then Lord Milner came in, rescued me and took me up to Mr Lloyd George.

'Mr Lockhart?' he said. He shook hands and stepped back in order to scrutinise me more carefully. '*The* Mr Lockhart?' I looked foolish. Then, having made me the centre of attraction, he continued very slowly, so that everyone could hear: 'From the wisdom of your reports I expected to see an elderly gentleman with a grey beard.' He patted me on the back, asked me my age, muttered something about youth and Pitt being Prime Minister at twenty-four, and we sat down to business. Another meeting was started, this time with Mr Lloyd George presiding. My diary tells me that at the time I thought he looked tired and old. He was, however, remarkably active and adroit in his handling of the meeting. He asked me a few questions about Lenin and Trotsky. A fresh question followed almost before I had time to answer the previous one. I saw that his own mind was made up. He had been greatly impressed, as Lord Milner told me afterwards, by an interview with Colonel Thompson of the American Red Cross, who had just returned from Russia and who had denounced in blunt language the folly of the Allies in not opening up negotiations with the Bolsheviks. The questions ended, Mr Lloyd George stood up, referred briefly to the chaotic conditions in Russia and to the necessity of getting into touch with Lenin and Trotsky, emphasised the need for tact, knowledge and understanding, and finished up by stating that

* A member of the extreme wing of the Social-Revolutionaries.

Mr Lockhart was obviously a man whose right place at that moment was in St Petersburg and not in London. I was then told I could go.

That afternoon I had another meeting with Lord Milner and Lord Carson. This time Viscount Cecil (then Lord Robert Cecil) was present, and I had a very difficult quarter of an hour. Lord Robert was then Under-Secretary for Foreign Affairs. He was supremely sceptical of the usefulness of establishing any kind of relations with the Bolsheviks, and, as a sidelight on his subsequent development as an internationalist, it is worth putting on record that the man, who since the war has sat so often round the same table in Geneva as Litvinov* and Lunacharsky,† was at that time the most convinced of all responsible English statesmen that Lenin and Trotsky were paid agents of Germany, working deliberately for German ends, with no policy and no ambitions of their own. I was still in the dark regarding my fate.

That night Lord Milner and Lord Robert left for Paris, and I went home to spend Christmas with my father and mother, having been told to leave my telephone number and to hold myself in readiness in case I might be required to go on my travels again.

On New Year's Day I was back at the offices of the War Cabinet. A scheme was being evolved. It was certain that I was to return to Russia almost at once. In what capacity I was not told.

Three days later all my doubts were put at rest. I was to go to Russia as head of a special mission to establish unofficial relations with the Bolsheviks. Sir George Buchanan was returning home. I was to leave on the cruiser which was to fetch him from Bergen. My instructions were of the vaguest. I was to have the responsibility of establishing relations. I was to have no authority. If the Bolsheviks would give me the necessary diplomatic privileges without being recognised by the British Government, we would make a similar concession to Litvinov, whom the Bolsheviks had already appointed Soviet Ambassador in London.

The situation bristled with difficulties, but I accepted it without hesitation. The first essential was to acquire a suitable introduction to Lenin and Trotsky and to establish a *modus vivendi* with Litvinov.

* Maxim Litvinov (1876–1951), Russian Ambassador in London 1917–18.
† Anatoly Lunacharsky (1875–1933), Commissar for Education 1917–29.

Thanks to Rex Leeper, both tasks succeeded beyond my expectations. Leeper was on friendly terms with Rothstein, subsequently Bolshevik Minister in Teheran and then an official translator in our own War Office. I had a long talk with Rothstein, the substance of which I carefully noted in my diary. Rothstein, who had lived for years in England, was an intellectual armchair revolutionary. He said Trotsky's ambition was not a separate peace but a general peace. He pointed out that if he were Lloyd George he would accept Trotsky's offer of a Conference unconditionally. England would be the chief beneficiary. The Russian stipulations about self-determination would fall through with an ineffective protest from Trotsky, and England and Germany could arrange the colonial questions between them. Germany would agree to almost all other terms – that is, no annexations and no contributions. She might even be prepared to compromise on the Alsace-Lorraine question. In any case, it was absurd for England to prolong the war for the sake of Alsace-Lorraine. There was nothing easier to destroy than sentimental causes which are not rooted in a people itself, and we should have to consider very seriously whether we should get a better peace nine months hence.

At the time such proposals would have been regarded as treason. Today, to a world which is groaning under the burden of the peace treaties, they do not seem so unreasonable. Incidentally, it is interesting to note that Rothstein was only six weeks out in his prediction of the end of the war.

I avoided any discussions of a general peace, brought the subject back to Russia herself, and elaborated my proposals for opening up negotiations with his friends. I expressed a genuine sympathy with Russia's desire for peace, pointing out that she might have great difficulty in concluding a separate peace with Germany and that even unofficial contact between the English and Russian Governments would be as useful to the Bolsheviks as to us.

We parted on good terms, Rothstein promising to use his influence with Litvinov to provide me with the necessary recommendation to Trotsky. A few days later the whole affair was arranged over the luncheon table at a Lyons shop in the Strand. The two contracting parties were represented by Litvinov and Rothstein on the Russian side and Leeper and myself on the English side. There was to be no recognition – at any rate for the present. Unofficially, both Litvinov and I were to have certain diplomatic privileges, including the use of ciphers and the right to a diplomatic courier.

It was an amazing meal. Outside, the January sky was like lead and the room, poorly lit at the best of times, was grey and sombre. Leeper and I were just thirty. Litvinov was eleven years our senior. Rothstein was a year or two older than Litvinov. Both men were Jews. Both had suffered persecution and imprisonment for their political convictions. Yet Litvinov, whose real name was Wallach, was married to an Englishwoman. Rothstein had a son – a British subject – in the British army.

The success of that luncheon was made by Rothstein, who supplied to the conversation the necessary mixture of banter and seriousness which afterwards I was to find so useful in my negotiations with the Bolsheviks in Russia. Small, bearded, with dark lively eyes, he was a kind of intellectual cricket, whose dialectical jumps were as bewildering to us as they were amusing to himself. There was certainly nothing bloodthirsty in his revolutionary make-up. If the British Government had only left him in peace, I believe he would be living quietly in England to this day. Litvinov, heavily built, with broad forehead, was more sluggish and slower witted. My impression of him was not unfavourable. In so far as a Bolshevik can be said to differentiate in his degrees of hate of bourgeois institutions, he certainly regarded German militarism as a greater danger than English capitalism.

After a nervous beginning the course of our negotiations ran smoothly, and there and then, on the rough linen of a standard Lyons table, Litvinov wrote out my letter of recommendation to Trotsky. I give it herewith in Rothstein's translation:

Citizen Trotsky,
    People's Commissary for Foreign Affairs.

DEAR COMRADE,
    The bearer of this, Mr Lockhart, is going to Russia with an official mission with the exact character of which I am not acquainted. I know him personally as a thoroughly honest man who understands our position and sympathises with us. I should consider his sojourn in Russia useful from the point of view of our interests.

My position here remains indefinite. I learnt of my appointment only from the newspapers. I hope a courier is bringing me the necessary documents without which the difficulties of my position are greatly increased. The Embassy, Consulate, and Russian Government Committee have not yet surrendered. Their relations to me will be determined by the relations of the British Government.

I wrote the other day to the Ministry for Foreign Affairs, asking for a meeting in order to regulate certain practical questions (the viséing of passports, use of ciphers, military convention, etc.), but have not received any reply. I presume the question of my recognition will not be settled until the arrival of Buchanan.

The reception accorded me by the Press is quite satisfactory. I am making the acquaintance of the representatives of the Labour movement. I have issued an appeal to the English working-men in all the Socialist papers. Even the bourgeois Press readily accords me its pages to explain our position.

I shall write more fully by the first courier. I have not received an answer from you to my telegram of January 4th, new style,* No. 1. I request you very much to confirm the receipt of all telegrams and to number your telegrams.

The ciphers will, I trust, be delivered to me by the courier. Greetings to Lenin and all friends. I press your hand warmly.

Yours,

M. LITVINOV.

Rothstein begs me to greet you.

London, January 11th (new style), 1918.

The luncheon closed on a humorous note. As we were ordering a sweet, Litvinov noticed on the menu the magic words: 'pouding diplomate'. The idea appealed to him. The new diplomat would eat the diplomatic pudding. The Lyons 'Nippy' took his order and returned a minute later to say there was no more. Litvinov shrugged his shoulders and smiled blandly. 'Not recognised even by Lyons,' he said.

My last days in England were not solely occupied by Litvinov and Rothstein. There was the personnel of my mission to engage. I was given almost a free hand. As my chief assistant I wanted Rex Leeper, whose knowledge of Bolshevism would have been invaluable.

* See Editorial Note, p. xvii.

Almost at the last moment, however, he decided to remain at home, where he thought he could serve a more useful purpose by maintaining contact with Litvinov, and by interpreting the peculiar mentality of the Bolsheviks to the mandarins in Whitehall. Subsequent events were to prove the wisdom of his action. Although at the time I regretted his decision, I was to be grateful later for his presence in England, when I ran my neck into the noose in Moscow. As a substitute for Leeper I took Captain Hicks, who had recently returned from Russia, where he had done useful work as a poison gas expert. A man of great personal charm, he was popular with Russians and understood their mentality. He was, too, a good linguist with a first-class knowledge of German and a working acquaintance with Russian. His views on the situation were in tune with my own. I never regretted my decision. He was a most loyal colleague and devoted friend. As my commercial expert I took with me Edward Birse, a Moscow businessman, who had talked Russian from his cradle. Edward Phelan, a brilliant young official of the Ministry of Labour and today a prominent figure in the International Labour Office in Geneva, made up the full complement of my mission. As I was taking ciphers with me, I was also recommended to engage the services of a reliable orderly. This necessitated a letter from the War Cabinet and an interview with General Macready, the Adjutant-General. The interview was invigorating. General Macready had views on Russia. Standing before the fireplace of his room in the War Office, he delivered them in a series of snorts. An orderly for Russia! What the devil was the use of taking soldiers to Russia! Did the boys in the Foreign Office never read history? Couldn't they realise that when an army of ten millions had once broken it could not be reformed inside a generation? All military propaganda in Russia was useless and a sheer waste of money and manpower.

The general's views were eminently sensible. They would have saved unnecessary bloodshed and millions of money, if they had prevailed in Whitehall during 1918. I agreed with them and between the snorts endeavoured to tell him so. I explained to him that my mission was diplomatic and not military and that my object was to establish contact with the men who at that moment were negotiating a separate peace with Germany. I obtained my orderly – a six-foot-two ex-Irish guardsman, who was drunk when he joined me at the station, slept himself sober during the journey to Edinburgh, drank himself drunk again the next morning, offered to fight me for half a crown in Princes Street, and lost himself on the way to Queensferry. We never saw him again.

I had, too, a long round of interviews with the various officials at the Foreign Office: Lord Hardinge, Eric Drummond, George Clerk, Don Gregory, John Buchan, Ronnie Campbell and Lord Robert Cecil – the last-named still supremely sceptical and still convinced that Trotsky was a German in disguise. During these first eleven days of January I derived a minor thrill from the English Press. My mission was vested with a certain amount of secrecy. There had been, however, the usual leakage. There were paragraphs, facetious or flattering according to the views of the particular newspaper, about the young man from Moscow. One evening paper excelled itself by declaring that I had been appointed Ambassador to Russia, that the choice had lain between Mr Arthur Henderson and myself, and that my knowledge of Russia had turned the scales in my favour.

Lord Milner I saw almost daily. Five days before my departure I dined alone with him at Brooks's. He was in his most inspiring mood. He talked to me with a charming frankness about the war, about the future of England, about his own career, and about the opportunities of youth. He was bitter about the Foreign Office, called Mr Balfour* a harmless old gentleman, and castigated other prominent permanent officials who are still living. Before he died, he said, he would like to have six months at the Foreign Office. He would begin with a broom – no, he would start with a fire. He would have liked to see Lord Robert Cecil as Foreign Secretary, with Sir Eyre Crowe as his assistant.

About the war he was inclined to be pessimistic. As he gave me my final instructions about my mission, he pointed out the gravity of the situation. If the submarine menace were not speedily averted, a decision could not be long delayed. He envisaged the possibility and even the probability of a peace by negotiation. As far as Russia was concerned, things were so bad that it did not matter very much what I did. My main task must be to do as much harm to the Germans as possible, to put a spoke in the wheels of the separate peace negotiations, and to stiffen by whatever means I could the Bolshevik resistance to German demands. All the information I could obtain as

* Arthur Balfour (1848–1930), Foreign Secretary 1917–19. He had been Prime Minister 1902–11.

to the real nature and strength of the Bolshevik movement would be extremely valuable. If I was in any difficulty, I was to telegraph to him direct.

I find it hard to write of Lord Milner in anything but superlatives. He never shone in the market-place of politics. He had none of the tricks of the politician. Certainly, he was no orator as Mr Lloyd George is. But in a Cabinet, most of whose members were profoundly ignorant of everything outside England, his wide range of knowledge, his capacity for real work, and his comprehensive grasp of administrative detail made him invaluable. To Mr Lloyd George he was the indispensable collaborator, who could be relied upon to read every paper, to sift every scheme, and to form an unbiased and detached view of every problem that was put before him. His nobleness of mind, his entirely natural charm of manner, his lofty idealism, the complete absence of ambitious scheming or of anything approaching self-conceit in his character, and his broad and vigorous patriotism made him the ideal inspirer of youth. With young men, too, he was at his best. He liked to surround himself with them. He believed they should be given their chance. For to the end of his life this man, so gentle and understanding in manner and so tenacious in purpose, was deeply concerned with the future of England. He was, too, very far from being the jingo and the Conservative reactionary whom popular opinion at one time represented him to be. On the contrary, many of his views on society were startlingly modern. He believed in the highly organised state, in which service, efficiency, and hard work were more important than titles or money-bags. He had little respect for the aristocrat, who was effete, and none at all for the financier, who had made his money not by production but by manipulation of the market.

I must have been one of the last of the young men to worship at his feet, and there I have remained. I see no Milners in our public life at present – men who are prepared to serve the state disinterestedly and with no other ambition than to serve it well, and to this day, far more than the politicians or the millionaires, he stands out as an example to the country of the ideal public servant. In the life of every nation it is character which counts in the end, and among all the so-called great men of the world whom I have met there has been none who in this respect is fit to hold a candle to Lord Milner. My own conduct must have tried him highly. He had arranged my Russian mission, not because he had anything but a profound abhorrence of Bolshevism, but because he believed that I understood the Russian situation better than most Englishmen. He was probably disappointed when I seemed to go over body and soul to the Bolsheviks. He may have regarded my subsequent failure in Russia as a reflection on his judgement. But his attitude to me underwent no change. He was as kind to me when I returned as when I set out. I dined alone again at Brooks's with him on several occasions. I was a frequent visitor at his house in Little College Street. When I went abroad again, I kept in touch with him. He took an interest in my career, and it was on his advice (taken, unfortunately, too late) that I left the Foreign Office.

In one respect Lord Milner's promotion of my interests was detrimental to my prospects. I had been selected for this Russian mission not by the Foreign Secretary but by the War Cabinet – actually, by Lord Milner and Mr Lloyd George. The decision had been taken over the heads of the permanent officials, who chafed under the Lloyd George method of handling affairs and who resented having stray missions, headed by a junior Vice-Consul, foisted upon them.

I should have realised this at the time – indeed, I received a broad hint from Lord Robert Cecil – and with a proper humility should have placated the higher permanent officials. The Cecils and the Milners would depart with the end of the war. The Hardinges and the Tyrrells* or their equivalents would remain. I did see Lord Hardinge, before I left, and was, I hope, properly humble. But I confess that I gave this aspect of my new position little thought. Adventure tugs at the heart-strings of youth. I had been given the opportunity for a great adventure, and my one thought was to start on it at once. During the month which had just passed I had seen and met, and even been listened to by, the men who were in the very heart of affairs in London. I had been selected from among God knows what weird choice of candidates for a difficult and exciting mission. I had had a colossal stroke of luck. If my head had not been turned a little – and I do not think it was – there were sure to be kind friends who would say that it had been.

My departure was in the grand manner. With Litvinov's letter in my pocket and Lord Milner's blessing on my head, I travelled up to

* Charles, Lord Hardinge (1858–1944), and William George, Lord Tyrrell (1866–1947), senior civil servants.

Edinburgh on January 12th and stayed the night with my grand-mother, who cried affectionately over me. The next day, accom-panied by the other members of my mission and by my wife, who had come to see us off, I made my way to Queensferry. It was a glorious, sunny day, and, as we passed the tenth milestone, suddenly the Forth Bridge came into view and drawn up in two long rows behind it the assembled might of the British battle fleet.

We arrived at the Hawes Inn in time for luncheon. The Navy had now taken charge of us, and very little information was vouchsafed to us. Some time that afternoon we were to go on board the cruiser which was to take us to Bergen. Till dusk time lay heavy on our hands. I walked along the shore, looking at the great ships and won-dering when I should be home again. I had been brought up on *Kidnapped*. It was in this same salty old-fashioned Hawes Inn that Uncle Ebenezer and Captain Hoseason had made their plot to entice David Balfour on to the brig *Covenant* and to sell him into slavery on the American plantations. It did not seem a very happy omen. The day, too, was the thirteenth of the month. Action, however, soon banished the gloom from my thoughts. As the dusk grew into dark-ness, a young lieutenant came ashore and in a whisper informed us that we were to go aboard. There was a delicious secrecy and sense of mystery about the whole business. Soft-footed sailors spirited our luggage away. Then, silently, in single file, we crept down the steps of the jetty to the pinnace which was to convey us to the *Yarmouth*. At 6 p.m. we were on board. But it was not until dawn the next day that we raised anchor. Then, headed by the two destroyers which were to be our escort, we steamed slowly between the towering lines of the great battle-cruisers, down past the massive cylinders of the Forth Bridge, and out into the open sea.

The Great Adventure had begun.

If I had conveniently forgotten my sick-leave voyage from Moscow to London, the return journey remains as clearly stamped on my mind as if it were yesterday. There was neither monotony nor much tranquillity about it. I had become someone – or, at least, something – of minor importance, and the change in my status was reflected in the different attitude towards me of those two great barometers of worldly significance: the Press and our own Legations abroad. On my first night on board the *Yarmouth* I dined alone in solemn state with the captain, a tall, well-built man with a strong face and a quiet, self-reliant manner. He was a grandson of W. G. Grace, the famous cricketer, and is today an admiral. The rest of my mission dined in the wardroom. For many of us that was the last meal we had on board. As soon as we had passed May Island we ran into terrible weather with heavy seas and a raging wind. The cold, too, was bitter, and every half-hour or so we encountered a fresh blizzard. It was, in fact, the North Sea at its worst, and a light cruiser, cleared for action, was not the kind of ship best suited to face it. We could not go on deck. A goodly number of the crew and at least one officer were violently seasick. Hicks, Phelan and Birse were *in extremis*.

The next morning we arrived off the Norwegian coast, but the seas were too stormy and the blizzards too blinding to permit our making the entry into the fjord. During the night one of our destroyers, unable to keep head with the weather, had been forced to return home. For some time we had lost touch with the other owing to the wireless freezing.

I have never been seasick in my life, but I confess frankly that I was relieved both of discomfort and of a certain amount of fear when, after twenty-four hours of cruising off the Norwegian coast, we entered the Bergen fjord. Here we were met by Commodore Gade, the Commander-in-Chief of the Norwegian fleet. He had on board his steam yacht Sir George Buchanan, General Knox, Admiral Stanley, Captain Scale and Captain Neilson, who were returning to England. I had half an hour's conversation with the Ambassador, who was his usual charming self. This time, however, he looked ill and tired. The first ten months of the revolution had added ten years to his life.

Having said goodbye to the Ambassador and his suite, we had an excellent luncheon with Gade and at four o'clock were glad to stretch our legs on the firm ground of Bergen. The next morning we made the railway trip – the most wonderful in the world – from Bergen to Christiania. It was not to my mind so impressive in winter as in the autumn.

Christiania, whose merchants had grown fat on supplying ships and fish to the Allies, was very expensive and almost gay. Champagne began to flow at eleven o'clock in the morning and never ceased. The inhabitants, too, were very pro-British and, owing to the Norwegian loss of life from German submarines, violently anti-German. A few days before we arrived a German music-hall artist, who had been hissed by his Norwegian audience and who had expressed resentment, had been torn almost to pieces.

We had twenty-four hours at Christiania, and, although owing to the Russo-German peace negotiations I was anxious to push on as quickly as possible, the time passed pleasantly enough. I dined at our Legation and met Sir Mansfeldt Findlay, one of the tallest Englishmen in the world and certainly the tallest man in diplomacy. He was a good organiser and, aided by Charles Brudenell-Bruce, ran his huge Legation (Christiania, in peacetime a diplomatic backwater, had, owing to the blockade, the largest staff of any Legation or Embassy during the war) with great efficiency. In his political views he was an extreme Conservative, who would rather have lost the war than run the risk of social upheaval in England.

In Christiania, too, we met the first of the English refugees from Russia, members of our prosperous colonies in St Petersburg and Moscow, who in a night had seen their comfortable existence swept away before their eyes in the maelstrom of revolution. One conversation, in particular, I noted in my diary. It was with Reynolds, a well-to-do timber-merchant, who had been very intimate with members of the Embassy staff. He had lost everything, was very nervous, and was obsessed with only one idea: that we should make peace as soon as possible in order, in alliance with Germany, to restore order in Russia.

I recall this conversation because it was typical of the point of view we were to find among the Russian bourgeois in Moscow and St Petersburg during 1918. Yet in the face of these facts, all through this period our military experts were writing memoranda about the loyal Russians and about the restoration of the Eastern front. As if there were any Russians who thought of any other interests than their own or of any other front than the civil war front, once the Bolshevik revolution had started. This is not anti-Russian prejudice. It is plain common sense. An Englishman or a German, situated in similar circumstances, would have had the same thoughts and the same mental reactions. If there were Russians who accepted the English formula of restoring the Eastern front and who talked of the sanctity of their oath to fight until victory was assured, they did so, consciously or subconsciously, with their tongues in their cheeks. The one aim of every Russian bourgeois (and 99 per cent of the so-called 'loyal' Russians were bourgeois) was to secure the intervention of British troops (and, failing British, German troops) to re-establish order in Russia, suppress Bolshevism and restore to the bourgeois his property.

On our arrival at Stockholm we received news that civil war had broken out in Finland and that the chances of our getting through to St Petersburg were very small. I was determined, however, to push on, and, while Sir Esmé Howard (today Lord Howard and ex-Ambassador to the United States, then our Minister in Stockholm) telegraphed to the British authorities at Haparanda and Helsingfors to make all possible arrangements for our journey, I went off to see Vorovsky, the Bolshevik Minister, to arrange for a Russian train to meet us at the Finnish frontier.

I rather liked Vorovsky. He had a fine intellectual face with wistful grey eyes and a brown beard. He was thin, looked ascetic, and gave me the impression of a man of taste and refinement. He had beautiful hands and in Paris would have been taken immediately for an artist or a writer. I showed him my letter to Trotsky, and he promised to do everything he could to help me. He also gave me the latest news of the Russo-German peace negotiations at Brest-Litovsk. From my point of view they were encouraging. At first the Germans had wanted to conclude peace with the greatest possible despatch, but now, encouraged by the defection of the Ukrainians, who had gone over body and soul to them, they were trying to force the most impossible terms upon the Bolsheviks. The negotiations, Vorovsky said, were likely to be prolonged. If it were humanly possible, he would get us to St Petersburg in three days.

We arrived in Stockholm on Saturday, January 19th. It was Friday, January 25th, before we left for Haparanda and Finland.

Although the delay was irksome, our sojourn in Stockholm was not uninteresting. The town itself looked its best in its winter mantle of snow and clear blue sky. The weather was wonderful and the air like champagne. My hotel was besieged with visitors – mostly English and Russian refugees from Moscow and St Petersburg, who wanted me to protect their property or to take a message to their relatives. I lunched and dined with Sir Esmé Howard and through him met M. Branting, the Swedish Socialist Prime Minister. Branting, a massive and impressive figure of a man, was the convenor of the ill-fated Stockholm Socialist Conference, which had been frowned on by Mr Lloyd George and which had failed through the refusal of the British seamen to convey Mr Ramsay MacDonald and Mr Henderson across the North Sea. Branting still wanted to have his Conference and to include the Bolsheviks in his general invitation. Sir Esmé Howard, who in Stockholm probably had a better objective view of both sides in the war than any other diplomat elsewhere, rightly concluded that we had something to gain and nothing to lose from such a Conference, and supported Mr Branting's proposals. Like every other proposal which seemed to hint at peace, they came to nothing.

In Stockholm, too, I found some old friends – the volatile Lykiardopoulos, Guy Colebrooke, and that fine old Russian gentleman, General Wogak – and made some new ones, including Clifford Sharp, the brilliant editor of the *New Statesman*. 'Lyki', formerly a liberal, had now, like other Russian liberals, become very reactionary. He tried to strike terror into our hearts with tales of horror from Russia: how in Turkestan the population was killing off the old men and women and children because there was not enough to eat; how in Petrograd people were bartering a suit of clothes for a loaf of black bread. It was madness for us to proceed on our journey. England should reverse her policy and put her money on the monarchists. The Bolsheviks would not last another month!

More interesting was my dinner with Nobel – a member of the famous Swedish family. He had spent years of his life in St Petersburg and had large interests all over Russia. He had formed a more accurate estimate of the situation and was convinced that Bolshevism had not yet reached its apogee. Like all foreigners who had property in Russia he was anxious for a general peace and for an Allied-cum-German intervention against the Bolsheviks. He was one of the few people who at that time had visualised Bolshevism as a world-danger. With other Swedes he had joined a rifle club in order that he might take his place behind the bourgeois barricades in the event of a proletarian rising in Sweden.

Not all my time was passed in such serious and lugubrious conversations. More frivolous entertainment was provided by Sir Coleridge Kennard, who was the Legation secretary in charge of British propaganda in Sweden. Sir Coleridge is an Orientalist, a poet, and a romanticist. Obviously, he would have imaginative ideas on propaganda. The Swedish upper classses were pro-German. They were also sentimental and fond of late hours. Sir Coleridge conceived the fantastic but inherently sound plan of making them pro-Ally by providing Stockholm with a first-class British variety entertainment. He won over the benevolent Sir Esmé Howard to his scheme. He convinced Whitehall that English beauty and English talent were more potent political factors than subsidised leading articles in the Swedish Press. And he was given almost a free hand.

He was as proud of his cabaret as Mussolini is of his dramas, and we were not allowed to leave Stockholm without seeing it. It was a great experience. We dined in the magnificent Moorish hall of the Grand Hotel, and then, beneath a starlit sky with the moon shining on the icy waters of the fjords, we made our way to Rolf's, where Sir Coleridge held his court. Here for the first time I heard Miss Irene Browne sing 'Hello, My Dearie'. Here, too, Miss Betty Chester made her contribution to the Allied victory by a vivacity which drew roars of applause from the sentimental, punch-drinking Swedes. It was an excellent and most successful form of propaganda, for it paid its own way. For me it was to be the last link with Western civilisation for nine months.

The next day I received a message from Vorovsky requesting me to come to see him. He had received a telegram from St Petersburg. All arrangements had been made for our safe conduct from the Finnish frontier. He also gave me the latest news from Russia. It was disturbing. Shingariev and Kokoshkin, two ex-Ministers of the Kerensky Government, had been brutally murdered in their beds by sailors in the Marine Hospital in St Petersburg, to which they had been taken from the Petropavlosk Fortress. I had known both men intimately – more especially Kokoshkin, who was an old Moscow friend. Each belonged to the very best type of Russian. Their whole lives had been spent in disinterested public service. They were liberals, who had worked incessantly to help the downtrodden and oppressed, and it would have been hard to find two men in public life more free from personal ambition or self-seeking. The news of this butchery filled me with a sickening horror. The revolution was working out to pattern. Its chief victims were to be amongst those democrats who had trusted most in the common sense of the people. Even Vorovsky was shocked and seemed ashamed. Five years later he himself was to be shot down by the pistol of a Russian monarchist in the dining-room of the Beau Rivage Hotel in Lausanne.

That same evening, after a series of hurried farewells, we left for Haparanda, the Swedish frontier town on the northern extremity of the Gulf of Bothnia. The journey was tedious, lasting more than twenty-six hours. There were many delays, the engine puffing and snorting as though unwilling that we should go further. And, indeed, there would have been every justification for our turning back. Civil war had broken out in Finland between the Whites and the Reds. The Whites held the north. The Reds had seized control of Helsingfors. We should have to cross the line of fire between the opposing forces. The conductors and Swedish passengers on the train told us we should never get through.

On the morning of Saturday, January 26th, we arrived at Haparanda and, after some discussion and much uncertainty, we crossed over to Tornea on the Finnish side, where we spent the whole day debating our next decision. Having come so far, I was determined to push on. Thanks to the energy of Greener, the British passport-control officer, we succeeded in persuading the Finns to run a train, and at ten in the evening we set out into the unknown. Our fellow passengers were mainly Russian emigrants – former exiles of the Tsarist régime – who were returning to the new Paradise. Most of them were in a state of abject terror. Doubtless, they were afraid of the Finnish Whites, who at this stage of our journey were in complete control.

At eight o'clock the next night we arrived at Ruhimaki, where we were told that the bridge at Kuovala had been destroyed by White Guards and that we could not proceed further. We had a choice between returning to Stockholm or persuading the guard to make a detour and take his train to Helsingfors. We spent the night in the station and the next morning came on to Helsingfors to find the capital in a state of revolution. Desultory firing was going on in the square outside the station. On the platform we met Lednitski, a leading Polish lawyer, whom I had known in Moscow. He informed me that the hotels were crowded with refugees, that people were sleeping in threes and fours even in the bathrooms, and that we had no chance of obtaining accommodation. He offered to try to find rooms for us at the house of a Polish priest. When the firing seemed to have died down, I left Birse and Phelan in charge of our luggage and wandered off with Hicks and Lednitski to find the priest. The priest had no available accommodation. We left Lednitski with him and, armed with a map, set out on our long tramp back to the station. The weather was vile. There had been a thaw, and the snow, dirty and yellow, was soft and slushy. The firing in the side-streets sounded unpleasantly close. Then suddenly, as we mounted a hill and turned into a broad boulevard, we ran into a fleeing mob pursued by a detachment of sailors with a machine-gun. The sailors were spraying the street with bullets. The pursued had sought the shelter of the pavements. Some were rushing helter-skelter as fast as their legs could carry them. Others were trying to break open the locked doors of the shops and houses. Several corpses lay face downwards in the snow. The whole rush lasted only a few seconds, and Hicks and I, who were a fine mark in the middle of the road, had not time to turn back. We flopped on our faces in the snow. Very gingerly I held up a white handkerchief, while Hicks waved his British passport. The next few seconds seemed like eternity. The sailors, equally cautious, advanced very slowly with their machine-gun and pointed rifles. Fortunately, they were Russians, and my letter to Trotsky worked wonders.

The sailors, in fact, turned out to be a godsend. Satisfied regarding our bona fides, they took us to the station, where they gave strict orders for the safe custody of our baggage. Then they conducted us to the British Consulate. Here we met Grove and Fawcett, his Vice-Consul. They succeeded in fixing us up for the night in a small pension, and the next day Fawcett, who knew everyone in Helsingfors, persuaded the Red Finnish Government to give us a train and a safe conduct to the broken bridge on the other side of which we hoped to find a Russian train.

At seven o'clock the same evening we set out once more on our odyssey. Thanks to our Red safe conduct, we travelled very comfortably. Our train, at least, was heated, and the accommodation, if rough, was ample. We were favoured, too, by circumstances. The Finnish Reds were especially kind to us, because at that moment the White Finns were negotiating for German assistance.

When we came to the bridge we had a moment of trepidation. Rumour, however, had exaggerated, as usual, the extent of the destruction. The line, it is true, had been torn up. The arch of the bridge had been buckled. But the bridge itself was still standing and still passable on foot. At midnight we got out of our warm train into the freezing night. Then, with the aid of a lantern, we crept our way across the bridge. It was another eerie performance, but once again it was safely accomplished. The Red Finns who accompanied us – we had been provided with an armed escort – were both kind and efficient. In two shifts they carried our heavy luggage across the bridge for us. This was no mean feat, for we had provided ourselves with an abundance of stores, and our packing cases were both heavy and cumbersome. Not as much as a parcel was missing when the task was completed.

What was more, thanks to the intervention of the Finnish Reds, a train with steam up was waiting for us on the other side. We entrained at once and at seven on the following evening we arrived in St Petersburg without further incident or delay. We were the last British passengers to get through – the last British officials to make the journey from London to St Petersburg via Scandinavia until the end of the war.

It was a very different St Petersburg to which I had returned. The streets were in an appalling state. The snow had not been swept away for weeks, and the sleigh-drive from the Finland station on the north side of the river to the Embassy was like a ride on a scenic railway – without the security. The people in the streets were depressed and unhappy. Very dreadful, too, was the condition of the horses. They looked as if they had not had a square meal for weeks. Just before we came to the Troitsky Bridge, we passed a dead horse. It was frozen into the snow and had obviously been there for some days.

At the Embassy there was some confusion of thought and much division of opinion. Trotsky was at Brest-Litovsk endeavouring to make peace with the Germans, and no one seemed to know quite what was happening. The Embassy staff was split up into recognitionists and anti-recognitionists, and Lindley – now Sir Francis Lindley and Ambassador to Japan – who was in charge, steered an indecisive course between the two conflicting groups. Until we could find a suitable house, the members of my mission were quartered on different members of the other British missions in St Petersburg. My own good Samaritan was Rex Hoare, now British Minister in Teheran and then second secretary at the Embassy. A charming companion with a slow drawl, which belied an extremely active intelligence, Hoare was one of the few Englishmen who could take an objective view of the revolution. He was in favour of recognising the Bolshevik Government, and his views were in close accordance with my own. That night, as I sought to read myself to sleep, I found beside my bed a copy of Lord Cromer's* *Modern Egypt*. In it I came across an aphorism, which had guided Cromer's conduct in Egypt: '*Il faut s'accommoder aux circonstances et en tirer parti même de ce qui nous déplaît.*' It seemed an excellent guide for my own conduct in the difficult situation in which I now found myself.

The next day I had my first interview with Chicherin, who in Trotsky's absence at Brest-Litovsk was in charge of the Foreign Office. He received me in the same building in which Sazonov had

* As Consul-General in Egypt, Evelyn Baring, Lord Cromer (1841–1917), did much to reform Egyptian administrative, agricultural and financial policies.

formerly held sway. Petrov, a swarthy Jew, was present during our interview, and the serio-comic nature of the situation may best be illustrated by the fact that both men had been released from an English prison in order to return to Russia.

A Russian of good family, who long before the revolution had sacrificed a fortune for his Socialist convictions, Chicherin was a man of great culture. In his youth he had begun his career as an official of the Tsarist Foreign Office, and he spoke French, English and German with fluency and accuracy. He was dressed in a hideous yellow-brown tweed suit, which he had brought with him from England, and during the six months of our almost daily contact I never saw him in any other. With his sandy-coloured beard and hair and his sandy-coloured suit he looked like one of those grotesque figures made by children on the sea-shore. Only his eyes, small and red-rimmed like a ferret's, gave any sign of life. His narrow shoulders were bent with much toiling over his desk. Among a group of men who worked for sixteen hours out of the twenty-four, he was the most indefatigable and relentless in his attention to his duties. An idealist, whose loyalty to his own party was unshakeable, he was extraordinarily mistrustful of everyone outside it.

Our first interview was satisfactory, but vague. Later, when I knew my Chicherin better, I learnt that he never took a decision without reference to Lenin. On this occasion, however, he had evidently received instructions to be friendly. Indeed, the Bolsheviks, whose obvious policy was to play off the Germans against the Allies and the Allies against the Germans, welcomed my arrival. In the Bolshevik Press the importance of my mission and of my own position was wilfully exaggerated, and I was described, not only as the man of confidence of Mr Lloyd George, but also as an influential politician, whose sympathies were entirely with the Bolsheviks! This description of my standing caused some misunderstanding among the other Allied missions in St Petersburg. In particular, one American intelligence officer, whose chief contribution to the war was the purchase of a stack of documents, so palpably forged that even our own secret service would have nothing to do with them, reported to his Government that a dangerous English revolutionary had arrived in St Petersburg and was hob-nobbing with the Bolsheviks.

Chicherin was honest enough in his account of what was happening at Brest-Litovsk. He told me that the negotiations were going badly and that now was the great opportunity for England to make a friendly gesture towards Russia. Almost in the same breath he informed me that the Bolsheviks were now busily engaged in organising a new International, in which there would be no room for moderate Socialists like Branting and Henderson. This, in fact, was the beginning of the notorious Third International.

Another new acquaintance of these first days in the Bolshevised St Petersburg was Raymond Robins, the head of the American Red Cross mission, and brother of Elizabeth Robins, the well-known authoress. On the third evening of my arrival Rex Hoare invited him to dine with us, and we had a good talk. Robins, who was a philanthropist and a humanitarian rather than a politician, was a wonderful orator. His conversation, like Mr Churchill's, was always a monologue, but it was never dull, and his gift of allegory was as remarkable as it was original. With his black hair and his aquiline features, he had a most striking appearance. He was an Indian chief with a Bible for his tomahawk. He had stood as Roosevelt's Vice-President in the 'Bull Moose's' campaign for the American Presidency in 1912. Although a rich man himself, he was an anti-capitalist. Yet, in spite of his sympathies for the underdog, he was a worshipper of great men. Hitherto, his two heroes had been Roosevelt and Cecil Rhodes. Now Lenin had captured his imagination. Strangely enough, Lenin was amused by the hero-worship, and of all foreigners Robins was the only man whom Lenin was always willing to see and who ever succeeded in imposing his own personality on the unemotional Bolshevik leader.

In a less official sense Robins had a similar mission to my own. He was the intermediary between the Bolsheviks and the American Government and had set himself the task of persuading President Wilson to recognise the Soviet régime. He knew no Russian and very little about Russia. But in Gumberg, a Russo-American Jew, who for years had been in close touch with the Bolshevik movement, he had an assistant who supplied him with the necessary knowledge and arguments. And Gumberg's arguments in Robins's mouth made a most convincing case for recognition. I liked Robins. For the next four months we were to be in daily and almost hourly contact.

My first twelve days in St Petersburg were spent in an endless round of discussions with Chicherin and our own officials. My relations with Lindley, who as Chargé d'Affaires might reasonably have resented my intrusion into the political arena (as the official representative of the British Government he had, of course, no dealings with the Bolsheviks), were of the friendliest. I co-operated with him to the fullest extent, reporting everything to him, and consulted him about every step I took, and in this way what might have been an awkward and unpleasant situation was averted.

I made, however, little progress, and most of my telegrams to London remained unanswered. We were still completely ignorant of the true course of the negotiations at Brest-Litovsk, and Chicherin did little to enlighten our darkness. All that he would admit was that, while German militarism and British capitalism were equally hateful to the Bolsheviks, German militarism was for the moment the greater danger. Germany was now the centre of an anti-Bolshevik league. She was supporting the bourgeois cause in Finland, Romania, and the Ukraine. The Russian bourgeois were looking to her to intervene in Russia and to restore them to their former position. Here was a situation which the British Government could exploit to its own benefit. The Bolsheviks would welcome British support.

On February 9th I had an interview of a more intriguing nature. Various commissions of the Central Powers peace delegation were actually working in St Petersburg. Through a reliable channel I received a demand for an interview from one of the Bulgarian delegates. As I had nothing to risk in seeing him, I acceded to the request. In my diary he is entered merely as S. His name, I think, was Semidov. In a long and interesting conversation he told me that Bulgaria was ripe for peace and revolution and that with encouragement (which, I assume, meant money) from England there would be little difficulty in starting a movement to dethrone King Ferdinand and expel the pro-German Ministers. Obviously, the man may have been an *agent provocateur* sent to me by the Bolsheviks. In this case, however, the odds are that he was genuine. I reported the incident to London and heard no more about it.

While awaiting Trotsky's return from Brest-Litovsk, we took advantage of this respite to establish our mission in a large and well-furnished flat on the Palace Quay almost directly opposite the Peter and Paul Fortress and within a few hundred yards of the Embassy. There was, too, an excellent cellar, which we took over at a reasonable price. We could, in fact, have had a palace for next to nothing. The unfortunate aristocracy, deprived of everything, was only too glad to find a foreign official who could, even temporarily, safeguard its property.

As a house-warming I gave a luncheon party to which I invited the Embassy staff and other prominent British officials in St Petersburg. My chief guest was Robins. He arrived late, having just come from Lenin. He brought with him the news that Trotsky had refused to sign a shameful peace but that, as Russia could not fight, she would go on demobilising.

During luncheon Robins spoke little, but afterwards, when we assembled in the smoking-room, his tongue was loosed. Standing by the mantelpiece, his black hair smoothed back with characteristic gesture, he made a moving appeal for Allied support of the Bolsheviks. He began quietly, analysing the various Allied arguments against recognition and demolishing the ridiculous Allied theory that the Bolsheviks were working for a German victory. He drew a touching picture of a helpless people facing with courage and without arms the greatest military machine in history. We had nothing to hope from the demoralised Russian bourgeoisie, who were actually relying on German aid for the restoration of their rights and property. Then he began his eulogy of Trotsky. The Red leader was 'a four-kind son of a bitch, but the greatest Jew since Christ. If the German General Staff bought Trotsky, they bought a lemon.' As he worked up to his peroration, he became almost indignant over the folly of the Allies in 'playing the German game in Russia'. Then he stopped dramatically and took a piece of paper from the flap pocket of his uniform. I can see him now. Consciously or not, he had provided himself with an almost perfect setting. Before him a semicircle of stolid Englishmen. Behind him the roaring log-fire, its tongues of flame reflected in weird shadows on the yellow-papered walls. Outside, through the window, the glorious view of the slender spire of Peter and Paul with the great fire-ball of the setting sun casting rays of blood on the snow-clad waters of the Neva. Once again he pushed his hair back with his hand and shook his head like a lion. 'Have any of you read this?' he asked. 'I found it this morning in one of your "noospapers".' Then in a low voice, quivering with emotion, he read Major McCrae's poem:

> We are the Dead. Short days ago
> We lived, felt dawn, saw sunset glow,

Loved and were loved, and now we lie
  In Flanders fields.

Take up our quarrel with the foe:
To you from failing hands we throw
  The torch; be yours to hold it high.
  If ye break faith with us who die
We shall not sleep, though poppies grow
  In Flanders fields.

When he had finished, there was an almost deathly silence. For what seemed an eternity Robins himself turned away and looked out of the window. Then, squaring his shoulders, he came back to us. 'Boys!' he said. 'I guess we're all here for one purpose – to see that the German General Staff don't win this war.'

Three quick strides, and he was by my side. He wrung my hand. 'Goodbye, Lockhart,' he said. Four more strides, and he was gone.

As a dramatic performance Robins's effort was immense. Today, it sounds like emotional hysteria. Doubtless, too, he had rehearsed all his effects before his shaving glass in the morning. But at the moment his words made a deep impression on everyone who heard him. There was not a laugh or a smile. Even 'Benji' Bruce, with all his Ulster prejudices against revolution, was temporarily convinced that recognition or, at least, support of the Bolsheviks against German aggression was the right policy. General Poole, who afterwards commanded the ill-fated expedition to Archangel, was then of the same opinion.

Three days afterwards I had my first interview with Trotsky in the Russian Foreign Office. It lasted for two hours, during which we discussed all the modalities of Anglo-Russian co-operation. As one of the accusations levelled against me afterwards was that I had been infatuated from the first by Trotsky and was completely under his influence, I give my first impressions of him exactly as I entered them in my diary at the time:

February 15th, 1918. Had a two hours' conversation with L.D.T. [Lev Davidovich Trotsky]. He struck me as perfectly honest and sincere in his bitterness against the Germans. He has a wonderfully quick mind and a rich, deep voice. With his broad chest, his huge forehead, surmounted by great masses of black, waving

Right, Vaclav Vorovsky, Bolshevik Minister. *Below*, George Chicherin (left), Trotsky's aide in the Russian Foreign Office, and Maxim Litvinov (right), Russian Ambassador in London

Overleaf, Vladimir Lenin

hair, his strong, fierce eyes, and his heavy protruding lips, he is the very incarnation of the revolutionary of the bourgeois caricatures. He is neat about his dress. He wore a clean soft collar and his nails were carefully manicured. I agree with Robins. If the Bosche bought Trotsky, he bought a lemon. His dignity has suffered an affront. He is full of belligerent fury against the Germans for the humiliation to which they have exposed him at Brest. He strikes me as a man who would willingly die fighting for Russia provided there was a big enough audience to see him do it.

Trotsky *was* angry with the Germans. At that moment he was not quite certain what the German reaction would be to his famous declaration of 'no peace and no war', but he had a shrewd idea that it would be unpleaşant.

Unfortunately, he was also full of bitterness against the English. We had not handled Trotsky wisely. At the time of the first revolution he was in exile in America. He was then neither a Menshevik nor a Bolshevik. He was what Lenin called a Trotskist – that is to say, an individualist and an opportunist. A revolutionary with the temperament of an artist and with undoubted physical courage, he had never been and never could be a good party man. His conduct prior to the first revolution had incurred the severest condemnation by Lenin. 'Trotsky, as always,' wrote Lenin in 1915, 'is, in principle, opposed to the Socialist Chauvinists, but in practice he is always in agreement with them.'

In the spring of 1917 Kerensky requested the British Government to facilitate Trotsky's return to Russia. Common sense seemed to indicate one of two courses: to refuse, on the grounds that Trotsky was a danger to the Allied cause; or to allow him to return unmolested. As usual in our attitude towards Russia, we adopted disastrous half-measures. Trotsky was treated as a criminal. At Halifax, New Brunswick, he was separated from his wife and children and interned in a prison camp at Amherst with German prisoners for four weeks. His fingerprints were taken. Then, having roused his bitter hate, we allowed him to return to Russia. I am giving Trotsky's own account of the incident. I learnt afterwards that it was substantially correct. The outraged Trotsky came back to Russia, threw in his lot with the Bolsheviks, and relieved his injured feelings by writing a fiercely anti-British pamphlet entitled *A Prisoner of the*

English. Some trace of his resentment showed itself during our interview. I succeeded, however, in soothing him. The German danger was uppermost in his mind, and his last words, as I left him, were: 'Now is the big opportunity for the Allied Governments.'

I returned from my interview to our flat only to find an urgent message from Robins requesting me to come to see him at once. I found him in a state of great agitation. He had been in conflict with Saalkind, a nephew of Trotsky and then Assistant Commissar for Foreign Affairs. Saalkind had been rude, and the American, who had a promise from Lenin that, whatever happened, a train would always be ready for him at an hour's notice, was determined to exact an apology or to leave the country. When I arrived, he had just finished telephoning to Lenin. He had delivered his ultimatum, and Lenin had promised to give a reply within ten minutes. I waited, while Robins fumed. Then the telephone rang and Robins picked up the receiver. Lenin had capitulated. Saalkind was to be dismissed his post. But he was an old member of the party. Would Robins have any objection if Lenin sent him as a Bolshevik emissary to Berne? Robins smiled grimly. 'Thank you, Mr Lenin,' he said. 'As I can't send the son of a bitch to hell, "burn" is the next best thing you can do with him.'

This was the beginning of what was to be a hectic month. The Germans lost little time in replying to Trotsky's refusal to sign their peace terms and, to the consternation of the Bolsheviks, began to advance on St Petersburg. At first the Bolsheviks made some show of resistance. Orders were given in this sense to the fleet and to the Army. Trotsky himself, whom I was now seeing daily, informed me that, even if Russia could not resist, she would wage a partisan war to the best of her ability. Very soon, however, it became clear that, in the military sense of the word, there could be no resistance. The Bolsheviks had come into power on a peace slogan. A war slogan might easily bring about their ruin. The bourgeoisie was openly delighted at the prospect of the German advance, which had emboldened the anti-Bolshevik Press to attack the Bolsheviks with a frenzied fury. The determining factor was the attitude of the troops. On the rumour that the war was to be renewed desertions from the front assumed the proportions of panic flight, and, after an all-night sitting of the Commissars, a telegram was sent to the Germans capitulating entirely and asking for peace on any terms.

In the Bolshevik–Left Social-Revolutionary coalition, of which the Lenin Government was composed, there was a holy-war party. It included Bolsheviks like Petrov, Bukharin and Radek and, numerically, it was nearly as strong as the peace party. Lenin, however, was for peace. Without peace he could not consolidate his position. It was now that he formulated his policy of 'lavirovat' of which the best translation is the French *'reculer pour mieux sauter'*. Trotsky, as usual, steered a middle course. He wanted to fight. He considered that war was inevitable. If the Allies would send a promise of support, he informed me that he would sway the decision of the Government in favour of war. I sent several telegrams to London requesting an official message that would enable me to strengthen Trotsky's hands. No message was sent.

On February 23rd the German terms were received. They were considerably stiffer in their territorial demands than the Treaty of Versailles, and once again the ranks of the Bolsheviks were torn with dissension. The next day, after a fierce and passionate debate, the Central Executive Committee decided by 112 votes to eighty-six to accept the German terms. Lenin's cold, calculated logic dominated the meeting. There were, however, twenty-five abstentions. Among them was the vote of Trotsky, who during the discussion remained skulking in his room.

On the afternoon of the debate I telephoned to Trotsky. He had given me his private telephone number, and he answered the call himself. 'May I speak to Citizen Trotsky?' I asked. There was a growl of 'No' from the other end. But I had recognised his voice. 'Lev Davidovich,' I said quickly. 'This is Lockhart. I want to see you immediately.' There was a moment's silence. Then another growl:

'It's no use. But come at once if you like. I'm at Smolny.'

Smolny – in Tsarist days a seminary for young girls of good family – was the Bolshevik headquarters. It had a picturesque situation next door to a monastery – a pleasant blue and white building on the outskirts of the city. The institute itself was grey, with an entrance like a Greek temple. It reminded me of the old Royal Military College building at Sandhurst.

As I made my way past the armed guards who with machine-guns and fixed bayonets were posted before the gates, my pass, signed by Trotsky himself, was subjected to the closest scrutiny. Finally, I was taken to the commandant, a tall sailor, whom I was to meet again in less pleasant circumstances, and in a few minutes I was being piloted upstairs through a maze of corridors and classrooms to Trotsky's sanctum on the second floor. I made a mental note of the various notices still posted on the walls: Vth Class Dormitory, Linen Room, Drawing Class. Formerly these corridors had resounded to the gentle tramp of girls' slippers. Everything, one could be sure, had been immaculate; the only unseemliness a foolish giggle. Now all was dirt and confusion. Sailors, Red Guards, students and working-men lounged against the walls. None of them looked as if he had washed for a fortnight. Cigarette ends and crumpled news-sheets strewed the floors.

Trotsky's own room was an exception. Lofty and well-lit, it contained a red carpet. There was a fine birchwood writing desk. There was even a waste-paper basket. The habitual neatness of its occupant was everywhere manifest.

The occupant himself, however, was in the worst of tempers. 'Have you any message from London?' he asked, still scowling. I told him that I had not yet had a reply to my telegrams, but that, if the Bolsheviks would make a genuine effort to prevent half Russia from falling into German hands, I was confident that British support would not be withheld. 'You have no message,' he said. 'Well, I have. While you are here trying to throw dust in my eyes, your countrymen and the French have been intriguing against us with the Ukrainians, who have already sold themselves to the Germans. Your Government is working for Japanese intervention in Siberia. Your other missions here are plotting against us with all the bourgeois scum. Look at this,' he shouted. He seized a bundle of papers on his desk and thrust them into my hands. They were the alleged originals of forged documents which had already been shown to me. They were typed on paper with the stamp of the German General Staff. They were signed by various German staff officers including, I think, Colonel Bauer. They were addressed to Trotsky and they contained various instructions, which he as a German agent was to carry out. One instruction was an order to facilitate the passage by rail of two German submarines from Berlin to Vladivostok.

I had seen these documents before. They had been hawked round the Allied missions in St Petersburg for some time. One set of 'originals' had been bought by an American agent. Months afterwards it was discovered that these letters, purporting to come from such dif-

СОВѢТЪ НАРОДНЫХЪ
Комиссаровъ.

Петроградъ.

27 - февраля 1918 г.

№ 564

Прошу всѣ Организаціи, Совѣты и Комиссаров

вокзалов оказывать всяческое содѣйствіе членам

Англійской Миссіи гг. Р.Б. ЛОКАРТУ, В.Л.ГИК-

СУ и Д. ГАРСТИНУ.

Комиссар по иностранным Дѣлам _Л. Троцкій_

За Секретаря _Серг..._

P.S. Лицам предоставленіе записи

не подвергать ....

TRAVELLING PASS FURNISHED BY TROTSKY TO THE AUTHOR
(TRANSLATION OVERLEAF)

SOVIET OF THE PEOPLE'S COMMISSARS

———

Petrograd

27th February, 1918

No. 567

———

I request all Organisations, Soviets and Commissars of railway stations to give every assistance to the members of the English mission, Messrs R. B. Lockhart, V. L. Hicks and D. Garstin.

Commissar for Foreign Affairs,

L. TROTSKY.

Secretary,

SERGEYEV.

PS Personal stores of provisions not to be confiscated.

L. TROTSKY.

ferent centres as Spa, Berlin, and Stockholm, had been written on the same typewriter.

I smiled, but Trotsky was not to be placated. 'So this is what your agents waste their time and money on,' he hissed. 'Your intrigues here have only helped the Germans. I hope you are proud of your work. Your Foreign Office does not deserve to win a war. Your policy towards Russia right from the beginning has been indecisive and vacillating. Your Lloyd George is like a man playing roulette and scattering chips on every number. And now I have to put up with this. Do you know that, while your fools of spies are trying to prove that I am a German agent, my friends down there—' he waved his arm airily towards the room below where the Central Executive Committee was sitting, 'are calling me an Ententophile.' There was some justification for his attack. The British Government was entitled to regard Bolshevism as a scourge and an evil. It might make war on it or ignore it severely. But it was sheer folly to continue to regard it as a movement fostered solely for the furtherance of German ends. When I had told Trotsky that I had received no reply to my telegrams, I had been strictly truthful. I had, however, received messages from our Foreign Office. They still expressed Lord Robert Cecil's doubts and suspicions regarding Trotsky. If I had succeeded in convincing Whitehall that Trotsky was not a German staff officer in disguise, he was still a German agent. It was an unsatisfactory interview. The most I could extract from Trotsky was that, if peace were signed, it would be of short duration. The Bolsheviks had no intention of observing the German terms. He promised, however, to keep me fully informed. The same night Pokrovsky, Chicherin, and Karachan left for Brest-Litovsk to sign the peace. With the dislocation of the railway traffic and the Bolshevik genius for protraction the actual signing was to be delayed for another week.

In the meantime the uncertainty regarding the peace negotiations and the advance of the Germans towards St Petersburg had thrown the Allied Embassies into the wildest confusion. For hours on end there were long conferences regarding the policy to be pursued. Were the Embassies and missions to remain or were they to be evacuated? If they waited too long, they ran the risk of falling into the hands of the Germans. The decision to evacuate was forced by the action of the Germans, who refused to stop their advance until the Bolsheviks had actually signed the dictated peace treaty.

The decision having been taken, there remained the delicate task of obtaining Bolshevik visas for the large number of British officials and agents, many of whom were not entered on the diplomatic list. The Bolsheviks, who regarded the departure of the Allied Embassies in much the same manner as a gambler regrets the loss of an ace, were likely to make difficulties.

The securing of the visas was left to me, and, armed with a sheaf of passports, I drove down to the Foreign Office to try my luck. In the absence of Trotsky and Chicherin, I was received by Petrov, whose imprisonment in England had not increased his affection for British officials. After informing me that there could be no objection to the departure of bona fide diplomats, he referred me to Lutsky, an unpleasant Jewish lawyer, who was in charge of the passport department.

He was seated at his desk in a large room, the only other occupant of which was a girl typist, who sat at a small table in the corner. Lutsky's rudeness made me boil with rage. He was a rat, and I should have liked to shake him. I kept my temper while he went through my huge pile of passports. 'My orders are that only genuine diplomats may receive visas,' he said. 'All these people are not on the Embassy staff.' I explained patiently that my list was genuine and that the bearer of every passport was attached in some form or other to the Embassy. He scrutinised each photograph closely. To my relief he passed General Poole and various other officers who had been photographed in uniform. The pile was nearly finished, and I thought I was about to achieve a complete success. The rat, however, was enjoying his short reign. He was determined to let me feel his newly acquired power. He picked out a passport. 'I know this man,' he said. 'He is a spy. You are trying to deceive me in the same way as the French and Italians have done.' He stormed at me for a few minutes. 'For this dupery I shall refuse all visas.' I stood up, still keeping my temper under control. 'In that case,' I replied, 'please allow me to telephone to Trotsky. Here is his private telephone number and here is my pass to him signed in his own handwriting.' Lutsky hummed and hawed and changed his tune. 'Very well then,' he said, putting the rejected passport on one side, 'I shall stamp the others, but this one I shall not stamp.'

At this moment the Marchese Della Torretta, the Italian Chargé d'Affaires and later Italian Ambassador in London and Foreign

Minister under Mussolini, was announced. Lutsky sprang to his feet. In preparing for a new scene, he became almost friendly to me. Once again he went rapidly through my passports. He rejected several which belonged to members of the British colony and added them to the passport which he had already turned down. He called his typist. 'Sit down at my desk and stamp these passports,' he said, pointing to the large pile. 'The others are to be retained until further instructions.'

Then, puffing out his little chest, he advanced to the middle of the room to receive the Italian Marchese standing. The scene that followed was the most extraordinary that I have ever witnessed, perhaps the most extraordinary that has ever taken place between two representatives of foreign Governments. As soon as the Marchese entered the room, Lutsky overwhelmed him with a torrent of abuse. There had been some row about an Italian deputy called Count Frasso, who had been arrested by the Bolsheviks and who had been included in the Italian official passport list. There seemed no end to the epithets which Lutsky showered on the unfortunate Italian. 'Bandits', 'sneaks', 'sons of bitches' were among the mildest. Both men were of small stature. At first Torretta, gentle, correct and scrupulously polite, tried to remonstrate. His protests produced a further storm of violence. Torretta then became hysterical and almost tearful. His face went a ghastly white. With his silver-grey hair and his short black coat he reminded me of the Rabbit in *Alice in Wonderland*. His hands clutched nervously at his trouser legs. Then he, too, began to scream. It seemed only a matter of seconds before the two men must come to blows.

The scene fascinated me, but I had work of my own to do. Among my rejected passports was the passport of Terence Keyes, a brother of Admiral Keyes and a colonel in our intelligence service. I knew that he had been engaged in various anti-Bolshevik schemes. If his passport were to be held up, things might be awkward. In the meantime the girl was stamping my passports with one eye on her work and the other on the drama which was taking place before us. She was pretty. I talked to her gently, and she smiled. I continued to talk, and, as we talked, I began to fiddle with the passports. As I was whispering to her, I slipped Keyes's passport into the large pile. And, God bless her blue eyes, she stamped it!

Just as her work was finished, I heard Lutsky flinging his last word at Torretta: 'Not a single Italian is to leave,' and, crestfallen and crumpled, the Marchese crept out of the room. Thoroughly satisfied with himself, Lutsky came over to his desk. I had the viséd passports, Keyes's among them, under my arm. The half-dozen rejected ones were still lying on his table. 'May I go now?' I said politely.

'Certainly,' he replied.

I walked away and then turned back.

'I think I had better take the rejected passports as well,' I said. 'Their owners may get into trouble without them.'

He shrugged his shoulders. In his mind he was still fighting his battle with Torretta. 'Take them,' he said, and, picking them up slowly, I made a dignified exit.

That night the British and French officials (there were, of course, no Italians) left by special train for Bieloostrov and the Finnish frontier. Petrov, who was Acting Commissar for Foreign Affairs, went down on the engine for a final revision of the passports. There was trouble with the French, but all our party, including Terence Keyes, passed the frontier without a hitch.

If my mission in Russia failed in every other respect, it was at least successful in this, that it saved some forty or fifty British officials from the indignities and humiliations that were heaped upon their French and Italian colleagues.

There was a pleasant curtain to this passport drama. On the day after the departure of the Embassies Lutsky was arrested for granting visas to French subjects who were not entitled to them. He was accused of having accepted French money. That night I dined well on an affair that was well ended. I had used no bribes – only my innate Celtic persuasiveness and a pair of Russian eyes.

The Allied Embassies left on February 28th. The next day I went to Smolny and had my first interview with Lenin.

I felt a little forlorn. My own position was now vaguer than ever. But I had decided to remain at my post for two reasons. The Bolsheviks had not yet signed the peace terms. They probably would do so, but even then the peace was likely to be of short duration. Here was a position which I might usefully exploit. Secondly, so long as the Bolsheviks held the reins of government in Russia, I felt that it would be foolish to cut off all contact with them and to leave the field open to the Germans. I was convinced that their internal strength was far greater than most foreign observers realised, and that there was no other power in Russia which was capable of replacing them.

This, indeed, was the fundamental difference between Whitehall and myself. The consensus of official opinion in London seemed to be that Bolshevism would be swept away within a few weeks. My instinct told me that, weak as the Bolsheviks were, the demoralised forces of the anti-Bolsheviks in Russia were still weaker. In the intensity of the civil strife which was now developing, the Great War had ceased to have any significance to all classes of Russians. In so far as Germany was our main enemy (and at this state few Englishmen regarded Bolshevism as a serious menace to Western civilisation), we had nothing to gain by stimulating civil war. If we took sides against the Bolsheviks, we should be backing the weaker horse and would have to employ large forces to ensure even a temporary success.

In informing Lindley of my desire to remain, I made use of these arguments. He made no objection. I therefore sent back to England Phelan and Birse, who in the situation which had now arisen could be of little service to me, and asked for Rex Hoare, whose views were in sympathy with my own and whose steadying influence would have been of great value to me. He was willing to stay on, but Lindley, perhaps rightly, decided that, as my mission was nominally an unofficial one, he was not justified in allowing me to retain the services of a professional diplomat. He was quite willing that I should take on any official who was willing to remain and who was outside the permanent staff of the Embassy. There were several volunteers, and from them I selected Denis Garstin, a brother of the well-known novelist* and a young cavalry captain, who spoke Russian with tolerable accuracy. Other English officials who remained were Captain Cromie, the naval attaché, who was determined not to let the Baltic fleet fall into the hands of the Germans, Woodhouse, the Consul, Major McAlpine and Captain Schwabe of General Poole's mission, and various officers and officials of our intelligence services. They were entirely independent of me and supplied their own reports to London.

With Lindley's departure I was, therefore, left to my own resources. Moreover, the route through Finland was now closed, and for the next six months I was to be shut off from all communication with England except by telegraph. Robins, too, had joined the American Embassy in its flight to Vologda and had informed me by telephone that in all probability the Ambassador and his staff would leave the next day for America via Siberia. If I could receive any encouragement from Lenin he would remain and do his best to persuade the American Ambassador to follow his example.

It was, therefore, with a sinking feeling in my heart that I went to Smolny that morning to see the Bolshevik leader. He received me in a small room on the same floor as Trotsky's. It was untidy and bare of all trappings except a writing desk and a few plain chairs. It was not only my first interview with Lenin. It was the first time that I had set eyes on him. There was nothing in his personal appearance to suggest even faintly a resemblance to the superman. Short of stature, rather plump, with short, thick neck, broad shoulders, round, red face, high intellectual forehead, nose slightly turned up, brownish moustache, and short, stubbly beard, he looked at the first glance more like a provincial grocer than a leader of men. Yet in those steely eyes there was something that arrested my attention, something in that quizzing, half-contemptuous, half-smiling look which spoke of boundless self-confidence and conscious superiority.

Later I was to acquire a considerable respect for his intellectual capacity, but at that moment I was more impressed by his tremendous will-power, his relentless determination, and his lack of emotion. He furnished a complete antithesis to Trotsky, who, strangely silent, was also present at our interview. Trotsky was all temperament – an individualist and an artist, on whose vanity even I

* Crombie Garstin (1887–1930), author of such novels as *The Owl's House* (1923), *High Noon* (1925) and *The West Wind* (1926).

could play with some success. Lenin was impersonal and almost inhuman. His vanity was proof against all flattery. The only appeal that one could make to him was to his sense of humour, which, if sardonic, was highly developed. During the next few months I was to be pestered with various requests from London to verify rumours of serious dissensions between Lenin and Trotsky – dissensions from which our Government hoped much. I could have given the answer after that first interview. Trotsky was a great organiser and a man of immense physical courage. But, morally, he was as incapable of standing against Lenin as a flea would be against an elephant. In the Council of Commissars there was not a man who did not consider himself the equal of Trotsky. There was not a Commissar who did not regard Lenin as a demigod, whose decisions were to be accepted without question. Squabbles among the Commissars were frequent, but they never touched Lenin.

I remember Chicherin giving me an account of a Soviet Cabinet meeting. Trotsky would bring forward a proposal. It would be violently opposed by another Commissar. Endless discussion would follow, and all the time Lenin would be writing notes on his knee, his attention concentrated on some work of his own. At last someone would say: 'Let Vladimir Ilyich [Lenin's Christian name and patronymic] decide.' Lenin would look up from his work, give his decision in one sentence, and all would be peace.

In his creed of world-revolution Lenin was as unscrupulous and as uncompromising as a Jesuit, and in his code of political ethics the end to be attained justified the employment of any weapon. On occasions, however, he could be amazingly frank, and my interview was one of them. He gave – correctly as events proved – all the information for which I asked. It was quite untrue that the peace negotiations had broken down. The terms were such as one might expect from a militarist régime. They were scandalous, but they would have to be accepted. They would be signed preliminarily the next day and would be ratified by the overwhelming majority of the party.

How long would the peace hold? He could not say. The Government was to be transferred to Moscow to enable him to consolidate his power. If the Germans forced their hands and tried to install a bourgeois Government, the Bolsheviks would fight even if they had to withdraw to the Volga and the Urals. But they would fight on their own conditions. They were not to be made a cat's-paw for the Allies.

If the Allies understood this, there was an excellent opportunity for co-operation. To the Bolsheviks Anglo-American capitalism was almost as hateful as German militarism, but for the moment German militarism was the immediate menace. For that reason he was glad that I had decided to remain in Russia. He would give me all facilities, guarantee, as far as lay in his power, my personal safety, and grant me a free exit from Russia whenever I wanted to leave. But – he was sceptical about any possibility of co-operating with the Allies. 'Our ways', he said, 'are not your ways. We can afford to compromise temporarily with capital. It is even necessary, for, if capital were to unite, we should be crushed at this stage of our development. Fortunately for us, it is in the nature of capital that it cannot unite. So long, therefore, as the German danger exists, I am prepared to risk a co-operation with the Allies, which should be temporarily advantageous to both of us. In the event of German aggression, I am even willing to accept military support. At the same time I am quite convinced that your Government will never see things in this light. It is a reactionary Government. It will co-operate with the Russian reactionaries.'

I expressed my fears that, now that peace was a certainty, the Germans would be able to throw all their forces against the Western front. They might then crush the Allies, and where would the Bolsheviks be then? Even more serious was the danger that Germany would be able to relieve her starving population with grain forcibly exported from Russia. Lenin smiled. 'Like all your countrymen you are thinking in concrete military terms. You ignore the psychological factor. This war will be settled in the rear and not in the trenches. But even from your point of view your argument is false. Germany has long ago withdrawn her best troops from the Eastern front. As a result of this robber peace she will have to maintain larger and not fewer forces on the east. As to her being able to obtain supplies in large quantities from Russia, you may set your fears at rest. Passive resistance – and the expression comes from your own country – is a more potent weapon than an army that cannot fight.'

I went home in a thoughtful mood to find a batch of telegrams from the Foreign Office. They were full of complaints about the peace. How could I insist that the Bolsheviks were not pro-German, when they proposed giving half Russia away to Germany without firing a shot. There was, too, a strongly worded protest against Litvinov's activities in London. Would I warn the Bolshevik Government immediately that such conduct could not be tolerated. As I sat paraphrasing the sense of the protest into Russian, the telephone rang. It was Trotsky. He had received news that the Japanese were preparing to land troops in Siberia. What did I propose to do about it and how could I explain my own mission in the face of this open act of hostility? I queried the authenticity of his information and sat down again at my desk. My servant brought in yet another telegram. It was from Robins, advising me to come to Vologda. I got on to him by telephone, told him that I was going to see things through to the bitter end in St Petersburg, and requested him to inform his Ambassador about the Japanese imbroglio. Japanese intervention in Siberia would destroy all possibility of an understanding with the Bolsheviks. Common sense seemed to indicate that as a measure for reconstructing an Eastern front against Germany it was ludicrous. The final blow of a shattering day was a telegram from my wife – cryptically worded, but conveying unmistakably the information that my efforts were meeting with no sympathy in London. I was to be careful or my career would be ruined.

London had neither approved nor disapproved my decision to remain on after Lindley's departure. From the fact that the Foreign Office continued to bombard me with telegrams I concluded that it had acquiesced in the new situation. I indulged in a minor orgy of self-pity, which stiffened my obstinacy. Assuredly, my lot was a hard one. Then I went to bed and read the life of Richard Burton.* In the circumstances it was perhaps the most dangerous tonic I could have taken. Burton had fought against Whitehall all his life, and the results had been disastrous.

Life in St Petersburg during this period was a curious affair. The Bolsheviks had not yet succeeded in establishing the iron discipline which today characterises their régime. They had, in fact, made little attempt to do so. There was no terror, nor was the population particularly afraid of its new masters. The anti-Bolshevik newspapers continued to appear and to attack the Bolshevik policy with violent abuse. In particular Gorky, then editor of the *Novaya Zhizn*, excelled himself in denouncing the men to whom today he has given

* Sir Richard Burton (1821–90), explorer, principally in Africa.

his whole-hearted allegiance. The bourgeoisie, still confident that the Germans would soon send the Bolshevik rabble about its business, was more cheerful than one might have expected in such disturbing circumstances. The population was starving, but the rich still had money. Restaurants and cabarets were open, and the cabarets at any rate were crowded. On Sundays, too, there were trotting races before our house, and it was strange to contrast these beautiful, well-groomed horses with the starved and skeleton nags of the unfortunate 'droschke' drivers. The only real danger to human life during these early days of the Bolshevik revolution was furnished, not by the Bolsheviks, but by the anarchists – bands of robbers, ex-army officers, and adventurers, who had seized some of the finest houses in the city and who, armed with rifles, hand-grenades, and machine-guns, exercised a gangsters' rule over the capital. They lurked at street corners for their victims and were utterly unscrupulous in their methods of dealing with them. They were, too, no respectors of persons. One evening, on his way back from Smolny to the centre of the city, Uritsky, who was subsequently head of the St Petersburg Cheka, was pulled from his sleigh by bandits, stripped of all his clothes, and left to continue his journey in a state of nudity. He was fortunate to escape with his life. When we went out at night, we never went alone, no matter how short the distance. We walked, too, in the middle of the road, and we kept our finger tight on the gun in our overcoat pocket. Desultory firing went on all through the night. The Bolsheviks seemed quite incapable of dealing with this pest. For years they had been crying against the Tsarist suppression of free speech. They had not yet embarked on their own campaign of suppression.

I mention this comparative tolerance of the Bolsheviks, because the cruelties which followed later were the result of the intensification of the civil war. For the intensification of that bloody struggle Allied intervention, with the false hopes it raised, was largely responsible. I do not say that a policy of abstention from interference in the internal affairs of Russia would have altered the course of the Bolshevik revolution. I do suggest that our intervention intensified the terror and increased the bloodshed.

On Saturday, March 3rd, the preliminary peace was signed by the Russian delegates at Brest-Litovsk, and the next day a Congress of all the Soviets was summoned to meet at Moscow on March 12th, in

Lenin (centre) during a procession in Red Square, 1919. *Below*,
Lenin (centre) and members of the Council of the People's Commissars in session at Smolny, March, 1918

Left, Felix Dzerzhinsky, head of the Cheka. *Below left*, Joseph Stalin, and, *below right*, Anatoly Lunacharsky, Commissar for Education order to give the formal ratification. At the same time the Bolsheviks announced the formation of a new Supreme War Council and issued an order for the arming of the whole people. Trotsky was appointed President of the new Council, and Chicherin took his place at the Bolshevik Foreign Office.

I saw Chicherin on his return from Brest-Litovsk. He was dejected and therefore friendly. He informed me that the German terms had raised a feeling of resentment in Russia similar to that in France after 1870, and now was the most favourable moment for a demonstration of Allied sympathy. The peace was a dictated peace which Russia would break as soon as she was strong enough. This, indeed, was the attitude of every Commissar with whom I came into contact.

As St Petersburg was now to be evacuated by the Government, I asked Chicherin what arrangements he could make to house my mission in Moscow. As usual, he was all promises and vagueness. I therefore went to Trotsky, who, when he was in the mood, could get things done – and done quickly. I found him in a state of exaltation. His sense of the dramatic had adapted itself to his new office. Almost in a night he had become a soldier. His whole conversation breathed war. Ratification or no ratification, there would be war. At the small committee meeting of the leading Bolsheviks, which had already decided on ratification, he had abstained from voting. He would not attend the formal ratification in Moscow. He was remaining in St Petersburg for another week. He would be glad if I would remain with him. He would take me with him, when he left, and would be personally responsible for my comfort in Moscow. Preferring the virile action of Trotsky to the vacillations of Chicherin, I decided to stay on.

In spite of more trouble about Japanese intervention, the mention of which never failed to rouse the fire in Trotsky's eyes (incidentally, it made no appeal to the Russian bourgeoisie, who rightly concluded that it would not relieve their sufferings), my last week in St Petersburg was not unpleasant. I saw Trotsky every day, but otherwise I had less work than usual. The weather, too, was at its best, and we passed our time happily enough in entertaining our Russian friends.

It was at this time that I first met Moura Budberg, who was an old friend of Hicks and Garstin and a frequent visitor to our flat. She was then twenty-six. A Russian of the Russians, she had a lofty disregard for all the pettiness of life and a courage which was proof against all cowardice. Her vitality, due perhaps to an iron constitution, was immense and invigorated everyone with whom she came into contact. Where she loved, there was her world, and her philosophy of life had made her mistress of all the consequences. She was an aristocrat. She could have been a Communist. She could never have been a bourgeoise. Later, her name was to become linked with mine in the final drama of my Russian career. During those first days of our meeting in St Petersburg I was too busy, too preoccupied with my own importance, to give her more than a passing thought. I found her a woman of great attraction, whose conversation brightened my daily life. The romance was to come afterwards.

Cromie, our naval attaché, was another of her friends, and on his birthday Moura gave a little luncheon party to which we all came. It was during Maslennitsa, or Butter Week, and we ate innumerable 'bliny' (pancakes and caviare) and drank vodka. I wrote a doggerel verse for each guest, and Cromie made one of his witty speeches. We toasted our hostess and laughed immoderately. For all of us it was almost the last carefree hour we were to spend in Russia.

Of the four English guests at that luncheon I am the sole survivor. Cromie died gloriously, defending the Embassy from Bolshevik intrusion. Poor Denis Garstin, who had worked with all his boyish enthusiasm for an understanding with the Bolsheviks, was taken from me by the War Office and sent to Archangel, where he fell a victim to a Bolshevik bullet. Will Hicks, or 'Hickie', as everybody called him, died of consumption in Berlin in the spring of 1930.

It was a very peaceful St Petersburg during this last week. Never had it looked more beautiful, and its deserted streets added to its charm.

The centre of gravity had now been transferred to Moscow. Lenin had left on March 10th. It was not until the afternoon of the 15th that Trotsky informed me we were to leave on the following morning. He had just been appointed Commissar for War. At the very moment when his appointment was announced, the Congress of Soviets, which was to ratify the peace, had opened, and Lenin was making his historic answer to his pro-war critics: 'One fool can ask more questions in a minute than twelve wise men can answer in an hour.'

The next morning, having stored most of our heavy luggage in the

Embassy, we rose at seven and arrived at Smolny at eight, only to wait till ten before the Trotsky baggage train was ready. Most of that day we spent at the station, lolling about in the glorious sunshine and watching the seven hundred Letts, who furnished the Praetorian Guard of the new Red Napoleon, entrain. They looked a dour lot, but their discipline was excellent. The tediousness of our long wait was relieved by the drolleries of Bill Shatov, a cheerful scoundrel with a sense of humour. He had spent his years of exile in New York and had a rich fund of East-side stories. Most of them were at the expense of Russia and the Russians for whom, in spite of his Communist beliefs, he had a slight contempt. His appearance was even funnier than his yarns. A miniature Carnera,* he wore a suit of overalls over his ordinary clothes and sheepskin coat. The whole was surmounted by a large checked English cap. A pair of huge revolvers was strung from a belt at his hips. The general effect was a cross between a gunman and the rotund gentleman who furnishes the advertisement for Michelin tyres.

At last, at four o'clock, Trotsky arrived, resplendent in a khaki overcoat. We saluted, shook hands, and then he conducted us personally to our compartments. There were two of them, and, as, including our two Russian servants, we were only six strong, the accommodation was more than generous, more especially as the train was overcrowded. We travelled alone, but just before we reached Liuban we received a message from Trotsky. He would be glad if we would dine with him.

I shall remember that dinner to the end of my days. We dined at the head of a long table in the station restaurant. I sat on Trotsky's right and Hicks sat on his left. The fare was plain but good, a thick 'shtshi' soup,† veal cutlets with fried potatoes and sour gherkins, and a huge 'torte'. There was, too, beer and red wine. Trotsky, however, drank mineral water. He was in one of his genial moods and made an excellent host. Huge crowds, dumb and open-mouthed, watched us while we ate. The whole neighbourhood seemed to have assembled to see the man who had given peace to Russia and now did not want it. At the end of dinner I congratulated him formally on his appointment as Minister for War. He replied that he had not yet

* Primo Carnera (1906–67), Italian heavyweight boxer who won the world championship in 1933 and 1934.
† Russian cabbage soup.

accepted the post and that he would not accept it unless Russia were going to fight. At the time I believe he was sincere. Almost at the same moment the station-master came in and handed him a telegram. It was from Moscow. It contained the news that the Congress of Soviets had ratified the peace by an enormous majority.

We slept none the less soundly and arrived at Moscow the next morning without further incident.

At the station Trotsky gave another exhibition of good manners. He had secured rooms for us at the only hotel which was still functioning. He insisted on sending us off in his two cars, while he himself waited at the station.

5

In one sense I was glad to be back in Moscow. I knew nearly every stone of its cobbled streets. It was almost my home. I had spent more years of my life inside its walls than in any other city in the world.

Yet it was a new Moscow that I found. Many of my old Russian and English friends had left. Chelnokov had fled to the south. Lvov was in hiding. Most of the fine houses of the rich merchants were occupied by anarchists, whose outrages were even more daringly executed than in St Petersburg. The city, too, was abnormally gay with a gaiety that shocked me. The bourgeoisie was awaiting the Germans with impatience and was already celebrating in advance the hour of its relief. Cabarets flourished. There was even one in the Elite Hotel, which was now our headquarters. Prices were high, especially for champagne, but there seemed no lack of money among the guests, who nightly thronged the tables until the early hours.

I had, however, little time for moralising. Within twenty-four hours of my arrival I was plunged into a whirlpool of turbulent activity. I found Robins and his Red Cross mission at the Elite, where between us we had secured comfortable suites with sitting-rooms and bathrooms. General Lavergne and a large French military mission had also made Moscow their headquarters. General Romei was there with a smaller Italian mission. Major Riggs represented American military interests. If there was not to be the wildest confusion of opinion, it was essential that we should co-ordinate our efforts.

I called on all the Allied representatives, and at Romei's suggestion we had a daily conference in my rooms, at which Lavergne, Romei, Riggs and myself were always present. Robins also attended frequently. We succeeded in establishing a remarkably smooth co-operation. Almost to the bitter end we were in complete agreement regarding policy. We were watching the situation from the inside, and we realised that without Bolshevik consent military intervention would result only in a civil war, which, without very large Allied forces, would be disastrous to our prestige. Intervention with Bolshevik consent was the policy which we sought to carry out, and within ten days of my arrival we passed a common resolution condemning Japanese intervention as futile. In self-defence I should make it plain that all our actions were influenced by the situation on the Western front, where the great German March offensive was in full swing. We knew that the burning anxiety of the Allied High Command was to detach as many German soldiers from the West as possible. But taking every factor into consideration, we could not believe that this object could be attained by support of Alexeyev or Kornilov, who were at that time the forerunners of Denikin and Wrangel. These generals, like Skoropadsky, who was installed by the Germans as head of a White Government in Kiev, were not immediately interested in the war in the west. They may have been sincere in their desire to reconstitute an Eastern front against Germany, but, before they could do so, they had to deal with the Bolsheviks. Without strong foreign aid they were not powerful enough for this task. Outside the officer class – and it, too, was demoralised – they had no support in the country. Although we realised that the Bolsheviks would fight only if they were forced into war by German aggression, we were convinced that this situation might easily develop and that by a promise of support we might help to shape events in the form we desired. We could understand the resentment of the Allied Governments against the Bolsheviks. We could not follow their reasoning.

In this miniature Allied council Romei and I were independent. Romei reported direct to the Italian General Staff. He was not under the Italian Embassy. Since the departure of our own Embassy, I was alone. Lavergne, although the head of a military mission, was also military attaché. He was directly under the control of his Ambassador. Riggs was in an even more subordinate position. And the Allied Ambassadors were at Vologda, a little provincial town, hundreds of miles away from the centre of events. It was as if three foreign Ambassadors were trying to advise their Governments on an English Cabinet crisis from a village in the Hebrides. They were, too, strangely ill-fitted for their task. Francis, the American Ambassador, was a charming old gentleman of nearly eighty – a banker from St Louis, who had left America for the first time to be plunged into the vortex of the revolution. Noulens, the French Ambassador, was also a new arrival. He was a professional politician, whose attitude was determined by the prevailing policy of his own party in the French Chamber. Lavergne, too, had a Socialist on his staff – Captain Jean Sadoul, the well-known French barrister and former Socialist deputy. Sadoul, who was on friendly terms with Trotsky, was a legacy of Albert Thomas. He served Lavergne well and faithfully, but to Noulens he was like a red rag to a bull. Politician mistrusted politician. There was continual friction. Noulens held up Sadoul's correspondence with Thomas, and in the end his obstinacy and his oppression drove the unfortunate Sadoul into throwing in his lot with the Bolsheviks. Torretta, the Italian Chargé d'Affaires, knew Russia well and spoke the language. His Russia, however, was the Russia of the old régime. Even had he wished to do so, he was morally incapable of standing up against the virile and aggressive Noulens. Moreover, he had had that desperate interview with Lutsky. There was not much to be hoped for from Torretta.

Vologda, even more than London and Paris, lived on the wildest anti-Bolshevik rumours. Rarely a day passed without Lavergne's being ordered by his Ambassador to investigate some new evidence of Bolshevik pro-Germanism. Romei and I roared with laughter when Lavergne asked us if we had heard anything of a German Control Commission in St Petersburg. At the head of it was Count Frederiks, the former Court Minister of the Tsar. It was working behind the scenes, but it had complete control over the Bolshevik Foreign Office, and not a single foreigner could leave Russia without its permission. 'Another telegram from Vologda!' we said. But Lavergne did not laugh. These little excitements of M. Noulens had to be taken seriously, and, while Lavergne made enquiries on his own, down would go Sadoul to Trotsky to register an official protest against the establishment of such a mission. Trotsky would look blank. Sometimes he would be angry. At other times he would laugh and offer to write out a bromide prescription to calm the nerves of Their Excellencies of Vologda. His father had been a chemist, and his acquaintance with a drug store had enriched his vocabulary. Lavergne had to take the tedious journey to Vologda fairly frequently. Romei and I went only once. Romei's comment was that 'If we had put all the Allied representatives there in a cauldron and stirred them up, not one drop of common sense would have come out of the whole boiling.'

The month of March, 1918, was the period during which the Bolsheviks were most amenable to an understanding with the Allies. They were afraid of further German aggression. They had little confidence in their own future. They would have welcomed the assistance of Allied officers in training the new Red Army which Trotsky was now forming.

A coincidence of misfortune had provided us with a remarkable opportunity of supplying the Bolshevik War Minister with the Allied officers whom he required. A large French military mission, headed by General Berthelot, had just arrived in Moscow from Romania. Holding the view that it was better that the Red Army should be trained by Allied officers than by Germans, we proposed to Trotsky that he should make use of General Berthelot's services. The Red leader, who had already shown his goodwill by appointing a committee of Allied officers to advise him, accepted the proposal with alacrity. At the first meeting of this new committee, which was composed of General Romei, General Lavergne, Major Riggs and Captain Garstin, Trotsky made a formal request for help. General Lavergne accepted the invitation, and it was agreed that General Berthelot's mission should remain. We seemed to have secured a tactical advantage.

Two days later the whole scheme was wrecked. M. Noulens had intervened. General Lavergne was hauled over the coals for exceeding his powers, and General Berthelot and his staff of officers were ordered to return immediately to France. The barometer of Trotsky's temperament suffered a severe depression, and the *Izvestia* came out with a leading article declaring that 'only America had known how to treat the Bolsheviks decently and it was the Allies themselves who, by disregarding the wishes of the Russian people, were preventing the creation of a pro-Ally policy'.

If General Lavergne had his troubles, my own were just as great. With the help of our secret service agents the British Government had discovered a new pro-German scare. According to the reports it had received, Siberia was teeming with German regiments composed of war prisoners, who had been armed by the Bolsheviks. They were in control of a vast area. Here was a further proof that the Bolsheviks were handing over all Russia to the enemy. I received a querulous telegram pointing out the difference between my reports and the actions of the Bolsheviks.

I referred the matter to my Allied colleagues in Moscow. Common sense told me that the story was a mare's nest. Siberia, however, was far away. We could not quote the evidence of our own eyes. Robins and I, therefore, went down to the Commissariat for War to interview Trotsky. His reply was unequivocal. It was no use his issuing a denial. We should not believe him. We must go – and see for ourselves. There and then he offered full facilities to anyone we liked to send to carry out an investigation on the spot.

Ill as I could spare him, I decided to send Hicks, my most reliable assistant. He left that night together with Captain Webster, an officer of the American Red Cross mission. Trotsky carried out his promise. He gave to both officers a personal letter instructing the local Soviets to give them the fullest assistance. They were to be allowed to go anywhere and to see everything.

Hicks was not to return for six weeks. During that time he travelled all over Siberia, inspecting the prison camps and carrying out his investigations with great thoroughness. His telegrams to me contained some startling information, especially regarding Semenov, the Cossack general, who behind the Chinese frontier was waging a brigand warfare against the Bolsheviks. But of armed German or Austrian war-prisoners in Siberia he had seen no trace.

I paraphrased his reports and ciphered them to the War Office. The immediate reaction of London was a telegram from the War Office ordering Hicks to return to England at once. I was in a quandary. I had a shrewd idea why Hicks had been recalled. Moreover, I could not spare him. I had already more work than I could cope with, and no one on my staff was an expert cipherer. At the end of a long day's work I had to sit up late and take a hand in the ciphering myself. I sent a telegram to the Foreign Office pointing out my difficulties. At the same time I added that Hicks had been sent to Siberia on my responsibility and that, if he were to be recalled, there was no other course than for me to ask for my own recall. I received a private telegram from George Clerk, whose kindness and patience with my shortcomings I remember with gratitude, informing me that Hicks could remain.

The incident closed, but it did not increase my popularity in London. Within four days I received two alarming telegrams from my wife. The second ran as follows: 'Have fullest information. Do nothing rash. Am anxious about your future career. I understand your personal feelings but hope to see you soon. Would be better for you. Please acknowledge immediately, also wire about no sympathy here.'

The meaning was unmistakable. I knew from whom my wife had received her information. I was to throw in my hand and come home. I kept a stiff upper lip and my troubles to myself.

Quite apart from the major question of policy, life at this moment was full of minor excitements. There were perpetual pinpricks between the British and Russian Governments – pinpricks which served to confuse the real issue. We had small missions all over Russia, and each mission had a different policy. At the same time we were making every kind of protest against the Bolshevik confiscation of Allied property. The Bolsheviks retaliated by attacks on the war aims of the Allies and attempts to influence British Labour in their favour. Litvinov, in particular, was making himself a nuisance in London. In this game of protest and counter-protest I was a sadly battered shuttlecock between the battledores of the two Governments.

Nevertheless, there were rays of light in this murky situation. The German successes on the Western front had alarmed the Bolsheviks. They were prepared to go so far as to agree to Allied intervention in the event of renewed aggression by the Germans. The atmosphere in Moscow at this stage may best be illustrated by the fact that in its account of the March fighting on the Western front the Bolshevik Press suppressed all German bulletins. The bourgeois Press published them in full.

The Germans, too, seemed to be playing into our hands in Russia. Their attitude towards the Bolsheviks was truculent and overbearing. They made numerous protests against our presence at Murmansk, which we still occupied, and for form's sake the Bolshevik Foreign Office sent me several notes, which in accordance with its practice of so-called open diplomacy were published in the official Press. I took the notes to Chicherin. 'What am I to do with them?' I asked. He replied that it would help if we would take the local Soviet into greater consideration. 'Otherwise', he said cynically, 'you can put them in your waste-paper basket.'

Trotsky, although almost in despair over the attitude of the Allies, was no less friendly. 'Just when we are on the verge of going to war,' he said, 'the Allied Governments do everything they can to help the Germans.' In the history of the Jews, which at that time was – not without reason – my bedside literature, I found the prayer of Bar Cochba, the Jewish 'Son of the Star', in his struggle against the Romans in AD 132. 'We pray Thee not to assist our enemies: us Thou needst not help.' The words were almost the same as those which Trotsky addressed to me daily.

It was at this time that Trotsky gave me one remarkable proof of his physical courage. I was talking to him in the Commissariat for War in the square behind the Cathedral of the Saviour. Suddenly, a startled assistant burst into the room in a state of panic. There was a large crowd of armed sailors outside. They had not been paid or their pay was insufficient. They wanted to see Trotsky. If he did not come, they would storm the place.

Trotsky rose at once, his eyes blazing, and went down into the square. I watched the scene from the window. He made no attempt to satisfy the sailors. Instead, he lashed them with a withering blast of invective. They were dogs totally unworthy of the fleet, which had played such a glorious part in the revolution. He would look into their complaints. If they were justified, they would be rectified. If not, he would brand them as traitors to the revolution. In the meantime they were to go back to their barracks or he would disarm them and take away their privileges. The sailors slunk away like beaten curs, and Trotsky returned to me to resume his conversation where he had left off. Was Trotsky another Bar Cochba? At any rate he was very bellicose.

Lenin, whom Robins saw frequently, was more guarded, but he, too, was prepared to go a long way to secure the friendly co-operation of the Allies.

Nor were the other Commissars behindhand in their evidence of friendliness. I had established smooth-working relations with Karachan, who, together with Chicherin and Radek, formed a kind of triumvirate at the Bolshevik Foreign Office. An Armenian, with dark, waving hair and a well-trimmed beard, he was the Adonis of the Bolshevik Party. His manners were perfect. He was an excellent judge of a cigar. I never saw him in a bad temper, and during the whole period of our contact, and even when I was being denounced as a spy and an assassin by his colleagues, I never heard an unpleasant word from his lips. This is not to imply that he was a saint. He had all the guile and craft of his race. Diplomacy was his proper sphere.

Radek, however, was our chief delight among the Commissars. A Jew, whose real name is Sobelsohn, he was in some respects a grotesque figure. A little man with a huge head, protruding ears, clean-shaven face (in those days he did not wear that awful fringe which now passes for a beard), with spectacles, and a large mouth with yellow, tobacco-stained teeth, from which a huge pipe or cigar was never absent, he was always dressed in a quaint drab-coloured Norfolk suit with knickers and leggings. He was a great friend of Ransome,* the correspondent of the *Manchester Guardian*, and through Ransome we came to know him very well. Almost every day he would turn up in my rooms, an English cap stuck jauntily on his head, his pipe puffing fiercely, a bundle of books under his arm, and a huge revolver strapped to his side. He looked like a cross between a professor and a bandit.

Of his intellectual brilliance, however, there was no doubt. He was the virtuoso of Bolshevik journalism, and his conversation was as sparkling as his leading articles. Ambassadors were his game and Foreign Ministers his butts. As Assistant Commissar for Foreign Affairs he received the Ambassadors and Ministers in the afternoon, and the next morning, under the thinly disguised pseudonym of Viator, he attacked them in the *Izvestia*. He was a Puck full of malice and with a delicious sense of humour. He was the Bolshevik Lord Beaverbrook.

When the German Embassy arrived, he sorely tried the patience of the Kaiser's representatives. For, in those days, at any rate, this little man was violently anti-German. He had been at Brest-Litovsk, where he had taken an impish delight in puffing the smoke of his vile cheroot into General Hofmann's face. He had voted on every occasion against peace. Hot-headed and impulsive, he chafed under the restraint which from time to time had to be placed on his conduct by his more cautious colleagues. And, when he came to us and was rewarded with a half-pound tin of navy tobacco, he would air his grievances with scintillating abandon. His satirical shafts were aimed at all and sundry. He spared nobody – not even Lenin, and certainly not the Russians. When the peace was ratified, he exclaimed, almost in tears: 'My God, if we had had any other race but Russians behind us in this struggle, we should have upset the world.' He had a poor opinion of both Chicherin and Karachan. Chicherin was an old woman. Karachan he described as the 'osel klassicheskoi krasoty' – the donkey of classical beauty. He was an

* Arthur Ransome (1884–1967), then a foreign correspondent for both the *Observer* and the *Manchester Guardian*. He was later to marry Trotsky's secretary, Evgenia Shelepin, and find success through writing children's novels, most notably *Swallows and Amazons* (1931).

amusing and entertaining comedian and, kept in proper check, the most dangerous propagandist that the Bolshevik movement has so far produced.

During our first two months in Moscow Robins and I enjoyed a privileged position. We had no difficulty in seeing the various Commissars. We were even allowed to be present at certain meetings of the Central Executive Committee. On one occasion we went to hear the debate on the new army. In those early days the Bolshevik Parliament held its meetings in the main restaurant of the Metropole Hotel, which had been renamed the 'First House of Soviets'. The deputies were seated in chairs set out in rows as for a concert. The various speakers spoke from the little pulpit from which formerly Konchik, the leader of the orchestra, had stirred countless bourgeois souls with the sobbing of his violin. On this particular occasion the chief speaker was of course Trotsky. As a demagogic orator Trotsky is wonderfully effective until he loses his temper. He has a fine command of language, and the words stream from his mouth in a torrent, which never seems to abate. At its highest pitch his voice sounds almost like a hiss.

That night he was at his best. He was the man of action reporting the first progress of his great achievement – the creation of the Red Army. There was just sufficient opposition – in March and April there were still several Mensheviks in the Central Executive Committee – to rouse him to a great effort but not to make him lose his control, and he demolished his opponents with vigour and obvious relish. The enthusiasm he aroused was remarkable. His speech was like a declaration of war. He himself was an incarnation of belligerent hate.

Before the debate began, Robins and I were given tea and biscuits and were introduced to various Commissars whom we had not yet met: the mild-mannered and silky-tongued Lunacharsky; Bukharin, diminutive in size but a man of great personal courage and the only Bolshevik who was not afraid to criticise Lenin or to cross swords with him in a dialectical duel; Pokrovsky, the eminent Bolshevik historian; Krylenko, an epileptic degenerate, the future Public Prosecutor, and the most repulsive type I came across in all my connections with the Bolsheviks. These four men, together with Lenin and Chicherin, represented the purely Russian element in a hotchpotch of Jews, Georgians, Poles and other nationalities.

During the debate we sat at a side table with Radek and Gumberg, Robins's Jew-American assistant. Lenin came into the hall several times. He sat down and chatted with us for a few minutes. He was, as usual, in a good humour – indeed, I think of all the public figures I have met he possessed the most equable temperament – but he took no part in the debate. The only attention he paid to Trotsky's speech was to lower his voice slightly in his own conversation.

There were two other Commissars whom I met that night for the first time. One was Dzerzhinsky, the head of the Cheka and a man of correct manners and quiet speech but without a ray of humour in his character. The most remarkable thing about him was his eyes. Deeply sunk, they blazed with a steady fire of fanaticism. They never twitched. His eyelids seemed paralysed. He had spent most of his life in Siberia and bore the traces of his exile on his face. I also shook hands with a strongly built man with a sallow face, black moustache, heavy eyebrows, and black hair worn *en brosse*. I paid little attention to him. He himself said nothing. He did not seem of sufficient importance to include in my gallery of Bolshevik portraits. If he had been announced then to the assembled party as the successor of Lenin, the delegates would have roared with laughter. The man was the Georgian Dzhugashvili, known today to the whole world as Stalin, the man of steel.

Of these new acquaintances the one who made the deepest impression on me was Lunacharsky. A man of brilliant intellect and wide culture, he has been more successful than anyone in converting bourgeois intellectuals to Bolshevism or to tolerance of the Bolshevik régime. It was he who brought back Gorky to the Bolshevik fold, to which, perhaps without knowing it, he had always belonged. It was he, too, who insisted on the preservation of the bourgeois arts, who provided protection for the treasures of the Russian museums, and who is primarily responsible for the fact that today Moscow has still its opera, its ballet, and its famous Art Theatre. It was also Lunacharsky, who, as an original adherent to the Orthodox faith, started the 'Bolshevising' movement inside the Russian Church. A brilliant speaker, he advanced many original arguments in support of his revised religion. It was during that first year of Bolshevism that he made his famous speech in which he compared Lenin's persecution of the capitalists with Christ's expulsion of the moneylenders from the Temple, finishing with the startling peroration that 'if Christ were alive today, he would be a Bolshevik'.

Robins and I had one more thrilling experience during this period of March and April, 1918. One of Trotsky's first tasks as Commissar for War had been to rid Moscow of the anarchist bands who were terrorising the city. At three in the early morning of April 12th he carried out a simultaneous raid on the twenty-six anarchist nests. The venture was a complete success. After a desperate resistance the anarchists were evicted from the houses they had occupied, and all their machine-guns, their rifles, their ammunition, and their loot were captured. Over a hundred were killed in the fighting. Five hundred were arrested. Later in the day on Dzerzhinsky's invitation, Robins and I made a tour of the different fighting areas. We were given a car and an armed escort. Our cicerone was Peters, Dzerzhinsky's Lettish assistant and my future gaoler-in-chief.

The anarchists had appropriated the finest houses in Moscow. On the Povarskaya, where the rich merchants lived, we entered house after house. The filth was indescribable. Broken bottles littered the floors, the magnificent ceilings were perforated with bullet-holes. Wine stains and human excrement blotched the Aubusson carpets. Priceless pictures had been slashed to strips. The dead still lay where they had fallen. They included officers in guards' uniform, students – young boys of twenty – and men who belonged obviously to the criminal class and whom the revolution had released from prison. In the luxurious drawing-room of the House Gracheva the anarchists had been surprised in the middle of an orgy. The long table which had supported the feast had been overturned, and broken plates, glasses, champagne bottles, made unsavoury islands in a pool of blood and spilt wine. On the floor lay a young woman, face downwards. Peters turned her over. Her hair was dishevelled. She had been shot through the neck, and the blood had congealed in a sinister purple clump. She could not have been more than twenty. Peters shrugged his shoulders. 'Prostitutka,' he said. 'Perhaps it is for the best.'

It was an unforgettable scene. The Bolsheviks had taken their first step towards the establishment of discipline.

If we lived in a state of chronic crisis, life was not without its relaxations. Thanks to the American Red Cross, we were well supplied with stores and tobacco. Hicks, too, was an excellent organiser, and in the days when the going was still good he provided us with a cellar which nearly lasted out our stay. We dined in our rooms, entertaining our colleagues and making as brave a show as we could in return for the more sumptuous hospitality which their larger numbers and their superior accommodation enabled them to offer. After dinner there was generally a game of poker with the Americans. Robins did not play. He read his Bible or talked to me. But his staff did. My fellows were no match for them, and, when I took a hand in the game, I, too, had to pay for my education. There was an Irish-American called O'Callaghan, whose equal as a poker-player I have yet to discover. He was a confirmed pessimist. Every time he played he would take out his watch and say: 'The luck changes at twelve o'clock, when it gets worse.' His own luck or skill never changed. He took our money with unfailing regularity.

On Sundays we went to the ballet. Except that the Imperial box was crowded with 'comrades', the performance was the same as in Tsarist days, and excellent it was. For a few hours we could forget our troubles, and, watching the same scenery and the same dancers, I found it hard to remember that we were in the middle of the greatest revolution the world has ever known. Then the curtain would go down. The orchestra would strike up 'The International', and we returned to the grim realism of the time in which we lived. In the space of a few months 'The International' was the third national anthem I had heard played by the same orchestra.

When the spring came, we made excursions into the country, picnicked in the woods and played rounders in the fields. It was our only form of exercise. Our favourite resort was Archangelskoe, the beautiful country home of Prince Yusupov. It was strange to see the place deserted. The peasants had taken over the land, but, as far as we could see, they had not touched the house, and everything seemed intact. After Moscow the solitude was vastly soothing. There was no traffic on the roads, and, once we were clear of the outskirts of the city, we rarely saw a living soul. The absence of traffic, in fact, was a danger which nearly brought me to disaster. Coming back one

Moura Budberg

Above left, Arthur Ransome, then a foreign correspondent for the *Observer* and the *Manchester Guardian*, and, *above right*, secret agent Sidney Reilly. *Left*, Yakov Sverdlov, President of the Central Executive Committee night after dusk, we ran into a toll-bar. The turnpike keeper had gone to sleep. Fortunately, we were not going very fast, and beyond a smashed windscreen our car suffered no damage. My hands, however, were badly cut by the broken glass, and I bear the scars of the adventure to this day.

We even went to a cabaret – a cellar called the 'Podpolye' in the Okhotny Riad. It was a stupid escapade, for the place was illegal, and if we had been caught we should have looked foolish. The hall was crowded with bourgeois of the richer class. There was an excellent stage, tables on the floor, and a row of boxes at the end. Prices were high, but there was champagne on every table. We took a box and sat down to listen to a first-class entertainment such as only Russians can provide. It was here that I heard for the first time Vertinsky, a decadent young genius, whose songs, written and sung by himself, expressed the disillusionment of the Russian intelligentsia. One song, in particular, made a deep impression on me: 'Ya Nye Znaiu Zachem' ('I Do Not Know Why'). It was an anti-war song, and Vertinsky, his face powdered a deathly white, sang it with immense effect. I can remember only the first few lines:

> I do not know why
> or for what purpose.
> Who sent them to death
> With relentless, untrembling hand.
> Only it was all so useless,
> So pitiless . . .

The song was encored again and again. It reflected the mood of an anti-Bolshevik audience which had lost its soul and its morale. It was the song of a class which had already abandoned all hope – a class which would go almost to any length to avoid death by fighting. Yet only that morning I had received a telegram from the Foreign Office giving the view of a British military expert that all that was required in Russia was a small and resolute nucleus of British officers to lead the 'loyal Russians' on to victory.

As I sat reflecting on the hard fate of the man on the spot, there was a sudden rush at the door and a stern roar of 'hands up!' Twenty men in masks had entered the room and were covering the audience with Browning pistols and revolvers. There was a deathly stillness.

Quickly and without fuss, four of the bandits went through the pockets of the audience, collecting money, jewellery and everything of value. Most of them wore officers' uniform – whether with right or not I had no means of determining. When they reached our box, the leader noticed the English uniforms of Captain George Hill and Garstin. I had already handed over my watch and notecase. The man saluted. 'You are English officers,' he said. With my arms still stretched towards Heaven, I answered 'Yes'. He returned me my money and my watch. 'We do not rob Englishmen,' he said. 'I apologise for the state of my country which forces me to adopt this manner of earning our living.'

We were in luck. Fortunately, we were never in a position to repeat the experiment. When Trotsky exterminated the anarchists, he closed the cabarets as well.

As far as Moscow was concerned, we Allies were a not unhappy family. Lavergne and Romei were splendid companions, and, during the eight trying months we were together, we never had a quarrel or a cross word. Romei, in particular, was a great stand-by. He was the most stolid Italian I have ever met. He faced every crisis with complete objectiveness and could always be relied upon to give a common-sense solution to every problem. He had no illusions about the collapse of Russia as a fighting machine and opposed himself resolutely to any scheme of adventure.

With the other British missions in Russia my relations were not so good. I maintained as close a contact as possible with Cromie, the naval attaché, and was able to assist him in his work by bringing him into touch with Trotsky. He was a gallant and extremely efficient naval officer, but was without experience of political work. Occasionally, too, I saw McAlpine, a former Treasury official and a man of first-class intellect. His headquarters were in St Petersburg. He, too, was able to take an objective view of the situation and remained to the end a convinced opponent of intervention. There were, however, other British officials, who I knew disapproved of my policy and, without knowing what I was doing, intrigued against me. The truth is that our various missions and remnants of missions were at sixes and sevens. There was no one in a position of authority, and, although the Foreign Office addressed me in their telegrams as 'British Agent, Moscow', and the Bolsheviks insisted on labelling me 'British Diplomatic Representative', I was completely in the dark regarding the work of a whole group of British officers and officials for whose presence in Russia and for whose protection my position with the Bolsheviks was the only guarantee.

There was no British policy, unless seven different policies at once can be called a policy. And, for the furtherance of this vagueness, the Foreign Office insisted on keeping my own position as vague as possible. If in the House of Commons some irate interventionist wished to know why in the name of decency the British Government maintained an official representative with a Government of cut-throats, who boasted of their determination to destroy civilisation, Mr Balfour or his Under-Secretary would then reply quite truthfully that we had no official representative accredited to the Bolshevik Government. On the other hand, when some revolutionary-minded liberal charged the British Government with the folly of not maintaining an accredited representative in Moscow in order to protect British interests and to assist the Bolsheviks in their struggle with German militarism, Mr Balfour would reply, with the same strict regard for the truth, that in Moscow we had a representative – an official with great experience of Russia – who was charged precisely with these duties.

Obviously, the British Government was faced with a problem of immense difficulty. It was not in a position to send large forces to Russia. If it supported the small officer armies in the south, it ran the risk of driving the Bolsheviks into an unholy league with the Germans. If it supported the Bolsheviks, there was, at the beginning at any rate, a serious danger that the Germans would advance on Moscow and St Petersburg and set up their own pro-German bourgeois Government. (Personally, I should have preferred this course, as it would have drawn more German troops into Russia. Without German military support no bourgeois Government could have maintained power for a month. The Bolsheviks would always have mastered the forces of the anti-Bolshevik Russians.) Moreover, it was physically impossible for our Government to keep pace with the situation, which changed radically every forty-eight hours. That British Ministers were unable to see any sign of order in the prevailing chaos was natural enough. Where they were to blame was in listening to too many counsellors, and in not realising the fundamental truth that in Russia the educated class represented only an infinitesimal minority, without organisation or political experience and without any contact with the masses. It was the crowning folly of Tsarism that outside its own bureaucracy it had sternly repressed every political outlet. When Tsarism collapsed, the bureaucracy collapsed with it, and there was nothing left but the masses. In Moscow, with one's fingers on the pulse of the events, everyone except the most obstinate traditionalist could realise that here was a cataclysm which had shattered all previous conceptions of Russia. London, however, continued to regard it as a passing storm, after which the glass would return to 'set fair'. The most dangerous of all historical aphorisms is the catch-phrase: '*plus ça change, plus c'est la même chose*.' During the spring and summer of 1918 it was constantly on the lips of the British pro-interventionists. History has its ebbs and flows, but unlike the tide the ebb comes slowly and, rarely, if ever, in one generation.

Another heavy weight on my shoulders during this period was my contact with my old political friends of pre-revolutionary days. Those who had remained in Moscow came to see me. They came, some in anger, some in sorrow, and some in friendship. They could be divided into three classes: those who were in favour of general peace; those who were in touch with the White generals in the south and who believed in the so-called Allied orientation; and those who realised sadly that the Bolsheviks had come to stay. I do not include the out-and-out pro-Germans in this classification. They did not come to see me.

These interviews were a source of genuine grief to me. These men had been my friends and colleagues in the task of promoting Anglo-Russian friendship. To refuse them help seemed almost like treachery. With the advocates of a general peace – the idea was that we should make peace with Germany and allow the Germans to deal with Bolshevism – my task was comparatively simple. I could only shake my head sorrowfully and say that in the light of the situation on the Western front this object seemed unattainable. Nevertheless, they persevered, and, when the German Embassy arrived in Moscow, one prominent Russian informed me that he had consulted the German Ambassador and was in a position to arrange a private interview for me with him at the Russian's house. I referred the matter to the Foreign Office and was instructed to have nothing to do with the proposal.

Much more trying was my position with the advocates of Allied intervention. Situated as I was, I was not in a position to offer them any promise of help or of support. Nor did I do so, although for the sake of information I maintained a more or less regular contact with them. I was visited, too, by various emissaries from General Alexeyev, General Kornilov, and, later, General Denikin, but, as I was surrounded by *agents provocateurs* and could not be certain of their bona fides, I was severely non-committal in my answers.

The third class, whom I may call the realists, were few in number. They included men like Avinov, the former Assistant Minister of the Interior, and young Muraviev, ex-secretary of Izvolsky* and a brother of the first Lady Cheetham. Avinov, a man of great intelligence and objectivity, was the most understanding of all my friends. He was a man whom no one could help liking. His manners were as charming as his culture. His wife, born a Countess Trubetskaya, belonged to one of the oldest families in Russia. The revolution had destroyed everything he held dear in life. But, prescient beyond most of his compatriots, he saw clearly. And in the course of a brilliant exposé of the revolutionary movement he told me sadly that the Bolsheviks were the only Government that had shown the slightest sign of strength since the revolution, that in spite of its dictatorial tyranny its roots were in the masses, and that the counter-revolution had no chance of success for years to come.

We had, too, other visitors in the form of stranded English missions returning from Romania and the south. There was Le Page, a self-possessed and bearded naval officer, who had the arduous task of maintaining relations with the Russian fleet in the Black Sea. There was de Candolle, a railway expert, who had been engaged on a mission in Romania. On his return home through Moscow, he left me his assistant, Tamplin, whom I added to the strength of my own mission. A little later, I picked up Lingner, who had been employed on a propaganda mission in Tiflis and who, in order to reach Moscow, had completed a real odyssey of dangerous adventure. Both Tamplin, who spoke Russian perfectly, and Lingner, who had a good business head, were of great help to me. Nor must I forget to mention Arthur Ransome, the correspondent of the *Manchester Guardian*, who, if not a member of our mission, was something

* Alexander Petrovich Izvolsky (1856–1919), diplomat. He played a key role in bringing about the Triple Entente between France, Russia and Great Britain.

more than a visitor. He lived in our hotel and we saw him almost daily. Ransome was a Don Quixote with a walrus moustache, a sentimentalist, who could always be relied upon to champion the underdog, and a visionary, whose imagination had been fired by the revolution. He was on excellent terms with the Bolsheviks and frequently brought us information of the greatest value. An incorrigible romanticist, who could spin a fairy-tale out of nothing, he was an amusing and good-natured companion. As an ardent fisherman who had written some charming sketches on angling, he made a warm appeal to my sympathy, and I championed him resolutely against the secret service idiots who later tried to denounce him as a Bolshevik agent.

Our most exciting visitors, however, were the Germans, whom we saw frequently but never greeted. As a direct result of the peace of Brest-Litovsk the Germans had appointed Count Mirbach Ambassador in Moscow. He was due to arrive on April 24th. The first of a long series of duels began on April 22nd, when the Bolsheviks roused me to fury by requisitioning forty rooms in my hotel for the new Ambassador and his staff. Most of the rooms were on the same floor as my own.

White with passion, I went to Chicherin and protested vigorously against this insult. Chicherin was apologetic, but impotent. I stormed and I blustered. Chicherin looked up wearily, his ferret-eyes blinking with amazement at this fierce outburst from so good-natured a person as myself. He wrung his hands, pleaded for time, promised that the intrusion would be only for a few days, and excused himself on the ground that there was no other accommodation available.

In despair I went to Trotsky, who, at any rate, could be relied upon to give a decision. He was not to be found. He had, however, an extremely able and tactful secretary, Evgenia Petrovna Shelepin, who is now an English subject and the wife of Arthur Ransome. I told her that I must speak to Trotsky immediately and that the matter was one of the utmost urgency. Within five minutes I was speaking to him on the telephone. In the most vigorous Russian I could command I told him that I would not tolerate this insult, and that unless the requisition order were rescinded at once, I should move myself, my mission, and my baggage to the station and camp there, until he gave me a train. I demanded an immediate answer.

Trotsky, who was in the middle of a Commissars' meeting at the Kremlin, took my outburst splendidly. He agreed that our position would be intolerable. He promised to take immediate action. He was as good as his word. Half an hour later he telephoned to me to say that the matter had been settled. He had given categorical orders that other quarters – he did not know where – were to be found for the Germans. For several days they were lodged uncomfortably in a second-rate hotel. Then they moved to a magnificent private house in the Denezhny Pereulok. This minor triumph I owed entirely to Shelepin. I rewarded her later, when she wanted to leave Russia, by giving her a British passport – an illegal act, for which I hope I shall not be held responsible today.

On April 26th Count Mirbach presented his credentials at the Kremlin. He was received, not by Lenin, but by Sverdlov, the President of the Central Executive Committee. The proceedings were formal and acidly polite. In his speech Sverdlov said: 'We greet in your person the nation with whom we concluded the Treaty of Brest-Litovsk.'

The staff of the German Embassy was composed almost entirely of Russian experts. Mirbach himself had been Counsellor of the German Embassy in St Petersburg before the war. Riezler, his chief assistant, had had a long and varied experience of Russian politics. Hausschild, the First Secretary, was an old friend of mine. He had come to Moscow as Vice-Consul at the same time as myself. He was a man of sterling character. Until the outbreak of war he had always been pro-English.

Although they possessed so wide a knowledge of Russian affairs, I do not believe that the Germans were more successful in their dealings with the Bolsheviks than we were. Certainly, they made as many mistakes, and at no time was their position secure or happy. We went everywhere unarmed and unattended. The Germans never moved out of their quarters without a guard.

Their presence in Moscow, however, was a considerable embarrassment to us, and the Bolsheviks must have found a childish amusement in playing us off against each other. They did it very effectively. They herded us together in the same waiting-room at the Foreign Office. If they wished to annoy Mirbach they received me first. If the British Government had offended them in any way, they were suave to Mirbach and kept me waiting. If the Germans were too insistent in their demands, the Bolsheviks would threaten them with Allied intervention. When the Allies tried to force intervention on the Bolsheviks, they would draw an alarming picture of the dangers of a German advance on Moscow. As neither the Germans nor the Allies could make up their minds on a clear-cut policy towards Russia, Bolshevik diplomacy had all the advantages.

My meetings with the Germans at the Bolshevik Foreign Office caused me acute discomfort. Sometimes we were left together for nearly an hour, during which we turned our backs on each other and gazed out of the window or read the *Izvestia*. My most painful encounter was the first time I came face to face with Hausschild. He was alone in the waiting-room when I entered, and he came forward to greet me with a frank smile. I turned away as if I did not know him. It was an act which I have regretted ever since. Later, when I was arrested and in danger of my life, he put me to shame by associating himself with the diplomatic representatives of the neutral Powers in the demand for my release. Through the Swedish Chargé d'Affaires, he sent a friendly message to me when I was in prison. Today, he is dead, and I have never been able to repay my debt of gratitude or to apologise for my action.

There was one other visitor, who, like Arthur Ransome, became a permanency. This was Moura. Since saying goodbye to her in St Petersburg at the beginning of March, I had missed her more than I cared to admit. We had written to each other regularly, and her letters had become a necessary part of my daily life. In April she came to stay with us in Moscow. She arrived at ten o'clock in the morning, and I was engaged with interviews until ten minutes to one. I went downstairs to the living-room, where we had our meals. She was standing by a table, and the spring sun was shining on her hair. As I walked forward to meet her, I scarcely dared to trust my voice. Into my life something had entered which was stronger than any other tie, stronger than life itself. From then onwards she was never to leave us, until we were parted by the armed force of the Bolsheviks.

With the arrival of the German Embassy in Moscow the prospects of a renewal of the war between Germany and Russia began to diminish. The great opportunity for an understanding between the Bolsheviks and the Allies had been in February and March, when the Soviet Government was still uncertain what the Germans would do. By the beginning of May, Lenin's peace policy had made headway even among those Bolsheviks who were most opposed to the Treaty of Brest-Litovsk. Strangely enough, the Foreign Office, who in February and March had given me no encouragement, now began to show signs of approval. Thus I was urged to do my utmost to secure Bolshevik consent to an Allied military intervention in Russia.

The moment was not so favourable, but it had not entirely passed. There were still certain factors in our favour, of which the most important was the attitude of the German troops in the territory they had occupied. They had set up a bourgeois Russian Government in the Ukraine, whose first action was to restore the land to its former owners. This naturally provoked a peasant revolt which was suppressed with great cruelty. The Bolsheviks and Left Social-Revolutionaries, who came from the south, were furious and were doing everything they could to stimulate a partisan war against the Germans. The latter could take and hold the towns by their military strength. They never succeeded in controlling the countryside. Moreover, the military support, which the Germans had afforded to the White Finns in the Finnish civil war, was another factor to our advantage. Germany seemed to be taking the side of reaction. It was therefore natural that the forces of the Left should turn to us for aid.

Trotsky, too, was still talking of war as though it were inevitable. When I asked him if he would accept Allied intervention, he replied that he had already asked the Allies to make a proposition. He wanted safeguards about non-interference in Russia's internal affairs. I then said that, if the Allies would come to an agreement on this point, could we have a half-hour's conference to draw up a working arrangement. His reply was characteristic: 'When the Allies agree among themselves, it is not half an hour but a whole day that I shall give you.'

It is true that Lenin's views were less satisfactory. He, too, thought that war was inevitable and was in favour of an arrangement with the Allies. But he was determined to fix his own date of inevitability. I saw him for the last time on May 7th. He informed me frankly that to him it appeared clear that sooner or later Russia would become a battlefield for the two opposing Imperialist groups and that he was determined, for the sake of Russia herself, to prevent this for as long a period as was possible.

Nevertheless, right up to the end of June, there was a reasonable prospect of arriving at a *modus vivendi*. Unfortunately, although both the British and American Governments made some attempt to play with the idea of Allied intervention with Bolshevik consent, no definite policy was ever formulated. And in Vologda there was M. Noulens, the French Ambassador, intent only on one aim: to have no dealings with the cut-throats who had insulted him. On April 29th we had a meeting of the Allied representatives in my rooms. General Lavergne informed us that M. Noulens was in favour of intervention without Bolshevik consent and without asking for it. The general, who had been at Vologda, admitted that his Ambassador had been unable to advance a single military argument in favour of his proposal. Romei, Riggs and I again affirmed our adherence to a policy of co-operation with the Bolsheviks.

There were, too, minor frictions between the Bolsheviks and ourselves – frictions which played an important part in wrecking the working agreement we sought to achieve. Japanese intervention was one stumbling-block. At one moment we would be reporting favourable progress with Trotsky. The next day we would be back to where we were before. The Japanese had landed troops at Vladivostok. Scowls from Trotsky. All privileges to the British stopped. Telegrams to London. And after days of delay the answer would come that the incident was to be regarded as purely local.

Prospects of an agreement were not enhanced by a well-intentioned speech of Mr Balfour, who declared that the Japanese were coming to help the Russians. In a conversation with Ransome Lenin at once raised the question of 'which Russians', and in a shrewd analysis of the problem set out his reasons why Japanese intervention would benefit neither England nor Bolshevik Russia. He typed out his analysis and in his own handwriting added his attestation that it correctly represented his views. I reproduce the document in facsimile with an English translation on another page (1) as a specimen of

Одно изъ самыхъ слабыхъ мѣстъ въ рѣчи Бальфура есть заявленіе о
томъ,что японцы идутъ на помощь русскимъ.К а к и м ъ и м е н н о р у с-
с к и м ъ?.Въ нынѣшней Россіи есть одна сила,по своей природѣ предназ-
наченная не на жизнь,а на смерть противъ нападеній со стороны междуна-
_{для борьбы}
род-аго имперіализма - это власть Совѣтовъ.Первымъ же шагомъ тѣхъ
русскихъ,которымъ собираются "помогать" японцы,при возникновеніи слу-
хахъ о приближеніи послѣднихъ было требованіе упраздненія Совѣтской
власти.Въ случаѣ продвиженія японцевъ внутрь Сибири тѣ же "русскіе",
которымъ японцы собираются "помогать",будутъ требовать упраздненія
Совѣтовъ во всей. Сибири.Чѣмъ же Совѣтская власть можетъ быть замѣнена?
Единственное,что можетъ ее замѣнить,есть буржуазное правительство.
Но буржуазія въ Россіи достаточно уже ясно показала,что можетъ держаться
у власти лишь при помощи извнѣ.Если буржуазное правительство,опираю-
щееся на помощь извнѣ,удержится у власти въ Сибири,и Восточная Россія
будетъ потеряна для Совѣтской власти,то и въ Западной Россіи послѣдняя
будетъ до такой степени ослаблена,что врядъ ли долго.удержится,и ея
наслѣдникомъ явится буржуазное правительство,которое и здѣсь также
будетъ нуждаться въ помощи извнѣ.Держава,которая окажетъ эту помощь.
будетъ,конечно,не Англія.Легко понять,какія перспективы сулитъ такая
возможность.

Подтверждаю, что
это дѣйствительно моя
бесѣда с Рансомом и
разрѣшаю печать ея.
Москва 23/V 1918. Ленинъ.

STATEMENT BY LENIN ON JAPANESE INTERVENTION, WITH
FACSIMILE SPECIMEN OF HIS HANDWRITING
(TRANSLATION OVERLEAF)

One of the weakest spots in Balfour's speech is the statement that the Japanese are going to help the Russians. Which Russians? In Russia today there is one power, which by its nature is destined to wage a life-and-death struggle against the attacks of international Imperialism – that is the power of the Soviets. The first step, however, of those Russians whom the Japanese intend to 'help', as soon as they heard rumours of the advance of the latter, was to demand the abolition of the Soviet power. Should the Japanese move into Siberia, these same 'Russians' whom the Japanese are going to 'help' will demand the abolition of the Soviets throughout the whole of Siberia. What can take the place of the Soviet power? The only power that can take its place is a bourgeois Government. But the bourgeoisie in Russia has proved clearly enough that it can only remain in power with foreign help. If a bourgeois Government, supported by outside help, should establish itself in power in Siberia and eastern Russia become lost to the Soviet, then in western Russia the Soviet power would become weakened to such an extent that it could hardly hold out for long; it would be followed by a bourgeois Government which would also need foreign help. The power to give this help would, of course, not be England. It is easy to understand what avenues are opened up by this possibility.

I confirm that I really said this in a conversation with Ransome, and I give permission for it to be printed.

LENIN.
Moscow 23/vi/1918

Lenin's handwriting and (2) as an illustration of the workings of his mind.

Another source of trouble was the Czech army which, formed of Czech prisoners, had been fighting for Russia up to the period of the Bolshevik revolution. The Czechs, who were a well-disciplined and fully armed force, were under the control of French officers. My services, however, were requisitioned to secure their evacuation, presumably because of the privileged position I enjoyed with the Bolshevik Government. The evacuation was no simple matter. Not unnaturally, the Germans protested violently against the presence, on what was now neutral Russian territory, of a large force, which was to be used against them. Nevertheless, I succeeded in securing Trotsky's goodwill, and but for the folly of the French I am convinced that the Czechs would have been safely evacuated without incident. My task was not made easier by the last-minute requests of the British Government to use my influence to persuade Trotsky to divert the Czechs to Archangel. This, too, at a time when General Poole was already in north Russia, advocating a policy of intervention, which was subsequently adopted and which never amounted to anything more than an armed intervention against Bolshevism.

Ultimately, the Czechs were the cause of our final breach with the Bolsheviks. How I wish today that President Masaryk* had remained in Russia during this trying period. I am convinced that he would never have sanctioned the Siberian revolt. The Allies would have listened to him, and we should have been spared the crowning folly of an adventure which sent thousands of Russians to their deaths and cost the British taxpayer millions of pounds in money.

The sands were running out. We were drifting rapidly towards the inevitable tragedy. In Moscow, too, I was not alone in receiving no support from home. Robins had lost ground in Vologda. He had a formidable opponent in Summers, the American Consul-General in Moscow, who, married to a Russian of good family, was heart and soul for the old régime. When Summers died suddenly towards the end of April, there were slanderers who declared that he had been poisoned by the Bolsheviks and who looked askance at Robins. The

* Thomas Garrigue Masaryk (1850–1937), founder President of the Czechoslovakian Republic. He had gone to Russia in 1917 to recruit prisoners of war for the Czechoslovak Legion.

French, too, had put a spoke in Robins's wheel by playing on the American Ambassador's vanity. In his presence a member of the French Embassy had asked who was the American Ambassador – Francis or Robins – because they always said the opposite of each other. As a result of these intrigues Robins's position became intolerable, and early in May he left Russia in order to make a personal appeal to President Wilson. The night before he left he dined with us. He had been reading Rhodes's life and after dinner he gave us a wonderful exposition of Rhodes's character. Like Lord Beaverbrook, he possessed in a remarkable degree the talent of extracting exactly what he wanted from everything he read, and dramatising it afterwards in his conversation. He was a great personality and a man of sterling character and iron determination. His departure was a great loss to me. In the almost lone hand I was playing his moral courage had been an immense support.

Lavergne, too, willy-nilly, had been forced to adopt the Noulens policy. Even Romei, who as a soldier preferred action to inaction, was beginning to reach the stage when intervention even without Bolshevik consent seemed better than no intervention at all. At this stage the position was that President Wilson was still opposed to intervention without Bolshevik consent. The French were working vigorously for military support of the anti-Bolshevik forces. The British Foreign Office – I write Foreign Office intentionally, because the British War Office seemed to have a totally different policy – was pressing us hard for an immediate acceptance by the Bolsheviks of Allied military support. Presumably, although I do not think the conditions were ever laid down, they were prepared, in return for this consent, to guarantee to the Bolsheviks complete non-interference in Russia's internal affairs.

In this gloomy vacuum a ray of hope was suddenly propelled. Trotsky had been more than usually amenable. The Germans had been very aggressive in the south, and he had reacted in the usual belligerent manner. He had been conciliatory about Murmansk and about our stores at Archangel. He had even asked for a British naval mission to reorganise the Russian fleets and had offered to put an Englishman in charge of the Russian railways. I had telegraphed this news to London and for several days I received no answer. I was not astonished. The telegraph service was erratic, and delays and a break in the sequence of numbers were frequent. Then one evening I received a telegram, which was as long as a despatch. I sat up until late into the night deciphering it. It was from Mr Balfour. I learnt later that he had drafted personally nearly all the telegrams I received in Russia. I have no copy of this telegram. I cannot remember all its details, but its beginning and its end are firmly fixed in my memory. It began: 'There are three duties of a diplomat: one is to make himself *persona grata* to the Government of the country to which he is accredited. In this you have succeeded admirably. The second is to interpret to his own Government the policy of the Government of the country to which he is accredited. In this you have also been successful. The third is to interpret to the Government of the country to which he is accredited, the policy of his own Government. In this it seems to me that you have not been so successful.' Then followed a list of British grievances against Bolsheviks. When the list was completed, there was a sudden change. 'Since writing this,' the telegram went on, 'I have received your telegram informing me of Trotsky's request for British naval and technical experts. This is good news. If you can, indeed, persuade Trotsky to resist German penetration, you will have earned the gratitude of your own country and of all humanity.'

The telegram, although affording me fresh hope, was a little unkind. Admittedly, I had been unsuccessful in interpreting the policy of His Majesty's Government to the Bolsheviks. But for three months London had given me no indication of its policy or policies. In my reply I referred to my previous telegrams and requested humbly to be supplied with a more precise statement. It was not forthcoming. No naval mission was sent. No Englishman was appointed to the control of the Russian railways. But General Poole and a staff of officers were sent to Archangel and Murmansk.

Altogether May was a hectic and nerve-racking month. It began with an impressive parade of the Red Army on the Red Square. Trotsky took the salute in the presence of the foreign diplomatic representatives. Mirbach watched the review from his motor car. At first he smiled superciliously. Then he looked serious. He was the representative of the old German Imperialism. There was an unmistakable living force in the ill-clad, unorganised men who marched past him. I was impressed. The bourgeoisie, however, could not read the signs. They were obsessed with a strange story of a miracle, which had taken place that day. On the Nikolskaya the Bolsheviks had draped an icon with red bunting. As soon as they put it up, the cloth was miraculously torn.

On May 6th the American Ambassador paid a visit of several days to Moscow. I had several interviews with him and liked him. He was a kind, old gentleman, who was susceptible to flattery and swallowed any amount of it. His knowledge of anything beyond banking and poker was severely limited. He had a travelling spittoon – a contraption with a pedal – which he took with him everywhere. When he wished to emphasise a point, bang would go the pedal, followed by a well-aimed expectoration. During his Moscow visit he was responsible for a story which deserves to rank with Dumas's account of the loving couple plighting their troth under the shade of the 'Kliukva' (cranberry)! One afternoon Norman Armour, the efficient secretary of the American Embassy, came into the Ambassador's room.

'Governor,' he said, 'would you like to go to the opera tonight?'

'Nope,' was the reply, 'I think I'll play poker.'

'Do come, Governor,' said Armour. 'You really ought not to miss it. It's *Evgenie Onegin*.'

'Evgenny what?' said the Ambassador.

'Oh! you know,' replied Armour. 'Pushkin and Tchaikovsky.'

There was a crash from the pedal of the spittoon.

'What!' said the Ambassador ecstatically. 'Is Pushkin singing tonight?'

On May 7th, I had an excitement of a more disturbing nature. At six o'clock in the evening Karachan telephoned to me requesting me to come to see him. He had an extraordinary story to tell. That afternoon a British officer had walked boldly up to the Kremlin gate and had demanded to see Lenin. Asked for his credentials, he had declared that he had been sent out specially by Mr Lloyd George to obtain firsthand news of the aims and ideals of the Bolsheviks. The British Government was not satisfied with the reports it had been receiving from me. He had been entrusted with the task of making good the defects. He had not seen Lenin but he had been interviewed by Bonch-Bruevich, a Russian of good family and the closest personal friend of the Bolshevik leader. Karachan wished to know if the man was an impostor. The name of the officer, he said, was 'Relli'. I was nonplussed, and, holding it impossible that the man could have any official standing, I nearly blurted out that he must be a Russian masquerading as an Englishman or else a madman. Bitter experi-

Lenin and his sister,
Maria, on their way
to the Fifth All-
Russian Congress at
the Moscow Opera
House, July 4th, 1918.
Right, Maria Spiri-
donova, leader of
the Left Social-
Revolutionary Party
and later a prisoner in
the Kremlin alongside
the author

View of the Kremlin, with the chapel in the foreground. *Left*, Jacob Peters, Vice-President of the Cheka and the author's chief interrogator during his confinement ence, however, had taught me to be prepared for almost any surprise, and, without betraying my amazement, I told Karachan that I would enquire into the matter and let him know the result. That same evening I sent for Boyce, the head of the intelligence service, and told him the story. He informed me that the man was a new agent, who had just come out from England. I blew up in a storm of indignation, and the next day the officer came to me to offer his explanation. He swore that the story Karachan had told me was quite untrue. He admitted, however, that he had been to the Kremlin and had seen Bonch-Bruevich. The sheer audacity of the man took my breath away. I knew instinctively that on this occasion Karachan had adhered strictly to the truth. Now I was faced with the unpleasant and even dangerous task of saving a British agent, who, unless I denied him, might compromise me and for whose safety, although he was in no way subordinate to me, I felt myself in some measure responsible. Although he was years older than me, I dressed him down like a schoolmaster and threatened to have him sent home. He took his wigging humbly but calmly and was so ingenious in his excuses that in the end he made me laugh. Fortunately, I was able to arrange matters with Karachan so that his suspicions were not unduly aroused.

The man who had thrust himself so dramatically into my life was Sidney Reilly, the mystery man of the British secret service and known today to the outside world as the master spy of Britain.* My experiences of the war and of the Russian revolution have left me with a very poor opinion of secret service work. Doubtless, it has its uses and its functions, but political work is not its strong point. The buying of information puts a premium on manufactured news. But even manufactured news is less dangerous than the honest reports of men, who, however brave and however gifted as linguists, are frequently incapable of forming a reliable political judgement. The methods of Sidney Reilly, however, were on a grand scale, which compelled my admiration. We shall hear more of him before my story is ended.

About this time, too, I received a mysterious visit from a tall, clean-shaven Russian. He addressed me as 'Roman Romanovich'. I looked at him blankly. As far as I knew, I had never seen him before.

* See Robin Bruce Lockhart, *Reilly: Ace of Spies* (n/e, 1992) and *Reilly: The First Man* (1987).

'You do not recognise me?' he said.

'Frankly, no,' I replied.

He covered his chin and mouth with his hand. It was Fabrikant, a Social-Revolutionary and an intimate friend of Kerensky. The last time I had seen him, he had worn a beard! He was in dire trouble. Kerensky was in Moscow and wanted to leave Russia. The only way he could go was by Murmansk or Archangel. Fabrikant had been to see Wardrop, the British Consul-General, in order to obtain the necessary visa. Wardrop had refused to give it without first referring the matter to London. Several days might elapse before the answer came. There was an immediate opportunity of smuggling Kerensky out with a platoon of Serbian soldiers, who were returning home via Murmansk. Every hour he remained in Moscow exposed him to the danger of betrayal to the Bolsheviks. If the British refused to give him a visa, they might be responsible for his death. What did I propose to do about it?

I made up my mind very quickly. I dared not telephone to Wardrop lest our conversation might be tapped. If he had no authority to give a visa without reference to London, he was not likely to change his mind. I had no time to go to see him. I could not expose Fabrikant to the disappointment and even danger of sending him away and asking him to return. I had no authority to give visas. I was an Ishmaelite, to be owned and disowned as the British Government thought fit. I had no certainty that my visa would be accepted by the British authorities at Murmansk. We were living, however, in strange times, and I was prepared to go a long way to avoid endangering the unfortunate Kerensky's life. I therefore took the Serbian passport, which Kerensky had procured, wrote out a visa, and sealed my signature with the rubber stamp, which made apology for our official seal. That same evening Kerensky, disguised as a Serbian soldier, left for Murmansk. Not for three days, when I knew he must be safe, did I telegraph to London, reporting my action and my reasons for taking it. I was afraid that the Bolsheviks had a key to our ciphers.

My fears were not entirely groundless. Karachan himself had confessed to me that the Bolsheviks had made every attempt to procure the German ciphers. They had staged a raid on the German courier. He even suggested to me that, if our cipher experts could decipher them, he could furnish me with copies of the German telegrams. I suspect that my own popularity with the Bolsheviks was due to the fact that they knew from my telegrams that I was opposed to any form of intervention without Bolshevik consent.

Between May 15th and 23rd Cromie came down twice from St Petersburg to confer with me. He was anxious about the Black Sea fleet, which, owing to the German advance along the Black Sea coast, was now in imminent danger of capture. Together we went to see Trotsky. During Cromie's visit I had several interviews with the Red Minister for War, and, although he was now full of suspicions against the Allies, he was reassuring about the fleet and not un-friendly. After several days of negotiation he informed me that he had given orders for the destruction of the Black Sea fleet. A little later it was, in fact, blown up. This was the last interview I ever had with Trotsky. From now onwards his door was to be shut against me.

The next day (May 24th) was young Tamplin's twenty-first birth-day, and we gave him a dinner at Streilna, the restaurant outside the city where Maria Nikolayevna and her tziganes held their court. By what means I do not know, the place had escaped the vigilance of the Bolshevik authorities, and we were able to relax to our heart's con-tent. We were all a little excited. We felt instinctively that our stay in Russia was coming to an end, and the minor orgy, which I suppose every gypsy party must be called, was a welcome relief to the high tension of the previous weeks. We drank innumerable 'charochki', while Maria Nikolayevna sang to us as she had never sung before. She, too, realised that the days of her reign were numbered. One by one, she went through all our old favourites: 'Two Guitars', 'Once Again', 'To the Last Copeck', 'Black Eyes'.

> Po obichaiyu chisto-ruskomu;
> Po obichaiyu po-moskovskomu.
> Zit nye mozem my bez shampawskavo
> E bez penya, bez tziganskavo.

> [In the true Russian fashion,
> In the manner that is Moscow's.
> We cannot live without champagne
> Without our songs and our tziganes.]

The haunting minor chords of the guitars, the deep bass notes of Maria Nikolayevna's glorious voice, the warm stillness of the summer night, the rich fragrance of the lime-trees. How it all comes back to me like every experience which we cannot repeat.

There was one song which I have never heard from any other lips than Maria Nikolayevna's. In those days it was in tune with my own turbulent soul, and that night I made her repeat it again and again, until at last she laughed and kissed me on both cheeks. It was called 'I Cannot Forget', and it began:

> They say my heart is like the wind,
> That to one maid I can't be true;
> But why do I forget the rest,
> And still remember only you?

In English idiotic, but sung by Maria Nikolayevna in Russian a throbbing plaint of longing and desire.

We drank deep into the night. Hicks, Tamplin, Garstin, Hill and Lingner went out into the garden at different intervals to cool their heads, until I was left alone. When they returned, they found me sitting at the middle of the table – still erect and very serious and greeting them with a sigh: 'Roman Romanovich patchti pyan' – Roman Romanovich is almost drunk. It was *almost* true.

Their return broke the spell. I pulled myself together, and, when the dawn broke, I sent the others home and drove out with Moura to the Sparrow Hills to watch the sun rise over the Kremlin. It came up like an angry ball of fire heralding destruction. No joy was to come with the morning.

The next day I received news from St Petersburg that General Poole was expected in Archangel that evening. Colonel Thornhill, the former assistant military attaché, had already arrived in Murmansk and had paid a recent visit to St Petersburg. Although I had heard nothing of these movements from London – indeed, the Foreign Office were still pressing me (1) to secure the consent of the Bolsheviks to Allied military assistance, and (2) to expedite the departure of the Czech army from Russia – it was obvious that the interventionists were gaining ground.

I had further proof of their activities when on the same evening General Lavergne came to our daily meeting. He brought with him an invitation for me to go to Vologda to see the Allied Ambassadors. Mr Francis and M. Noulens wished to see if we could not co-ordinate our views and find a common formula.

Although I was scarcely in a position to refuse, I accepted with some reluctance. My visit to Vologda was to have an all-important influence on my career. Yet, although I realise today that it would have been better for me if I had remained in Moscow, this journey into the wilderness was a valuable experience.

Vologda itself was a sleepy provincial town with almost as many churches as inhabitants. As a connecting link with Moscow it was as useless as the North Pole. Its only advantage as a retreat for the Allied representatives was its proximity to Moscow.

On my arrival I called on M. Noulens, who received me with every mark of friendliness. After a short preliminary discussion I went off to dine with the American Ambassador, who was comfortably lodged in an old clubhouse and who was to be my host during my stay. The serious business was to be left until the next day.

My evening with the Americans had the merit of being amusing as well as instructive. Mr Francis was a charming host. At his house I met the Japanese Chargé d'Affaires, the Brazilian Minister, and the serious and still perturbed Torretta. We sat up late into the night, but Russia figured hardly at all in our conversation. From Francis I gathered that President Wilson was strongly opposed to Japanese intervention. Otherwise, he did not seem to have any decided views about Russia. Knowledge of Russian politics he had none. The only political entry in my diary for that evening is the laconic note: 'Old Francis doesn't know a Left Social-Revolutionary from a potato.' To do him justice, he made no pretence of professing to understand the situation. He was as simple and as fearless as a child. It never entered his head that he himself was in any personal danger. At dinner he asked me a few questions about life in Moscow. I answered him with commendable brevity, and the rest of the meal was devoted to chaffing the Brazilian Minister. This gentleman was the one joy of Vologda. I hope he is still alive and that he is still serving his country. He had reduced the art of diplomacy to a simple formula: do nothing, and promotion and honours are certain. He did his best to live up to his own formula. He slept all day and played cards all night. When the American Ambassador twitted him with doing no work, he turned the tables by wagering that his telegram bill was higher than the American's. His statement was correct. True it is that since February, 1917, he had sent only one telegram to his Government.

But it had cost over £1,000. He had translated and telegraphed to Rio the whole of Kerensky's first speech on the revolution! Having proved his case, he then proceeded to justify his philosophy. When he had entered the service as a young attaché, he had been full of zeal. He had gone to London as Second Secretary. He had worked strenuously on a report on the Brazilian coffee trade with England. He had made certain recommendations. His reward had been a reduction in rank and a transfer to the Balkans. When later he was transferred to Berlin, he resumed his zeal and furnished his Government with an admirable report on technical education in Germany. Once again he suffered a reduction in rank. Then wisdom came to him. Zeal had obviously no place in diplomacy, and he made up his mind to do nothing in future to remind his Government of his existence. From that moment his diplomatic career had been one long triumph and his promotion had been as regular as clockwork. The formula is not so absurd as the layman may imagine. It has stood more than one British diplomat in good stead.

As soon as dinner was over, Francis began to fidget like a child who wishes to return to its toys. His rattle, however, was a deck of cards, and without loss of time they were produced. The old gentleman was no child at poker. We played late, and, as usually happens when I play with Americans, he took my money.

The next day I lunched with the French Ambassador. There was nothing childish about M. Noulens. If he played poker, he played without cards. Politics – and politics viewed from the narrow, logical angle of a Frenchman – was his only game. General Lavergne had given him a copy of the report we had drafted on the military needs of the situation. It was based on the supposition that the Bolsheviks would give their consent to our intervention. Together we discussed the report. M. Noulens was flatteringly congratulatory. He agreed with the report. He had only one amendment to make. If the Bolsheviks would not give their consent, we must intervene without their consent. He advanced many arguments in support of this new formula. He referred to the critical situation on the Western front. He quoted telegrams from the French General Staff. The war would be lost or won on the Western front. And the French General Staff insisted on the necessity of some diversion in Russia which would prevent the Germans from transferring more troops from the east. It was essential that the various Allied representatives in Russia should present a united front. Dissensions in Allied policy had been the chief cause of delay in achieving victory. He would go far to obtain unity. He would accept our formula. He hoped I would agree to his amendment. I looked at Lavergne. I knew he had already capitulated. Romei had not come to Vologda, but he, too, had been subjected to pressure from Italian headquarters. As a soldier he was not likely to stand out against his own General Staff. I was alone. Robins had left. Sadoul, the French Robins, had been side-tracked. M. Noulens had taken away his right of telegraphing direct to Albert Thomas. Feverishly I tried to summarise my own position in my mind. Perhaps I could still pull off a big coup with Trotsky. Perhaps M. Noulens was cleverer than I realised. I was in a corner. If I refused to agree, M. Noulens would go ahead with his own policy. He would carry the Italians, the Japanese, and even Francis with him. If I consented, at least I should escape the stigma of having stood out against the united opinion of all the other Allied representatives. I capitulated.

In the blazing sunshine we walked across to the Ambassadors' meeting. Francis was in the chair, but Noulens dominated the proceedings. He was, in fact, the only Allied representative in Vologda who knew his own mind. He was at one with us regarding the number of troops that would be required for a successful intervention. Even with regard to the Czech army, which was then stretched like a serpent from the Volga to Siberia, he was strangely conciliatory. We discussed this question from all its angles and decided that the Czechs should be evacuated as soon as possible. After the meeting I said goodbye to M. Noulens. He was all smiles and affability. When, twenty-four hours later, I arrived in Moscow, I was met by Hicks with the news that there had been a serious clash in Siberia between the Bolsheviks and the Czechs. How the clash had arisen is unclear to me to this day. The report from the French officers, who were accompanying the Czechs, stated that the Bolsheviks, yielding to German demands, had tried to disarm the Czechs. The Czechs resisted and were now continuing their journey by the force of their own arms. The Bolsheviks maintained that at the instigation of the French the Czechs had made an unprovoked attack on the local Bolshevik authorities and had taken the law into their own hands. From which side the provocation came will probably remain a matter of dispute for all time. Nevertheless, what the result of this affair was to be was quite clear. The first plank in the platform of the intervention-ists had been laid.

I found Moscow in a state of siege. The Czech diplomatic council had been arrested. Numerous counter-revolutionaries had been rounded up and put in prison. The newspapers had been suppressed. There was an urgent request from Chicherin, begging me to use my influence to settle the Czech incident amicably. There was also a telegram from Cromie urging me to come to St Petersburg to see one of General Poole's officers who was arriving the next day.

I spent the next afternoon in interviewing Chicherin and Karachan. In the absence of details of what was happening in Siberia we were unable to make much headway about the Czech incident. That the Bolsheviks were anxious to settle the affair amicably was evident, but, as I had not time to receive instructions from London, I could only promise to do my best. My interview, however, left me with one clear impression. The suspicions of the Bolsheviks were now fully aroused. They were, as I had always believed, accurately informed about the activities of the French. They knew that General Poole had arrived in north Russia. Already they had a shrewd idea that the Czechs were to be the vanguard of an anti-Bolshevik inter-vention. I gave them the only answer I could: that the British Government's offer of military aid against Germany was still open. Chicherin laughed bitterly. The Allies were siding with the counter-revolutionaries. There was no choice for the Bolsheviks. They would oppose Allied intervention against Russia's wish in the same way as they would oppose German intervention.

The same evening, having decided that I could just afford the time, I left for St Petersburg. There I saw Cromie and McGrath, the English officer who had come out with General Poole. In one sense McGrath was reassuring. Some weeks before Trotsky, in a moment of depression, had suggested that I was merely a tool, used by the British Government to keep the Bolsheviks quiet while it was pre-paring an anti-Bolshevik coup. At the time I had been furiously indignant. Now I was perturbed. McGrath, however, set my mind at rest. The intervention plan, he said, was not very far advanced, and England had no policy at all as far as Russia was concerned. Nothing would be decided until Poole reported home.

If there was a negative comfort in this statement McGrath gave me several shocks. Poole himself was in favour of intervention.

Thornhill, who was at Murmansk, was a rabid interventionist. Moreover, Lindley, who had been our Chargé d'Affaires when I arrived in St Petersburg, was coming out again. This could mean only one thing. London had no confidence in me. I returned to Moscow in a state of dejection, aggravated by the humiliation that all St Petersburg should know of Lindley's pending arrival before my own Government had thought fit to inform me of the fact.

On my return to Moscow I found instructions from London regarding the Czech affair, and the same afternoon, together with my French and Italian colleagues, I went to the Russian Foreign Office. The proceedings were severely formal. Chicherin's room was long and bare of any furniture except the desk in the middle. We sat on wooden chairs facing him and Karachan. One by one, we read out our protests. Mine was the strongest. I told the two Commissars that for months I had done my best to bring about an understanding with the Allies, but that they had always put me off with evasions. Now, after promising a free exit to the Czechs, who had fought for the Slav cause and who were going to France to continue the fight against a foe who was still the Bolshevik enemy as well as ours, they had yielded to German threats and had wantonly attacked those who had always been their friends. I was instructed by my Government to inform them that any attempt to disarm the Czechs, or to interfere with them in any way, would be regarded as an act inspired by Germany and hostile to the Allies.

The Bolsheviks listened to our protests in silence. They were scrupulously polite. Although they had a case, they made no attempt to argue it. Chicherin, looking more like a drowned rat than ever, stared at us with mournful eyes. Karachan seemed stupidly bewildered. There was a painful silence. Everyone was a little nervous and none more than myself, whose conscience was not quite clear. Then Chicherin coughed. 'Gentlemen,' he said, 'I have taken note of what you said.' We shook hands awkwardly and then filed out of the room.

Our protest had made a profound impression. Months afterwards, when I was in prison, Karachan told me that both he and Chicherin had been completely surprised by the vehemence of my language. Their first suspicions of me had dated from that day. The suspicions were well founded. Almost before I had realised it I had now identified myself with a movement which, whatever its original object, was to be directed, not against Germany, but against the de facto Government of Russia.

I must explain the motives which had driven me into this illogical situation. For four and a half months I had opposed Japanese intervention and, indeed, every kind of intervention which had not received the sanction of the Bolsheviks. I had little faith in the strength of the anti-Bolshevik Russian forces and none at all in the feasibility of reconstituting an Eastern front against Germany. Moreover, I had been in close touch with the Czech Council. The Czech army, whose revolt had brought matters to a head, was composed of war-prisoners. They were Slavs, who, although technically Austrian subjects, had deserted in their thousands to the Russians at the beginning of the war. They bore no love to the Tsarist régime, which had always refused to recognise their separate nationality. They were democrats by instinct, and their sympathies were with the Russian liberals and the Social-Revolutionaries. They were not likely to co-operate smoothly with the Tsarist officers, who supplied the main strength to the armies of the anti-Bolshevik generals.

Why then had I given my adherence to a policy which seemed to hold out little promise of success and which was to expose me to widespread accusations of inconsistency? Although I desire to be strictly truthful, the answer is not easy. Fortunate indeed are the traditionalists, who accept the existing order of society in their cradle, and who solve every political problem by the simple formula of 'these men are my friends and those my enemies'. I could not see the situation in this light. I had been sent back to Russia mainly in order that I might keep the British Government informed about the real state of affairs. That task I had tried to fulfil to the best of my ability. I had no special sympathy for the Bolsheviks, nor did the numerous accusations of pro-Bolshevism augment unduly the obstinacy with which I strove to maintain an objective and unbiased view of the situation. At the same time, I could not help realising instinctively that, behind its peace programme and its fanatical economic programme, there was an idealistic background to Bolshevism which lifted it far above the designation of a mob movement led by German agents. For months I had lived cheek by jowl with men who worked eighteen hours a day and who were obviously inspired by the same spirit of self-sacrifice and abnegation of worldly pleasure which animated the Puritans and the early Jesuits.

If to realise that I was living in a movement which was likely to assume even greater proportions in history than the French revolution was to be pro-Bolshevik, then I am entitled to the label of pro-Bolshevism. I knew from my wife's telegrams – later they were to be confirmed from other sources – that my views were unpalatable to the British Government. I ought to have resigned and come home. Today, I should have been enjoying the reputation of a prophet who had predicted the various phases of the Russian revolution with remarkable accuracy.

I did not do so. It would be easy for me to say that my first duty was to my country, that, when my country had decided on another policy, I had no right to oppose it, and that to resign in the middle of the war would have been equivalent to deserting my post in the face of the enemy. I do not plead these excuses. They were not my motives. Three months later, when I was in prison, Karl Radek wrote a letter to Arthur Ransome, in which he described me as a '*carrièriste*', who, when he had seen that his own policy had no chance of being accepted, sought feverishly to regain the favour of his employers. This, too, although nearer the mark, is an unfair accusation. The motives for my conduct were two. Subconsciously, although I did not put the question to myself at the time, I was unwilling to leave Russia because of Moura. The other motive – and it was the all-compelling one, of which I was fully conscious – was that I lacked the moral courage to resign and to take a stand which would have exposed me to the odium of the vast majority of my countrymen.

There was perhaps one other more creditable motive. In my conceit I imagined that, if the Allies were bent on a military intervention in Russia, my special knowledge of the Russian situation would be of some value in aiding them to avoid the major pitfalls. I knew the Bolsheviks more intimately than any Englishman knew them at that time. I had had my finger on the pulse of events in Russia since January. The clamjamphrie of military experts, who from outside were screaming for intervention and who regarded the Bolsheviks as a rabble to be swept away with a whiff of grape-shot, was deprived by its geographical situation of that knowledge. Having gone over to intervention, I did my best to ensure that it would have at least some chance of success. To the last I opposed the theory that the 'loyal' Russians were capable of overthrowing the

Bolsheviks even if supported by Allied munitions and money and led by Allied officers. To the last I insisted on the need for large Allied forces, without which the whole scheme was bound to fail. I even devised a special formula: that the support which we would receive from the 'loyal' Russians would be in direct proportion to the number of troops we sent ourselves. For all the good I did I might have saved my breath for my own porridge. My volte-face had discredited me with everybody. The interventionists looked on me as an obstinate young mule, who had at last come over to their way of thinking. I was an obstacle which had been successfully removed. My views could now be safely disregarded. The Bolsheviks shared Radek's opinion of me. I had fallen between two stools. To this day I have suffered from my tumble. To the Bolsheviks I am the incarnation of counter-revolution. To the interventionists I am still the pro-Bolshevik who wrecked their plans!

The intervention itself did not take place until August 4th. The two months from June to August were a purgatory, during which our position gradually deteriorated. And, as a result of the increased danger which now threatened them, the Bolsheviks tightened up their discipline.

On June 10th 'Benji' Bruce arrived in Moscow. He had come to fetch his bride, the beautiful and charming Karsavina.* He brought me a large bundle of mail and my first real news from England. There was a letter from George Clerk, then Head of the War Department in the Foreign Office. It was full of nice things. Indeed, he and Colonel Kisch, who was then at the War Office, are almost the only senior officials who have been generous enough to sympathise with my attitude and to admit that my estimate of the situation had not been far wrong. Bruce, however, left me with no illusions regarding my unpopularity in England during the period of my so-called pro-Bolshevism. He informed me that in March I had nearly been recalled. He stayed only twelve hours in Moscow, but, in spite of the news he brought me, his visit was like a breath of wind coming over the desert. After being shut off from the world for five months I was thrilled by his account of the situation in England and on the Western front. Karsavina and he had a nightmare of adventure before reaching Murmansk. They had to travel without a Bolshevik permit. My powers to help them had ceased.

June was a dreary month. Perhaps because my conscience was uneasy, I lived in an atmosphere of suspicion. Trotsky would have no more dealings with us, and, although I continued to see Chicherin, Karachan, and Radek almost daily, we avoided the real issue in our conversations. With the alteration in the political attitude of the Bolsheviks came a change in our material position. We found it increasingly difficult to obtain supplies of fresh meat and vegetables. Without the tinned rations supplied to us by the American Red Cross mission we should have fared badly.

Through Hicks I increased my contact with the anti-Bolshevik forces. As far as we were concerned, they were represented in Moscow by an organisation called the 'Centre' which was subdivided into two wings of Left and Right, and by the League of the

* Tamara Platonovna Karsavina (1885–1978), ballerina.

Regeneration of Russia founded by Savinkov. There were constant bickerings between the two organisations. The Centre was in close touch with the White Army in the south. The White generals regarded Savinkov with suspicion. Indeed, about this period I received a letter from General Alexeyev in which he stated that he would sooner co-operate with Lenin and Trotsky than with Savinkov or Kerensky. Both organisations were agreed on one point only. They wanted Allied aid and Allied money. I saw one or two of the leaders, notably Peter Struve, a brilliant intellectual, who at one time had been a Socialist and had helped Lenin to frame his first Communist manifesto, and Michael Feodorov, a former Assistant Minister. Both were men of fine character. Both were unswervingly loyal to the Allies. I was, however, very guarded in my conversations with them. As far as I knew officially, the British Government had not yet decided on intervention. Until the decision was brought to my notice I gave no support to the Whites either in cash or in promises.

In this my attitude differed from that of the French, who, as I knew from their own admission, were supplying funds to Savinkov. Their promises, too, were extravagant. The Whites were led to believe that Allied military support would be forthcoming in decisive strength. The figure generally mentioned was two Allied divisions for Archangel and several Japanese divisions for Siberia. Encouraged by these hopes, the anti-Bolshevik forces began to increase their activities. On June 21st Volodarsky, the Bolshevik Commissar for Press Affairs in St Petersburg, was assassinated on his return from a meeting at the Obukhov works. The Bolshevik reply was swift. In his speech to the St Petersburg Soviet Uritsky, the head of the local Cheka, made a violent attack on England in which he accused the English of organising the dead Commissar's murder. The next day Shchastny, the Commander-in-Chief of the Baltic fleet, who had been a prisoner in the Kremlin, was condemned to death and shot. At the trial Trotsky distinguished himself by the violence of his language. The Terror was beginning.

I went to see Chicherin to protest against Uritsky's accusation. He put me off with semi-apologetic explanations. It was deplorable, but what else could we expect if we insisted on infringing Russia's neutrality. Russia wanted only to be left alone and to enjoy the fruits of her dearly bought peace. He was amusing about Trotsky, who, with his back to the wall, was always wanting to fight somebody and was now advocating strong measures against the Allies. 'It is strange', said Chicherin, 'how the military idea has gone to Trotsky's head. In March Lenin had to use his influence to prevent Trotsky from declaring war on Germany. Now it is Lenin's cool brain which is holding Trotsky back from declaring war on the Allies.'

Although the intervention appeared to be hanging fire, our stay in Moscow seemed near its end. None of us was very happy. Denis Garstin had already left us. He had been ordered to join General Poole at Archangel. He, too, had to leave clandestinely owing to the difficulty in securing a Bolshevik pass for him. He went with a sad heart. He would have liked to remain with us to the end. Poor boy! He was one of the first victims of the intervention. Still, we were not without optimism. Believing that the Allies would land in force, we were convinced that the Bolsheviks would be unable to offer a serious resistance. Even Ransome, whose opposition to intervention without Bolshevik consent had remained constant, told us that 'the show was over' and began to make preparations to leave. Before we ourselves were to be allowed to depart we were to have our fill of excitement.

One extraordinary adventure during this period was the murder of Count Mirbach, the German Ambassador. This assassination, accompanied as it was by an internal revolt against the Government, was the most dramatic political murder of modern times. As I myself was an uncomfortable eye-witness of the attempted coup d'état, I give my own account of the affair in full detail.

To understand the situation, the reader must remember that after the Bolshevik revolution in November,* 1917, the extreme wing of the Russian Social-Revolutionary Party joined hands with the Bolsheviks and co-operated with them in the formation of the new Government. They received a few posts in the various Commissariats, retained their places in the Soviets, and were strongly represented in the All-Russian Central Executive Committee, which, when the Congress of Soviets is not sitting, is the supreme legislative and executive power of the Russian Socialist Federative Soviet Republic. For the first eight months of its existence the Soviet Government was, in fact, a coalition.

As a party the Left Social-Revolutionaries were quite as extreme

* Or October by the then Russian calendar: see Editorial Note, p. xvii.

as the Bolsheviks in their hatred of capitalism and Imperialism. They were therefore as violent as the Bolsheviks in their denunciation of the Allies. In internal politics, while they differed from the Bolsheviks on agrarian questions, they upheld the Soviet system and supported the Bolsheviks in the prosecution of the civil war. Two members of the party, Colonel Muraviev, an ex-police officer, and Lieutenant Sablin, the son of the proprietor of the Korsh Theatre in Moscow, were during the first period of the Bolshevik régime the most successful military commanders of the new Government.

Unlike the Bolsheviks, however, the Left Social-Revolutionaries were not prepared to go to any lengths in their desire for peace. They had been opposed to the Brest-Litovsk peace and, although they retained their representatives in the Government, had never accepted it. They drew most of their support from the Ukraine, which had been occupied by the Germans, and the Germans were hard taskmasters who had installed a dummy reactionary Russian Government and restored the land to the Russian landowners.

The Left Social-Revolutionaries had not accepted this situation, and ever since the peace they had carried on a violent partisan war in the Ukraine against both the Russian landlords and the German troops of occupation. By both sides this miniature warfare was conducted with appalling cruelty. Goaded almost to despair by the sufferings of their compatriots in the Ukraine, the Left Social-Revolutionaries protested vigorously against the servile attitude of the Bolsheviks before the Germans and denounced the Bolshevik Commissars as Mirbach's lackeys. As even the official Press had to admit, almost daily, some fresh German breach of the Brest-Litovsk Treaty, considerable point was given to the caustic comments on the cringing tone of Chicherin's mild protests and the barely civil replies of the German Ambassador.

The real difference between the two Russian Government parties was that the Left Social-Revolutionaries regarded Germany as the chief menace to the revolution. The Bolsheviks, or rather Lenin, for he alone saw clearly in this confused atmosphere, were determined to do nothing which might endanger the fragile fabric of their peace. They were now more afraid of Allied intervention than of further aggression by the Germans. The two parties were of course at heart both anti-German and anti-Entente. The situation, however, was not without its comic side. While the Bolsheviks were publicly denouncing the activities of the Left Social-Revolutionaries in the Ukraine, they were supplying them secretly with the funds for their partisan warfare against the Germans.

There was one other grievance which further divided the two parties. Among the peasants the chief supporters of the Left Social-Revolutionaries were the Kulaks.* Partly in order to strengthen their own position in the country and partly to obtain more grain, the Bolsheviks had organised so-called Poverty Committees, composed of poorer peasants, who were encouraged to attack the richer Kulaks and to seize their grain.

Here obviously were dissensions, which were bound to come to a head. Secretly, the Left Social-Revolutionaries began to prepare fantastic plans for the overthrow of the Bolshevik Government and for a renewal of the war with Germany. By July 4th, the opening day of the Fifth All-Russian Congress, the political situation was ripe for the inevitable explosion.

For this Congress the Left Social-Revolutionaries had made special preparations. In spite of Bolshevik manipulation at the elections, they succeeded in returning about one-third of the eight hundred delegates present, and for the first time since November, 1917, the Bolsheviks were confronted, in their own carefully hedged-in Parliament, with a real official opposition.

The Congress took place in the Moscow Opera House. In the parterre, where once sat the 'balletomanes' and the richly bejewelled ladies of the Moscow plutocracy, now are ranged the official delegates: on the right, facing the stage, the Bolshevik majority, composed mainly of soldiers in khaki; on the left the Left Social-Revolutionary opposition, whose brawny arms and loose shirts proclaim their village origin.

On the high stage, from which Chaliapin first gave his immortal rendering of Boris, now sit the members of the Central Executive Committee – a motley gathering of about one hundred and fifty intellectuals with a strong predominance of Jews.

At a long table across the front of the stage is the Presidium, with Sverdlov, the President, in the centre. A Jew so dark that he might almost be suspected of 'colour', his black beard and his fierce black eyes make him look like some modern incarnation of the Spanish

* Landowners who opposed collectivisation. Suppressed by Lenin, they were later liquidated by Stalin.

inquisitors. On his left are Afanasiev, the Secretary of the Central Executive Committee, an insignificant young Jew with nervous twitching eyes, and Nakhamkis, the editor of the *Izvestia*, and better known to the public under his pseudonym of Steklov. At this table, too, sits Zinoviev, the President of the St Petersburg Commune. Clean-shaven and with an enormous forehead, he looks as intelligent as he is reputed to be. On the right of Sverdlov sit the Left Social-Revolutionary leaders: Kamkov, Karelin, both young Jews, clean-shaven, well-dressed, and clearly of the intellectual class; Cherepanov; and at the extreme end Maria Spiridonova, the thirty-two-year-old leader of the party. Very simply dressed, her dark hair brushed smoothly back over her head, and with pince-nez with which she toys continuously, she looks for all the world like Olga, the schoolmistress, in Chekhov's *Three Sisters*. In 1906, while still a girl, she had made herself famous by her assassination of Luzhinovsky, the notorious Councillor of the Government Administration of Tambov. She had been selected by her party to carry out this terroristic act, and in the middle of winter she waited for Luzhinovsky on the platform of the station at Borisogliebsk and fired on him with a revolver as he stepped out of the train. Her shots were successful, but an attempt to end her own life failed, and she was dragged from the platform and later raped by the Cossack soldiery. She had been condemned to death, but, yielding to a strong plea for mercy on account of her age, the Tsar had changed her sentence to one of penal servitude for life. The earnest, almost fanatical, expression in her eyes shows that her sufferings have affected her mind. She is more hysterical than practical, but her evident popularity with her own followers shows that she is still one of the few sentimental figures of the revolution.

Behind the Presidium table in serried rows are ranged the other members of the Central Executive Committee. Here are to be found the real Bolshevik leaders and the chief Commissars. They are present in full force from Trotsky to Krylenko, the scowling, twitching, Public Prosecutor. Only Dzerzhinsky and Peters are absent. These grim exponents of Bolshevik justice have no time for Congresses. Lenin, too, is late, as usual. He will slip in later, quietly, unobtrusively, but at the opportune moment.

In the boxes and galleries all around are the friends and supporters of the various delegates. Admission is by ticket only, and every entrance, every corridor, is guarded by groups of Lettish soldiers, armed to the teeth with rifle, pistol, and hand-grenade. In the great Imperial box are the representatives of the official Press. I take my place in the large parterre box on the right hand of the stage, together with Lavergne, Romei, and the other members of the Allied missions. Just above us are the representatives of the German, Turkish and Bulgarian Embassies. Fortunately for our enjoyment of the spectacle, we are not face to face.

From the first the atmosphere is charged with electricity. The opening day is devoted to speeches by minor delegates. The speeches are on strictly party lines. The three great crimes are the Brest-Litovsk peace, the Poverty Committees and the death sentence. The Left Social-Revolutionaries denounce all three. They support their denunciation of the peace treaty with bloodcurdling accounts of the German atrocities in the Ukraine. The Bolsheviks are on the defensive.

The real battle comes on the second day, when the heavy artillery on both sides is engaged. It is opened by Sverdlov, who wisely anticipates the Left Social-Revolutionary attack. He admits the horrors of the German occupation, but pleads that Russia is too weak to fight. He is less successful in his defence of the Poverty Committees. He scores a point over the Left Social-Revolutionary attitude towards the death sentence. The Left Social-Revolutionaries, he says, protested against the death sentence on Admiral Shchastny. At the same time they have co-operated closely with the Bolsheviks in the Extraordinary Commissions. One of their members is Vice-President of the Moscow Cheka, which has carried out numerous death sentences without any trial. Are they, then, to understand that the Left Social-Revolutionaries are against the death sentence in cases of trials but in favour of it when there is no trial. He resumes his seat amidst laughter and Bolshevik applause.

Spiridonova then rises, and from her first words one realises that this is no ordinary Congress, that today the Bolsheviks and the Left Social-Revolutionaries have come to the parting of the ways. She is obviously nervous. Her delivery, too, is monotonous, but, as she warms to her subject, she acquires a hysterical passion which is not unimpressive. Her attack is concentrated on the Poverty Committees. With pride she refers to the fact that her whole life has been dedicated to the welfare of the peasants. Keeping time to the rhythm of her sentences with an up-and-down movement of the right arm, she bitterly attacks Lenin. 'I accuse you', she says, addressing Lenin, 'of betraying the peasants, of making use of them for your own ends, and of not serving their interests.' She appeals to her followers: 'In Lenin's philosophy', she shrieks, 'you are only dung – only manure.' Then, working up to an hysterical peroration, she turns on the Bolsheviks: 'Our other differences are only temporary, but on the peasant question we are prepared to give battle. When the peasants, the Bolshevik peasants, the Left Social-Revolutionary peasants, and the non-party peasants, are alike humiliated, oppressed and crushed – crushed as peasants – in my hand you will still find the same pistol, the same bomb, which once forced me to defend—' The end of the sentence is drowned in a wild torrent of applause. A Bolshevik delegate in the parterre hurls an indecent assault at the speaker. Pandemonium ensues. Brawny peasants stand up in their seats and shake their fists at the Bolsheviks. Trotsky pushes himself forward and tries to speak. He is howled down, and his face blenches with impotent rage. In vain Sverdlov rings his bell and threatens to clear the theatre. Nothing seems more certain than that he will have to carry out his threat. Then Lenin walks slowly to the front of the stage. On the way he pats Sverdlov on the shoulder and tells him to put his bell away. Holding the lapels of his coat, he faces the audience – smiling, supremely self-confident. He is met with jeers and catcalls. He laughs good-humouredly. Then he holds up his hand, and with a last rumble the tumult dies. With cold logic he replies point by point to the criticisms of the Left Social-Revolutionaries. He refers with gentle sarcasm to their illogical and frequently equivocal attitude. His remarks produce another storm of interruption. Again Sverdlov becomes excited and grasps his bell. Again Lenin raises his hand. His self-confidence is almost irritating. Then, swaying slightly forward as he accentuates his points, but with strangely little gesticulation, he proceeds as calmly as though he were addressing a Sunday School meeting. To the taunts of servility towards the Germans he replies that the Left Social-Revolutionaries, in wishing to renew the war, are carrying out the policy of the Allied Imperialists. Coldly and without a trace of sentiment he defends the Brest-Litovsk Treaty, points out how bitter a humiliation it has been, but underlines the grim doctrine of necessity. He almost exaggerates the difficulties of the present situation, praises the courage of those who are fighting the battle of Socialism, counsels further patience, and promises a reward for that patience in a glowing picture of the future, when war-weariness must inevitably produce a revolution in all countries. Gradually the sheer personality of the man and the overwhelming superiority of his dialectics conquer his audience, who listen spellbound until the speech ends in a wild outburst of cheering, which, although many of the Left Social-Revolutionaries must know of the preparations for the morrow, is not confined to the Bolsheviks.

The effect on the Left Social-Revolutionaries, however, is only temporary. Lenin is followed by Kamkov, a brilliant orator who lashes himself into a passion of fury. His is a fighting speech, and I marvel at his foolhardiness. He spares no one. His peroration is magnificent in its dramatic emotion. He turns towards the box in which the Germans are sitting. 'The dictatorship of the proletariat', he thunders, 'has developed into a dictatorship of Mirbach. In spite of all our warnings the policy of Lenin remains the same, and we are become, not an independent Power, but the lackeys of the German Imperialists, who have the audacity to show their faces even in this theatre.'

In an instant the Left Social-Revolutionaries are on their feet shouting and shaking their fists at the German box. The theatre rings with roars of: 'Down with Mirbach! Away with the German butchers! Away with the hangman's noose from Brest!' Hurriedly Sverdlov rings his bell and declares the session closed, and in a fever of excitement the delegates stream from the hall.

One incident gives me cause for reflection. During Kamkov's speech a French intelligence officer in our box applauds fiercely. His attitude is typical of that of many of my Allied colleagues. They cannot realise that to both Bolsheviks and Left Social-Revolutionaries foreign intervention, whether by Germany or by the Allies, means counter-revolutionary intervention. When our own intervention took place it received no support from the Left Social-Revolutionaries.

The debate which had ended so dramatically on the evening of July 5th was not destined to be resumed on the Saturday afternoon of the 6th. The Congress, indeed, reassembled, but the Bolshevik leaders were absent. The stage revolution of yesterday had been transferred to the streets and to the barricades.

I went to the Opera House at four o'clock. It was a hot and sultry afternoon, and the atmosphere of the theatre was like a Turkish bath. The parterre was filled with delegates, but many of the seats on the platform were vacant. There was no Trotsky, no Radek. By five o'clock most of the other Bolshevik members of the Central Executive Committee had disappeared. The box allotted to the representatives of the Central Powers was empty. There was, however, a considerable number of Left Social-Revolutionaries including Spiridonova. She looked calm and composed. There was nothing in her manner to betray the fact that her party had already decided to put its whole existence to the supreme test of war.

Yet this was what had happened, although it was some time before we realised the truth. At six o'clock Sidney Reilly came into our box with the news that the theatre was surrounded by troops and that all exits were barred. He had only the vaguest idea of what had occurred. He knew, however, that there had been fighting in the streets. Something had gone wrong. Our apprehension was not diminished by a loud explosion in the corridor above us. A careless sentry had dropped a hand-grenade. Fearful that the Bolsheviks might search them before they were allowed to leave the theatre, Reilly and a French agent began to examine their pockets for compromising documents. Some they tore up into tiny pieces and shoved them down the lining of the sofa cushions. Others, doubtless more dangerous, they swallowed. The situation was too tense for us to appreciate its comic side, and, deciding that in this case inaction was the best policy, we sat down to await the dénouement with as brave a show of patience as we could assume.

Finally, at seven o'clock, we were relieved by Radek, who gave us the whole story. The Left Social-Revolutionaries had assassinated Mirbach, hoping thereby to provoke Germany into restarting the war. Headed by Sablin and Alexandrovich, the Vice-President of the Cheka, they had planned to arrest the Bolshevik leaders during the Congress in the theatre. Instead, they themselves had been caught in the trap which they had set for their opponents.

The story of their coup d'état may be told in a few words. At a quarter to three on the Saturday afternoon a motor car with two men drove up to the German Embassy in the Denezhny Pereulok. The Embassy itself was guarded by a detachment of Bolshevik troops. The occupants of the car, however, had no difficulty in obtaining an entrance, for they were provided with special passes signed by Alexandrovich in his capacity as Vice-President of the Cheka. A man named Blumkin, who for months had lived in the room next to me in my hotel, was the chief actor in the ensuing tragedy. Himself an official of the Cheka, he was received immediately by Riezler, the Councillor of the German Embassy. He informed Riezler that he must see Mirbach personally. The Cheka had discovered an Allied plot for the assassination of the German Ambassador. In view of Blumkin's credentials and the seriousness of his information, Dr Riezler himself took him into Count Mirbach's presence. When the Count asked him how the assassins proposed to act, Blumkin took a Browning from his pocket, replied, 'Like this,' and emptied his pistol into the body of the unfortunate Ambassador. Then, leaping out of an open window, he hurled a hand-grenade behind him in order to make doubly sure, and escaped.

In the meantime the Left Social-Revolutionaries had assembled such troops as they could persuade to support them in the Pokrovsky barracks. They included one unit of two thousand men who had been bought over by Popov, an agent of the Cheka, some disaffected soldiers from other regiments, and a few hundred sailors from the Black Sea fleet. For an hour they enjoyed a slight success. They arrested Dzerzhinsky. They captured the telegraph office. Then, however, their imagination failed them, and, beyond sending out telegrams all over the country to announce the success of their coup d'état, they did nothing. Towards evening they made a half-hearted attempt to approach the Opera House, but, finding it already surrounded by a strong detachment of Bolshevik forces, they retired to their headquarters. So feeble was their military effort that the vast majority of the Moscow population never realised until the next day that an attempted revolution was in progress.

In the meantime Trotsky had not been idle. He had called in two Lettish regiments from the suburbs. He had assembled his armoured cars. Within a few hours the Left Social-Revolutionary troops, opposed by overwhelming strength, laid down their arms. Some of the leaders escaped. Alexandrovich, however, was caught at the Kursk railway station and promptly shot. The Social-Revolutionary delegates in the Opera House were arrested without even a protest. The revolution, which was conceived in a theatre, ended in the same place.

The only effect of this *opéra bouffe* of the Left Social-Revolution-aries was to strengthen the hands of the Bolsheviks and the peace party. The repercussion in the country was insignificant. A few days later Muraviev, the Commander-in-Chief of the Bolshevik forces on the Volga, attempted to move his troops against Moscow. By this time, however, the failure of the coup d'état in Moscow was known, and he was arrested by his own men. He ended his life dramatically by shooting himself in the presence of the Simbirsk Soviet. Spiri-donova and Cherepanov were imprisoned in the Kremlin, where, later, I was to be their companion in misfortune. Blumkin, the assas-sin, escaped. Most of the rank and file, in order to save themselves from reprisals, went back on their leaders, condemned their action, and were readmitted into the Bolshevik fold.

This miserable affair, which should have been an object-lesson to the Allies in the sense that it proved beyond all doubt that Russia would do almost anything to avoid fighting either the Germans or the Allies, had certain reactions both on our own position and that of the Germans. The German Government was furious, but, con-vinced now of the certainty of Allied intervention, it did not declare war on the Bolsheviks. It demanded the right to send a battalion of German soldiers to guard its Moscow Embassy, but, when the Bol-sheviks refused this request, it confined its action to a diplomatic protest. The reaction in our own case was more comic. Two days after Mirbach's murder Radek came to see me and informed me that the Bolshevik Government wished to place a guard at my disposal. There was a broad grin on his face. He knew what my reply would be. I told him to put his guard where the Khyber Pass veteran had put the workhouse Christmas pudding. It was almost the last laugh we had together.

Our situation was, in fact, none too pleasant. During the Con-gress Lindley had arrived at Vologda, and his first telegram to me was vaguely alarming. It gave me, however, no indication either of policy or of the date of our intervention. The attempted counter-revolution was already uncomfortably near. Savinkov, egged on by French assurances of Allied help, had seized Yaroslavl, and Yaroslavl was between Moscow and Archangel, our only port of exit. Inciden-tally, Trotsky accuses me in his autobiography of having fomented and financed the Yaroslavl affair. This is wholly untrue. Never at any time did I furnish Savinkov with financial aid. Still less did I encourage him in any action he took. Trotsky, too, had issued an order that all French and British officers were to be refused travelling passes on account of their counter-revolutionary activities. Although technically this ukase did not apply to my mission, I knew that in practice there would be no difference. Moreover, there was great delay in the telegraph service to England, and I was never sure when this source of communication would be cut off from us altogether.

On the evening of July 17th I received from Karachan the official intimation of the murder of the Tsar and his family at Ekaterinburg. I believe that I was the first person to convey the news to the outside world. The only firsthand evidence of this crime that I can give concerns the official attitude of the Bolshevik Government. My own impression is that, alarmed by the approach of the Czech troops, who had now turned in their tracks and were at open war with the Bolsheviks, the local Soviet had taken the law into its own hands, and that the approval of the Central Government was subsequent. Certainly, there was no question of disapproval or disavowal. In its leading articles the Bolshevik Press did everything it could to justify the murder and reviled the Tsar as a tyrant and a butcher. It announced that it would begin immediate publication of his diaries. Later, a few instalments were published. All that they revealed was that the Emperor was a devoted husband and a loving father. When it was seen that their effect was to win sympathy for the Tsar, the instalments were stopped. Karachan, it is true, professed to be shocked and pleaded extenuating circumstances. He advanced the theory that the menace of Allied intervention was the direct cause of the Emperor's death. I am bound to admit that the population of Moscow received the news with amazing indifference. Their apathy towards everything except their own fate was complete, yet symptomatic of the extraordinary times in which we were living.

While this stark tragedy was taking place at Ekaterinburg, a drama, rich in its comic situations, was being enacted at Vologda. The Bolsheviks had sent Radek to this Allied Elysium in a last attempt to persuade the Allied Ambassadors to come to Moscow. Perhaps they were animated by a genuine desire to come to an amicable settlement. It is more probable that, realising that intervention was now inevitable, they desired to hold the Ambassadors in Moscow as hostages. For this delicate task they had chosen the Bolshevik Puck, and, if his effort failed, he richly satisfied his own sense of humour. He appeared before the Ambassadors with his revolver. He argued, cajoled, and even threatened. He interviewed them jointly and singly, but the Ambassadors stood firm. Then, in the evening, he went to the local telegraph office and gave an account of the failure of his mission by direct wire to Chicherin.

His joy-ride in Arcady had an amusing sequel. I received a word-for-word report of the Radek–Chicherin direct wire conversation from one of our secret agents. The document was so obviously genuine that the American Consul-General in Moscow sent a translation of it to his Ambassador. Without reading it, Francis put it in his pocket and took it to the Ambassadors' daily conference. 'Gentlemen,' he said, 'I have received an interesting document from Moscow. It is Radek's account of his negotiations with ourselves. I shall read it to you.' Fumbling with his pince-nez, he began: 'Ambassador Francis is a stuffed shirt-front.' It was only too true, but, coming from the Ambassador's lips, it was a little startling. Richer jests followed, and the climax came with the closing sentence: 'Lindley is the only man who has any sense. He practically admits that he considers Noulens's behaviour childish in the extreme.' Sir Francis Lindley has faced many difficult situations with unfailing courage and equanimity. I doubt, however, if he has ever felt quite so awkward as at that moment.

There was to be one more comedy before the final tragedy. On July 22nd an official British economic mission, composed of Sir William Clark, now British High Commissioner in Canada, Mr Leslie Urquhart, Mr Armistead, and Mr Peters of the Commercial Diplomatic Service, arrived in Moscow. They had come to discuss the possibilities of trade relations with the Bolsheviks. Their arrival staggered me. As far as I knew – and I had no certain knowledge – our intervention was only a matter of days. The Czech army was now advancing towards the west. It had taken Simbirsk and was then besieging Kazan. The Czechs were our Allies. In so far as we were supporting them we were supporting war against the Bolsheviks. Savinkov, too, was holding Yaroslavl, and Savinkov was being financed by the French. Moreover, at that very moment British troops must have been on their way to Archangel. Yet here was a British economic mission in Moscow breathing peace and commercial treaties to the Bolsheviks. Was there ever a more Gilbertian situation? Could I be surprised when, later, the Bolsheviks accused me of machiavellian duplicity and supplemented their denunciation of my crimes with well-documented references to Albion's perfidy. Alas! here was no guile or treachery. It was merely another example of one department in Whitehall not knowing what the other was doing. I took Sir William Clark to see Chicherin and Bronsky, the Trade Commissioner. I cannot say that I enjoyed the interview. Nor did I learn much from the English visitors. Sir William Clark knew nothing of the Allies' plans regarding Russia. Urquhart, who had mining interests in Siberia, was a convinced interventionist. I was glad when, after two days of abortive negotiations, they left for St Petersburg. Had they stayed twelve hours longer, they might have been detained indefinitely.

The next day, with startling suddenness, came the news that the Allied Embassies had left Vologda and had fled to Archangel. Although they issued a futile statement to the effect that their departure was not to be regarded as a rupture, the Bolsheviks rightly interpreted it as the prelude to intervention. Their flight, carried out without a word of warning to the Allied missions in Moscow, left me in an unenviable position. All too clearly I saw that the rôle of hostages, which had originally been destined for the Ambassadors, would now be reserved for us. Together with my French, American, and Italian colleagues I went to see Chicherin in order to feel our way. He was studiously polite and obviously anxious to avoid any act which would put the blame for any rupture of relations on the Bolsheviks. He pressed us to remain in Moscow and assured us that, whatever happened, we should be allowed to leave whenever we wanted to go. We gave a non-committal answer. We were still without any official intimation from our Governments. We took it for granted that the Allies had decided to land troops. We assumed that they would land in force at Archangel, Murmansk, and Vladivostok. We knew nothing for certain.

It was, however, clear that our own position in Moscow was no longer tenable, and I returned to my rooms to take the preliminary steps for our departure. The next few days were the most miserable of my whole stay in Russia. Moura had left Moscow some ten days before in order to visit her home in Estonia. Owing to the fighting on the Czech and Yaroslavl fronts travelling on the railways was now strictly controlled. I could not communicate with her. It seemed any odds on my having to leave Russia without seeing her again. For four days and nights I never slept. For hours on end I sat in my room playing patience and badgering the unfortunate Hicks with idiotic questions. There was nothing we could do, and in my despair my self-control left me and I abandoned myself to the gloomiest depression. Then on the afternoon of July 28th my telephone rang. I picked up the receiver. Moura herself was speaking. She had arrived in St Petersburg after six days of terrible adventure, during which she had crossed the no man's land between Estonia and Russia on foot. She was leaving that night for Moscow.

The reaction was wonderful. Nothing now mattered. If only I could see Moura again, I felt that I could face any crisis, any unpleasantness the future might have in store for me.

The sequence of events was now to be swift. On the day after Moura's return, General Eichhorn, the German Commander-in-Chief in Russia, was assassinated at Kiev. A young Moscow student called Donskoi, who was a member of the Social-Revolutionary Party, had carried out this act of terror. He had hired a cab and, passing the general, had hurled a bomb at him with fatal effect. I was sitting with Chicherin and Karachan when the news was conveyed to them by telephone. They made no concealment of their joy – especially Chicherin, who turned to me and said: 'You see what happens when foreigners intervene against the wishes of the people.' Their glee shocked me. My reason should have told me that in Bolshevik eyes the general was an oppressor, whose murderer was to be regarded as a liberator in just the same manner as bourgeois children are taught to admire Jael or Brutus. To the Bolsheviks German generals and English generals were in the same category as soon as they set foot on Russian soil. They were the agents of counter-revolution and, therefore, outside the law. Both Allies and Germans, however, made the mistake of regarding Russia solely in the light of their own conflict. At the German court-martial of Donskoi two days later the first two questions asked of the prisoner were: 'Do you know Lockhart? Do you know the head of the English mission in Moscow?'

On August 1st we received notice to leave our hotel. It had been requisitioned for the General Council of Russian Trades Unions. The Bolsheviks were showing their horns. No longer were we worthy of special consideration. Fortunately, I succeeded in obtaining occupation of my old flat in the Khliebny Pereulok, and we were able to avoid an awkward predicament.

On August 4th Moscow went wild with excitement. The Allies had landed at Archangel. For several days the city was a prey to rumour. The Allies had landed in strong force. Some stories put the figure at 100,000. No estimate was lower than two divisions. The Japanese were to send seven divisions through Siberia to help the Czechs. Even the Bolsheviks lost their heads and, in despair, began to pack their archives. In the middle of this crisis I saw Karachan. He spoke of the Bolsheviks as lost. They would, however, never surrender. They would go underground and continue the struggle to the last.

The confusion was indescribable. On the day after the landing I went to see Wardrop, our Consul-General, who had established his office in the Yusupov Palace close to the Red Gates. While I was talking to him, the Consulate-General was surrounded by an armed band. It was composed of agents of the Cheka. They sealed up everything, and everyone in the building was put under arrest except Hicks and myself. The special pass I had received from Trotsky still held good. This raid had an amusing aspect. While the Cheka agents were cross-examining our Consular officials downstairs, our intelligence officers were busily engaged in burning their ciphers and other compromising documents upstairs. Clouds of smoke belched from the chimneys and penetrated even downstairs, but, although it was summer, the Cheka gentlemen noticed nothing untoward in this holocaust. As we were to learn later, the Cheka was terrifying but far from clever.

At the same time a similar raid was carried out on the French mission and Consulate-General. Although the Italians and Americans were left alone, this outrage (it is true that in Bolshevik eyes our landing at Archangel was also an outrage against international law) could not be ignored, and the next day we all went to Chicherin to give formal notice of the rupture of relations and to demand our passports. Chicherin did not actually refuse. He seemed overwhelmed by the situation, and made his usual plea for time. The unfortunate Chicherin was, indeed, sorely harassed. Only that morning he had received a similar visit from Helfferich, who had succeeded Count Mirbach as German Ambassador. Helfferich, too, seemed to treat the Allied intervention as a serious menace to the Bolsheviks. He had no intention of sharing Count Mirbach's fate or of being caught in Moscow when the Allied troops marched in. The same night he took the train for Berlin, leaving only a small staff to carry on in Moscow.

Deserted now by both the Allies and the Germans, the Bolsheviks seemed to be in a hopeless position. The Czech army had captured Kazan, and, although the Bolsheviks had retaken Yaroslavl from Savinkov's Russians, they seemed incapable of offering any serious opposition to the large Allied force which was supposed to be advancing from Archangel. For forty-eight hours I deluded myself with the thought that the intervention might prove a brilliant success. I was not quite sure what we should be able to do when we reached Moscow. I could not believe that a bourgeois Russian Government could be maintained in Moscow without our aid. Still less did I believe that we could persuade any considerable number of Russians to renew the war with Germany. In the circumstances the intervention was bound to assume an anti-Bolshevik rather than anti-German character. It was, therefore, likely that our occupation of Moscow would last indefinitely. But, with the adequate forces, which I assumed we had at our disposal, I had no doubt of our being able to reach the Russian capital.

Disillusionment was to follow swiftly. On August 10th the Bolshevik newspapers splashed their front page with headlines announcing a great Russian naval victory over the Allies at Archangel. I regarded this report as a joke or, at best, as a feeble attempt on the part of the Bolsheviks to stimulate the courage of their own followers. But that afternoon, when I saw Karachan, I had misgivings. His face was wreathed in smiles. The dejection of the previous days had gone, and his relief was too obvious to be put down to play-acting. 'The situation is not serious,' he said. 'The Allies have landed only a few hundred men.'

I smiled sceptically. Later, I was to discover that his statement was only too true. The naval victory was a myth. The Bolsheviks had sunk an Allied barge in the Dvina. But the account of the strength of the Allied forces was literally correct. We had committed the unbelievable folly of landing at Archangel with fewer than twelve hundred men.

It was a blunder comparable with the worst mistakes of the Crimean War. In the chaotic state of Russia it was obvious that, if intervention was to be a success, it must start well. It had begun as badly as it could, and no individual gallantry could ever repair that initial mistake. The plan of the pro-interventionist Russians was to hold the line of the Volga with the Czechs and to join up with the Allies in the north and with Generals Alexeyev and Denikin in the south. The latter had been advised to proceed via Tsaritzin to Samara, while it was hoped that the Allies would be able to advance almost unopposed to Vologda and Viatka. The weakness of our landing force in the north resulted in the loss of the Volga line and in the temporary collapse of the anti-Bolshevik movement in European Russia.

All my worst fears were speedily justified.

In the absence of a strong lead from the Allies the various counter-revolutionary groups began to quarrel and bicker among themselves. The accuracy of my dictum that the support we would receive from the Russians would be in direct proportion to the number of troops we sent ourselves was speedily proved. The broad masses of the Russian people remained completely apathetic.

The consequences of this ill-conceived venture were to be disastrous both to our prestige and to the fortunes of those Russians who supported us. It raised hopes which could not be fulfilled. It intensified the civil war and sent thousands of Russians to their death. Indirectly, it was responsible for the Terror. Its direct effect was to provide the Bolsheviks with a cheap victory, to give them a new confidence, and to galvanise them into a strong and ruthless organism. To have intervened at all was a mistake. To have intervened with hopelessly inadequate forces was an example of spineless half-measures which, in the circumstances, amounted to a crime. Apologists for this policy maintain that it served a useful purpose in preventing Russia from falling into the hands of Germany and in detaching German troops from the Western front. By June, 1918, there was no danger of Russia being overrun by Germany. The effect of the intervention on the German situation in the west was insignificant. The fact remains that, whatever may have been the intentions of the Allied Governments, our intervention was regarded by those Russians who supported it as an attempt to overthrow Bolshevism. It failed, and, with the failure, our prestige among every class of the Russian population suffered.

Karachan's optimism was a bitter disillusionment, but now that the intervention had begun I had to do my best to aid it. My efforts during August were concentrated (1) on securing our own departure, and (2) on furnishing financial assistance to the Russians who were supporting us.

As far as our own departure was concerned, we had reached a deadlock. Chicherin had assumed an attitude which was typical of Bolshevik diplomatic finesse. Of course we could have our passports. We could leave as soon as we liked. But where did we intend to go? The Germans were in control in Finland. The Turks were in Constantinople. He did not suppose we should like to make the long 'trek' to the Afghan or Persian frontiers. Yet these seemed the only exits.

I cut short this long rigmarole. 'What about Archangel?' I asked. He washed his hands apologetically. 'The English counter-revolutionaries are at Archangel,' he said. 'We cannot let you go there.' We seemed to be checkmated. It was only too likely that we should be held in Moscow as hostages. There was only one hope: that the Finnish–German bourgeois Government would guarantee us a safe conduct through Finland. We put ourselves in the hands of the diplomatic representatives of the neutral Powers, who at once began negotiations with the Finnish and German Governments.

I took advantage of this period of waiting to supply financial aid to the pro-Ally organisations, who were badly in need of funds. For weeks the French had furnished this aid single-handed, and my refusal to co-operate in this work had been a sore point with Alexeyev's and Denikin's political representatives. Now that we had reached an open rupture with the Bolsheviks, I contributed my share. Although the banks were closed and all dealings in foreign exchange illegal, money was easily available. There were numerous Russians with hidden stores of roubles. They were only too glad to hand them over in exchange for a promissory note on London. To avoid all suspicion, we collected the roubles through an English firm in Moscow. They dealt with the Russians, fixed the rate of exchange, and gave the promissory note. In each transaction we furnished the English firm with an official guarantee that it was good for the amount in London. The roubles were brought to the American Consulate-General and were handed over to Hicks, who conveyed them safely to their destined quarters.

Apart from this excitement the days passed drearily. There was almost no other work that we could do. With the exception of a small pocket code for emergency messages we had destroyed all our ciphers and all our documents. We had a daily meeting of the Allied representatives at the American Consulate-General, which was now our safest refuge. For, strangely enough, although the United States had associated itself with this landing at Archangel, the Bolsheviks showed no animosity against the Americans. Their name was always excluded from the official protests against the alleged atrocities by the French and British troops in north Russia. They were never mentioned in the violently anti-French and anti-British articles in the Moscow Press.

We made plans for our departure – the negotiations with the

Finnish and German Governments were proceeding slowly but not unsatisfactorily. At immense expense the French kept a train waiting with steam up so that we might leave without a moment's delay. From the British in St Petersburg we were completely cut off. Through the Dutch Legation I sent Cromie a message informing him that I could do nothing to help him and that he had better conduct his own negotiations for the departure of himself and the other British officials. I had several discussions with Reilly, who had decided to remain on in Moscow after our departure.

It was an extraordinary situation. There had been no declaration of war, yet fighting was proceeding on a front stretching from the Dvina to the Caucasus. We were unable to leave Moscow, yet our liberty of action inside the city was almost unrestricted. On the other hand, we knew little of what was going on outside. All that seemed clear was that the Bolsheviks were holding their own.

We struggled successfully against dejection. We dined with the French, and they with us, and played bridge. We renewed our unsuccessful encounters with the Americans at poker. Here I must pay my tribute to Poole, the American Consul-General, and to Wardwell, the head of the American Red Cross mission. They would have had little difficulty in arranging their own departure. Yet they stood solidly by us to the end.

In the afternoons we had strenuous football matches at the British Consulate-General. There was one historic encounter between the British and the French, for which even General Lavergne, complete in shirt, military riding breeches, braces, and military boots, turned out. He performed prodigies of valour, his silver hair sparkling gaily in the August sun. Sadoul, the French Socialist deputy, who was afterwards to join the Bolsheviks, kept goal. As there was no referee, the charging was terrific. The French had several heavyweights, and, shod as we were with tennis shoes, we suffered several casualties. The result, however, was the same as at Waterloo – this time without the aid of the Germans, and, the victory clinched, we carried the general off the field to toast his health in Russian beer. It was the last game of football I ever played.

A few days after this international contest – on August 15th, to be exact – I received a visit which was to cause international diversions of a more serious nature. I was lunching in my flat, when the bell rang and my man announced two Lettish gentlemen. One was a short, sallow-faced youth called Smidchen. The other, Berzin, a tall, powerfully built man with clear-cut features and hard, steely eyes, called himself a colonel. He was, in fact, in command of one of the Lettish regiments which formed the Praetorian Guard of the Soviet Government. Smidchen brought a letter from Cromie. Always on my guard against *agents provocateurs*, I scrutinised the letter carefully. It was unmistakably from Cromie. The handwriting was his. The text referred to a previous communication which I had addressed to him through the Swedish Consul-General. The expression that he was making his own arrangements to leave Russia and hoped 'to bang the "dore" before he went out' was typical of this very gallant officer. Above all, the spelling was his. No forger could have faked this, for like Prince Charles Edward, Frederick the Great, and Mr Harold Nicolson, poor Cromie could not spell. The letter closed with a recommendation of Smidchen as a man who might be able to render us some service.

I asked the two men what they wanted. Berzin did most of the talking. He explained that while the Letts had supported the Bolshevik revolution, they could not fight the Bolsheviks' battles indefinitely. Their one ambition was to return to their own country. As long as Germany was powerful this was impossible. On the other hand, if the Allies, as now seemed likely, were to win the war, it was clear that the Allies and not Germany would have the final word regarding the future of Latvia. They were therefore determined not to put themselves wrong with the Allies. They had no intention of fighting against General Poole's forces at Archangel. If they were sent to that front, they would surrender. Could I arrange matters with General Poole so that they would not be shot down by the Allied troops?

It was an interesting and plausible proposal. It would have to be considered seriously, but, before holding out any encouragement, I wanted to consult my colleagues. I told the two conspirators that, while I understood their reluctance to fight against the Allies, I was not in a position to help them. I was not in touch with General Poole. Moreover, I was expecting to leave Russia at any moment. Their best plan would be to send their own messenger to General Poole. In this connection I might be able to assist them. I arranged for them to call on me at the same time the next day.

That afternoon I thrashed out the whole matter with General

Lavergne and M. Grenard, the French Consul-General and subsequently French Minister to Yugoslavia. We decided that, while we must be very careful not to compromise our own position in any way, it was probable that the Letts had no desire to fight against the Allies. There could be little harm in encouraging them to send a messenger to General Poole. We would assist them in this matter. As the negotiations for our own departure were now nearing a happy conclusion, we would put them in touch with Sidney Reilly, who was staying on. Reilly could keep an eye on their movements and help to stimulate their reluctance to oppose our troops. The next day I saw the two Letts, gave them a paper saying 'please admit bearer, who has an important communication for General Poole, through the English lines', and put them into touch with Reilly.

Two days later Reilly reported that his negotiations were proceeding smoothly and that the Letts had no intention of being involved in the collapse of the Bolsheviks. He put forward a suggestion that after our departure he might be able, with Lettish help, to stage a counter-revolution in Moscow. This suggestion was categorically turned down by General Lavergne, Grenard, and myself, and Reilly was warned specifically to have nothing to do with so dangerous and doubtful a move. Reilly then went 'underground' – that is, into hiding – and, until he escaped to England, I never saw him again.

For another fortnight our enforced idleness continued. Our departure, so the neutral diplomats informed us, was now decided in principle. The actual date would be fixed at any moment. We packed our clothes, deciding rightly that we should have to travel light, and with heavy heart I resigned myself to the abandonment of all the belongings in my flat – my collection of Oriental books, my furniture, and my wedding presents. One night we went out to 'Streilna' to say goodbye to Maria Nikolayevna, our gypsy queen. 'Streilna' had been closed, but we found her in her 'dacha' close by. She wept over us copiously, sang a few of our favourite songs to us in a low voice, which was scarcely louder than a whisper, and, kissing me on both cheeks, begged us to remain with her. She saw tragedy ahead of us. She would disguise us, hide us and feed us, and arrange for our departure to the south. Her advice, as sound as it was well meant, could not be taken. She came to the gate to see us off, and we said goodbye beneath the giant firs of the Petrovsky Park with the harvest moon casting ghostly shadows around us. It was an eerie and emotional farewell. We never saw her again. Vaguely I heard that she died a few years ago in poverty.

The tragedy which she had foreseen came with a pistol shot. On Friday, August 30th, Uritsky, the head of the St Petersburg Cheka, was murdered by a Russian *Junker* called Kannegiesser. The next evening a Social-Revolutionary, a young Jewish girl called Dora Kaplan, fired two shots point-blank at Lenin as he was leaving Michelson's factory, where he had been speaking at a meeting. One bullet penetrated the lung above the heart. The other entered the neck close to the main artery. The Bolshevik leader was not dead, but his chances of living were at a discount.

I received the news within half an hour of the actual shooting. It could hardly fail to have serious consequences, and, with a premonition of our impending fate, Hicks and I sat up late, discussing in low whispers the events of the day and wondering how they would affect our own unenviable situation.

We went to bed at one o'clock, and, worn out by months of strain, I slept soundly. At 3.30 a.m. I was awakened by a rough voice ordering me to get up at once. As I opened my eyes, I looked up into the steely barrel of a revolver. Some ten armed men were in my room. One man, who was in charge, I knew. He was Mankov, the former commandant of Smolny. I asked him what this outrage meant. 'No questions,' he answered gruffly. 'Get dressed at once. You are to go to Lubyanka No. 11.' (Lubyanka No. 11 was the headquarters of the Moscow Cheka.) A similar group of Cheka agents was dealing with Hicks, and, while we dressed, the main body of the invaders began to ransack the flat for compromising documents. As soon as we were ready, Hicks and I were bundled into a car and, with a gunman on each side of us, were driven off to the Cheka headquarters. There we were put into a square small room, bare of all furniture except a rough table and a couple of plain wooden chairs.

After a long wait I was taken along a dark corridor. The two gunmen, who accompanied me, stopped before a door and knocked. A sepulchral voice said: 'Come in,' and I was brought into a long, dark room, lit only by a hand-lamp on the writing table. At the table, with a revolver lying beside the writing-pad, was a man, dressed in black trousers and a white Russian shirt. His black hair, long and waving as a poet's, was brushed back over a high forehead. There was a large wrist-watch on his left hand. In the dim light his features looked more sallow than ever. His lips were tightly compressed, and, as I entered the room, his eyes fixed me with a steely stare. He looked grim and formidable. It was Peters. I had not seen him since the day he had accompanied Robins and myself on our tour of inspection of the anarchists' strongholds.

'You can go,' he said to the two gunmen, and then there was a long silence. At last he turned his eyes away and opened his writing folder. 'I am sorry to see you in this position,' he said. 'It is a grave matter.' He was scrupulously polite, but very serious. I asked for information, pointing out that I had come to Moscow on the invitation of the Soviet Government and that I had been promised full diplomatic privileges. I made a formal protest against my arrest and demanded to speak to Chicherin.

He ignored my protests. 'Do you know the Kaplan woman?' I did not, but I decided that in the circumstances it was better to answer no questions. I repeated as calmly as I could that he had no right to question me.

'Where is Reilly?' was his next question. Again I made the same answer.

Then he produced a paper from his folder. It was the pass to General Poole which I had given to the Letts. 'Is that your writing?' he asked.

Yet again I replied with studious politeness that I could answer no questions.

He made no attempt to bully me. He fixed me again with a long stare. 'It will be better for you if you speak the truth,' he said.

I made no reply. Then he rang a bell, and I was taken back to Hicks. Again we were left alone. We hardly spoke and, when we did, we talked trivialities. We realised that our conversation was likely to be overheard. I had only the vaguest idea of what had happened. It was obvious, however, that the Bolsheviks were trying to link us up with the attempt on Lenin's life. This manoeuvre did not disconcert me. The attempt on Lenin might be an indirect consequence of Allied intervention, but we had had nothing to do with it. I was more uneasy about the mention of Reilly's name and the production of my pass to Poole. I guessed that there had been a hitch somewhere and that my two Lettish visitors were *agents provocateurs*.

As, holding the lapels of my coat, I tried to review the situation in my mind, I suddenly felt in my breast pocket a notebook, which contained in cryptic form an account of the moneys I had spent. The Cheka agents had ransacked my flat – they were probably searching it at that moment, but they had not thought of searching the clothes we had put on when we were arrested. The notebook was unintelligible to anyone except myself. But it contained figures, and if it fell into Bolshevik hands they would find some means of rendering it compromising. They would say that the figures represented movements of Bolshevik troops or moneys I had spent on fomenting counter-revolution. That notebook preyed on my mind. How was I to be rid of it? We might be searched at any moment. In the circumstances there seemed only one solution to the problem. I asked permission of our four sentries to go to the lavatory. It was granted, but the affair was not so simple. Two gunmen accompanied me to the door, but, when I started to close it, they shook their heads. 'Leave it open,' they said and took up their stand in front of me. It was an embarrassing moment. Should I take the risk or not? Fortunately, the decision was made for me by the insanitary conditions of the place. There was no paper. The walls were smeared with stains of human excrement. As calmly as I could, I took out my notebook, tore out the offending pages and used them in the manner in which the circumstances dictated. I pulled the plug. It worked, and I was saved.

I went back to Hicks and sat down to wait. At six in the morning a woman was brought into the room. She was dressed in black. Her hair was black, and her eyes, set in a fixed stare, had great black rings under them. Her face was colourless. Her features, strongly Jewish, were unattractive. She might have been any age between twenty and thirty-five. We guessed it was Kaplan. Doubtless, the Bolsheviks hoped that she would give us some sign of recognition. Her composure was unnatural. She went to the window and, leaning her chin upon her hand, looked out into the daylight. And there she remained, motionless, speechless, apparently resigned to her fate, until presently the sentries came and took her away. She was shot before she knew whether her attempt to alter history had failed or succeeded.

At nine o'clock in the morning Peters himself came in and informed us that we could go home. We were discharged. We heard afterwards that he had been uncertain how to act and had telephoned to Chicherin for instructions. Chicherin had protested against our arrest.

It was Sunday morning and it was raining. We found an old 'droschke' and, tired and dejected, we made our way home. The flat was all upside down. The cook and our two men servants had disappeared. Moura, we learnt from the porter downstairs, had been taken off to the Cheka.

On the way home we had bought a paper. It was full of bulletins about Lenin's condition. He was still unconscious. There were, too, violent articles against the bourgeoisie and against the Allies. But there was no mention of our arrest, no effort to incriminate us in the assassination of Uritsky or the attempt on Lenin.

After a bath and a shave I went round to the Dutch Legation to see Oudendijk, the Dutch Minister, who was now in charge of our interests. He was a little man who had spent most of his life in China. His wife was English, and he spoke our language perfectly. I found him in a state of great agitation. There had been a terrible tragedy in St Petersburg. On the same day as I had been arrested, a band of Cheka agents had burst into our Embassy there. The gallant Cromie had resisted the intrusion and, after killing a Commissar, had been shot down at the top of the staircase. All British officials in St Petersburg had been arrested.

With a sinking feeling in my heart I went to find Wardwell. I was anxious about Moura and my servants, and hoped that he would be able to secure their release. He promised to do his best, and his quiet assurance did much to restore my self-control. He had been unable to see Chicherin, but had been promised an interview for the next day. He, too, was unaware of what lay behind these arrests. He supposed that, as a result of the attempt on Lenin's life, the Bolsheviks had lost their heads. He was afraid that the threat of a Red Terror, which now filled the newspapers, would soon be put into execution.

As I walked back to my flat I was struck by the emptiness of the streets. Such people as went about their business did so with quick steps and furtive glances. The street corners were guarded by little groups of soldiers. A new fear was abroad. In forty-eight hours the whole atmosphere of the city had changed. The next day, unable to bear the suspense about Moura's fate any longer, I went down to the Foreign Office and demanded to see Karachan. I was received at once. Avoiding all political discussion, I went straight to the point.

Whatever grievances the Bolsheviks might have against me, it was inhuman that they should seek to hit at me through the arrest of Moura. I appealed to his decency and begged him to release her. He promised to do what he could. It was my thirty-first birthday, and I spent it alone with Hicks, who prepared us a meal of coffee, black bread, and sardines.

On the Tuesday we read the full tale of our iniquities in the Bolshevik Press, which excelled itself in a fantastic account of a so-called Lockhart Plot. We were accused of having conspired to murder Lenin and Trotsky, to set up a military dictatorship in Moscow, and by blowing up all the railway bridges to reduce the populations of Moscow and St Petersburg to starvation. The whole plot had been revealed by the loyalty of the Lettish garrison, whom the Allies had sought to suborn by lavish gifts of money. The whole story, which read like a fairy-tale, was rounded off with a fantastic account of my arrest. I had been surprised, it was stated, at a conspirators' meeting. I had been taken to the Cheka and, as soon as my identity was established, I had been immediately released. An equally fantastic story described the events in St Petersburg. Cromie's murder was depicted as a measure of self-defence by the Bolshevik agents, who had been forced to return his fire. Huge headlines denounced the Allied representatives as 'Anglo-French Bandits', and in their comments the leader-writers shrieked for the application of a wholesale terror and of the severest measures against the conspirators.

At first I was inclined to regard this outburst as a typical Bolshevik attempt (1) to excuse their murder of Cromie, which I felt sure they had never intended, and (2) to galvanise their own supporters and to strike terror into the heart of would-be counter-revolutionaries in Moscow itself. Reilly, whose name figured largely in the plot, had disappeared. Unless he had completely lost his head, the whole story was a tissue of invention.

I found that Poole, the American Consul-General, took a more serious view of the conspiracy. He was inclined to regard Reilly as an *agent provocateur*, who had staged this plot for the benefit of the Bolsheviks. One account of the conspiracy mentioned a project whereby Lenin and Trotsky were not to be murdered, but were to be led through the streets of Moscow in their shirts. This fantastic proposal could have emanated only from Reilly's fertile imagination. I

243

laughed at Poole's fears. Later, I was to know much more of Reilly than I did at that time, but my estimate of his character did not alter. He was then in his forty-sixth year. He was a Jew with, I imagine, no British blood in his veins. His parents came from Odessa. His real name was Rosenblum. The name of Reilly he had taken from the second name of his first wife's father, an Irishman called Callahan. How he became a British subject I do not know to this day. Prior to the war he had spent most of his time in St Petersburg, where he had earned considerable sums of money as a commission agent in various forms of business. He was a man of great energy and personal charm, very attractive to women and very ambitious. I had not a very high opinion of his intelligence. His knowledge covered many subjects, from politics to art, but it was superficial. On the other hand, his courage and indifference to danger were superb. Moreover, Captain Hill, his associate in his dangerous plan to remain on in Moscow after our departure, was a man whose loyalty was beyond suspicion. He was as brave and as bold as Reilly. He spoke Russian just as well. If there had been any double-crossing by Reilly, Hill would hardly have failed to detect it. Ridiculous as this story was, I found nevertheless that through Poole it had gained some credence in England. When two months later I reached London, I had to go bail with the Foreign Office for Reilly's bona fides when, after a series of hairbreadth escapes, this remarkable man succeeded in making his way to Bergen. I did so without the slightest hesitation.

But, although I never questioned Reilly's loyalty to the Allies, I was not sure – indeed, I am not sure to this day – how far he had gone in his negotiations with the Letts. He was a man cast in the Napoleonic mould. Napoleon was his hero in life and at one time he possessed one of the finest collections of Napoleana in the world. He saw himself being left alone in Russia and the prospect of playing a lone hand may have inspired him with a Napoleonic design. In conversation afterwards he always denied most of the Bolshevik allegations. His own theory was that Berzin and the other Letts, whom he saw, were at first sincere in their desire to avoid fighting against the Allies. When they realised that the Allied intervention was not serious, they went back on him and betrayed him to save their own skins. Be this as it may, the so-called Allied plot was to have serious consequences for all of us.

Reilly's subsequent career was curious. On his return to England, he speedily established himself with Mr Churchill and the advocates of post-war intervention, and went to south Russia as a British agent with Denikin's forces. When that venture ended in disaster, Reilly allied himself with Savinkov, who was then besieging the statesmen of England and France with requests for support for his so-called 'Green' movement. Reilly, who was a lavish spender, exhausted his financial resources on Savinkov. He became hard up and, in a last desperate endeavour to re-establish his fortunes, set out for Russia in 1926 on some counter-revolutionary scheme alleged to be organised by ex-Guards officers. His subsequent fate is not known with certainty. The Bolsheviks announced that he had been shot while trying to cross the Finnish frontier. Such evidence as is available would seem to prove that he walked into a Bolshevik trap, that his Guards officers, whom he met abroad, were really Cheka agents, and that he was taken to a 'dacha' outside Moscow and then shot.

After this long digression, which contains the whole truth, so far as I know it, about the so-called Lockhart Plot, I must return to my own situation in Moscow. The account of the Allied conspiracy had appeared in the Russian papers of September 3rd. In spite of the serious nature of the allegations I was left at liberty throughout that day. I discovered later that there was considerable difference of opinion in Bolshevik official circles regarding the procedure to be observed towards me. There were several Commissars who were not prepared to swallow the whole of the Cheka's story without some dilution. The next day I determined to approach Karachan again in order to make a last appeal for Moura, who was still in prison. He was not unfriendly. I told him that the story in the Soviet Press was a tissue of lies, and he laughed good-humouredly. 'Now you know', he said, 'what we have to put up with from your newspapers.' He was, however, not very hopeful about Moura, and, deciding on desperate remedies, I made up my mind to approach Peters himself. I walked up from the Russian Foreign Office to the Lubyanka and asked to see him. My request caused some excitement and much whispering among the guards in the entrance hall. It took me half an hour to gain admission and still longer to obtain access to Peters. When he received me, I tackled him at once about Moura. I told him that the conspiracy story was a fake and that he knew it. Even if there were a grain of truth in it, Moura knew nothing about it. I begged him to release her at once. He listened to me patiently and promised that my assurance of her innocence would receive every consideration. Then he looked me straight in the face. 'You have saved me some trouble,' he said. 'My men have been looking for you for the last hour. I have a warrant for your arrest. Your French and English colleagues are already under lock and key.' This last statement was not strictly accurate. Some of them had avoided capture by what was to prove the one comic expedient in our ignominious situation. But this I shall recount later. As far as I myself was concerned, this time I was to be a prisoner in all seriousness.

My term of imprisonment lasted for exactly one month. It may be divided into two periods: the first, which lasted five days and was marked by discomfort and fear; the second, which lasted for twenty-four days and may be described as a period of comparative comfort accompanied by acute mental strain.

In Lubyanka No. 11, a former insurance company's office, I was kept in a room which was used for the registration and preliminary examination of minor criminals. It had three windows, two of which looked on to an inside courtyard. It was furnished with a table, four wooden chairs, and an old, broken-down sofa, on which, if I was fortunate, I was sometimes allowed to sleep. Generally, I slept on the floor. The real hardship, however, was that the room was never empty, never dark. Two sentries were on guard all the time. The work of the minor Commissars, who used the room, never ceased by night or day. Most of these men were Letts or Russian sailors. Some of them were not unfriendly. They regarded me with a kind of detached interest, spoke to me occasionally, and gave me the *Izvestia* to read. Others again were surly and hostile. At night Peters would send for me, and I would have to go through a kind of bantering cross-examination. I cannot say that he treated me unfairly. The want of sleep was a severe strain, and for that reason I found his midnight questions trying. They were mostly urgent appeals to tell him the whole truth in my own interests. He would inform me that my colleagues had confessed (one French agent did write an anti-Ally letter which was published in the Bolshevik Press), and he would urge me to do the same if I wished to avoid being handed over to the revolutionary tribunal. He was, however, neither brutal nor even impolite. As between prisoner and gaoler, our relations were pleasant. He himself was married to an English-woman, whom he had left in England. He seemed interested in my romance with Moura. Occasionally, too, he would come into my room and ask if I were being properly fed. The food – tea, thin soup, and potatoes – was not sustaining, but I made no complaint. On the second day, he brought me two books to read: Wells's *Mr Britling Sees It Through*, and Lenin's *State and Revolution*. My one comfort was the official Bolshevik newspapers, which my gaolers took a propagandist joy in supplying to me. Certainly, as far as my own case was concerned, they were far from reassuring. They were still full of the Lockhart Plot. They contained numerous resolutions, passed by workmen's committees, demanding my trial and execution. They gave, too, full prominence to foreign comment on the plot. The German Press, in particular, did itself proud. During the war it had suffered much from similar accusations of undiplomatic conduct, notably, in the von Papen case,* and now it made the most of our alleged misdemeanours, which were described as the most scandalous in the history of diplomacy. There were, too, discouraging reports of Bolshevik victories over the Czechs and the Allies, and still more fearsome accounts of the Terror, which was now in full force. It was not these details which relieved my anxiety. From the first day of my captivity I had made up my mind that, if Lenin died, my own life would not be worth a moment's purchase. Only one thing could save me: an overwhelming victory of the Allied armies in France. Knowing the Bolshevik passion for peace at almost any price, I felt that such a victory might moderate the Bolshevik attitude towards us. And the *Izvestia*, to my relief, contained not only bulletins of Lenin's health but also news from the Western front. Both were comforting. By September 6th Lenin was pronounced to be out of danger. In the west the Allied advance was meeting with real success.

From Peters I learnt that my colleagues had been herded together in the Butirky prison. I alone had been singled out for solitary confinement. It was an additional strain.

Two macabre incidents marked the period of my detention in the Cheka. On the third day a bandit was brought into my room. He was a tall, powerful fellow not more than twenty-five. I was a silent witness of his cross-examination, which was very different from anything I had experienced at Peters's hands. At first he laughingly asserted his innocence. No man was a more loyal supporter of the Soviet régime than he. No man had observed the decrees more scrupulously. The accusations of banditry and smuggling, with which he had been confronted, were the acts of counter-revolutionaries, who were seeking to destroy him. He made a brave show, but the Commissar paid no attention. With relentless reiteration he

* Franz von Papen (1879–1969), who, while working as the German military attaché in Washington in 1915, was accused of espionage and subsequently expelled from the United States.

repeated his question: Where were you on the night of August 27th? The bandit blustered, became confused, lied, and, when he saw that the Commissar knew he had lied, began to weep and plead for mercy. The Commissar laughed and scribbled something on a piece of paper. He tossed it to the sentry, while the bandit still grovelled before the table. The sentries tapped him on the shoulder, and in an instant his manner changed. Realising that his doom was sealed, he sprang to his feet, hurled one sentry against the wall, and made a dash for the door. One of the Bolsheviks put his foot out, and the bandit fell sprawling on the floor. He was seized and, still scuffling and shouting curses at his captors, was dragged out of the room.

The second incident, more terrifying in its effect upon my nerves, took place on my last day in Lubyanka No. 11. I was reading in the afternoon, when Peters came into the room. I went over with him to the window to talk. When he had a free moment, he liked discussing England, the war, capitalism and revolution. He told me strange tales of his experiences as a revolutionary. He had been in prison in Riga in Tsarist days. He showed me his nails as a proof of the torture which he had undergone. There was nothing in his character to indicate the inhuman monster he is commonly supposed to be. He told me that he suffered physical pain every time he signed a death sentence. I believe it was true. There was a strong streak of sentimentality in his nature, but he was a fanatic as far as the clash between Bolshevism and capitalism was concerned, and he pursued his Bolshevik aims with a sense of duty which was relentless.

As we were talking, a motor van – a kind of Black Maria – pulled up in the courtyard below, and a squad of men, armed with rifles and bandoliers, got out and took up their places in the yard. Presently, a door opened just below us, and three men with bowed heads walked slowly forward to the van. I recognised them instantly. They were Shcheglovitov, Khvostov, and Bieletsky, three ex-Ministers of the Tsarist régime, who had been in prison since the revolution. There was a pause, followed by a scream. Then through the door the fat figure of a priest was half-pushed, half-carried, to the Black Maria. His terror was pitiful. Tears rolled down his face. His knees rocked, and he fell like a great ball of fat on the ground. I felt sick and turned away. 'Where are they going?' I asked. 'They are going to another world,' said Peters drily. 'And that man', he said, pointing to the

priest, 'richly deserves it.' It was the notorious Bishop Vostorgov.*
The ex-Ministers formed the first batch of the several hundred victims of the Terror who were shot at that time as a reprisal for the
attempted assassination of Lenin.

That same night Peters sent for me. 'Tomorrow', he said, 'we are
sending you to the Kremlin. You will be alone and you will be more
comfortable.' In my presence he rang up the Commandant of the
Kremlin. 'Are Citizen Lockhart's rooms ready?' he asked peremptorily. The answer was obviously in the negative. 'Never mind,' said
Peters, 'give him Bieletsky's.' Bieletsky was one of the ex-Ministers
who had been shot that afternoon. The allusion seemed ominous.
The Kremlin was reserved only for the most unfortunate political
prisoners. Hitherto, not one had left it alive.

I was taken to the Kremlin on the evening of September 8th. I was
placed in an apartment in the Kavaleriisky Korpus. My new quarters
were clean and comfortable. They consisted of a small hall, a sitting-
room, a diminutive bedroom, a bathroom – alas! without a bath –
and a tiny kitchen. The rooms in former days had served as a flat for
one of the ladies-in-waiting. Unfortunately, the windows on both
sides opened on to corridors, so that I had no fresh air. Unfortunately, too, I was not alone, as Peters had promised I should be. I had
a companion in misfortune, the Lett, Smidchen, who was the cause
of all our troubles and who was alleged to be my accomplice and
agent. We spent thirty-six hours together, during which I was afraid
to exchange a word. Then he was taken away. I never heard what
happened to him. To this day I do not know whether he was shot or
whether he was handsomely rewarded for the part he had played in
unmasking the 'great conspiracy'. There was one other drawback to
my new prison. On both sides of my quarters I had sentries: one for
each window. They were changed every four hours, and, as each
change had to come into my rooms to certify that I was there, I was
woken up every night at ten, two and six.

My sentries were mainly Letts, but there were also Russians, Poles
and Hungarians. I had also an old man – a former servant of the

* Archpriest Ioann Vostorgov (1864–1918), Orthodox cleric. In the summer of 1918 he was arrested by the Bolsheviks for allegedly promoting
anti-Semitic propaganda, and was executed in August of that year following further charges of counter-revolutionary activity, whereupon he was
declared a martyr.

Kremlin – who did my rooms. He was as kind as he dared to be, but our conversation was limited and confined strictly to requests for the Bolshevik newspapers and for hot water for my samovar. From the *Izvestia* I learnt that the Allied Governments had sent a fierce note to the Bolsheviks, demanding our immediate release and holding them separately and jointly responsible for our safety. By way of reprisal England had arrested Litvinov and thrown him into prison. Chicherin had replied to this protest with a note which set out our alleged misdeeds at great length, but which contained an offer to let us go free in exchange for Litvinov and other arrested Russians in France and England. Chicherin's offer was to some extent reassuring. As, however, other sections of the official newspaper continued to announce that I was to be tried for my life, I was still far from certain of my release and even of my personal safety.

My food in the Kremlin was the same as in Lubyanka No. 11 – soup, tea and potatoes. Peters apologised for it, stating that it was the same as that supplied to himself and his assistants. From what I had observed during my stay in the Cheka headquarters, his statement was true.

One of my first acts, after my arrival in the Kremlin, was to write to Peters on behalf of Moura and my staff. Once again my appeal was to his sense of decency. I told him my staff was in no way responsible for anything I might or might not have done. As far as Moura was concerned, I asked him what satisfaction he could have in making war on women. On the third day he came to see me. He informed me that in all probability I should be handed over to the revolutionary tribunal for trial. He had, however, released Moura. What was more, he had given her permission to bring me food, clothes, books and tobacco. Provided it was written in Russian and given to him open, he offered to take a note from me to her. At the same time he gave instructions to the Commandant of the Kremlin that I was to have two hours' exercise daily in the open air. He was in a magnanimous mood. Lenin was now well on the way to recovery. The news from the Bolshevik front was excellent. The Bolsheviks had recaptured Uralsk from the Czechs. Kazan was on the eve of capitulation.

Peters was true to his word. That afternoon I had concrete proof of Moura's release in the form of a basket with clothes, books, tobacco, and such luxuries as coffee and ham. There was, too, a long letter from her. Of course, it contained no news of any sort, but it arrived sealed. It was not to be read by the prying eyes of my guards. Peters himself had stamped it with the official seal of the Cheka with a footnote signed in his own bold handwriting: 'Please deliver this letter in sealed form. It has been read by me. – Peters.' This strange man, whose interest I had somehow aroused, was determined to show me that a Bolshevik could be as chivalrous in small matters as any bourgeois.

The clothes and the food – but especially the clothes – were a real boon. I had not taken off my suit or washed or shaved for six days. I was not to be relieved of my anxiety for another fortnight. Only the night before, Krylenko, the Public Prosecutor, had spoken at a meeting and, amid loud cheers, had announced that the Allied conspirators were to be tried by him and that the criminal Lockhart would not escape his proper punishment. From now on, however, my prison life was to be tolerably comfortable.

Naturally, time lay heavy on my hands. Gradually, however, I evolved a kind of routine, which made the day pass more rapidly. As soon as I was dressed, I sat down to play a Chinese patience. (With my clothes and books Moura had enclosed a pack of cards.) I played a kind of game with myself. With Celtic superstition I said to myself that, if I did not get it out, the day would end in disaster. It was an unhealthy excitement in which I gambled my life against the cards. Fortunately for my peace of mind, I never failed to get the patience out. Some days, however, it was late in the afternoon before I succeeded.

My card-playing ended, I read. The books I read during my three weeks in the Kremlin included: Thucydides, Renan's *Souvenirs d'Enfance et de Jeunesse*, Ranke's *History of the Popes*, Schiller's *Wallenstein*, Rostand's *L'Aiglon*, Archenholtz's *History of the Seven Years' War*, Beltzke's *History of the War in Russia in 1812*, Sudermann's *Rosen*, Macaulay's *Life and Letters*, Stevenson's *Travels with a Donkey*, Kipling's *Captains Courageous*, Wells's *The Island of Doctor Moreau*, Holland Rose's *Life of Napoleon*, Carlyle's *French Revolution* and Lenin and Zinoviev's *Against the Current*. I was a serious young man in those days.

The preparation of my meals was another pastime. After luncheon there was my walk in the Kremlin grounds. My first walk was on September 11th. It was the day on which the Bolsheviks recaptured Kazan, and the Kremlin was a riot of flags and red bunting. In the early days of the Bolshevik régime the Kremlin was a fortress to which visitors were rarely, if ever, admitted. Even at the time of my friendliest relations with the Bolsheviks I had never crossed its threshold. My interviews with Lenin, Trotsky, Chicherin and the other Commissars had always been outside its walls. Now I was able to see the changes which had taken place since the October revolution. The giant monument to Alexander II on the parade ground had been dragged down from its huge pedestal. The cross which marked the spot where the Grand Duke Serge had been blown up had been removed.

My sentry on that first day was a Pole. He walked beside me with loaded rifle and was talkative and not unfriendly. He informed me that he had frequently accompanied the Tsarist ex-Ministers on their walks and that few prisoners who entered the Kremlin came out alive. The betting among his comrades was two to one on that I would be shot.

On the whole, my sentries were decent, sensible fellows, who made no attempt to jeer at me. During my whole period of captivity I struck only one really nasty one – a sour-faced curmudgeon, who swore at England, cursed me as an assassin, and refused to allow me even to send a message to the Commandant. He was a Hungarian. The Letts were the best. Most of them were contemptuous of the Russians, whom they regarded as inferiors. One Lett informed me that, if Russia could have put a million non-Russian troops into the trenches, she could not have failed to win the war. Every time the Letts advanced, he said, they were let down by the Russians, who failed invariably to support them. He despised, too, the dirt and laziness of the Russian troops. On the other hand, he had a wholesome respect for the Bolshevik leaders, whom he regarded as supermen.

Not all my sentries were Bolsheviks. They were divided into three classes: first, the ardent Communists, who convinced one by their sincerity and by their devotion to their cause. Of these there were not many. Secondly, the sheep who went with the crowd – Bolshevik today, Menshevik tomorrow. And, thirdly – and these were the most numerous – the sceptical, who believed that in Russia anything was possible and everything bad. All, however, were convinced that the revolution had come to stay. Even those Letts who were anxious to return to Latvia laughed at the possibility of a successful counter-revolution. To them counter-revolution meant the restoration of the land to the landowners.

These walks were a welcome relief to the monotony of my existence. They kept me from thinking about myself, and, although at first I could not refrain from indirect questions to my guards regarding my own fate, the answers I received soon discouraged further attempts to satisfy my morbid curiosity. Every day during my walk I paid a visit to a little church built in the wall of the Kremlin. It had a little garden round it and a famous icon called 'Our Lady of Unexpected Joy'. Before the war, inspired by the attractiveness of the title, I had written a short story about it, which was published in the *Morning Post*. Now it was to be for three weeks the shrine of my daily prayers.

After my first week in the Kremlin, Karachan came to see me. He was reticent about my own case. He, too, hinted that a public trial was inevitable. He also informed me that René Marchand, a member of the French mission, had furnished the Bolsheviks with full proofs of an Allied meeting at the American Consulate-General. At this meeting the Allied representatives had discussed such measures as blowing up railway bridges and cutting off Moscow and St Petersburg from their sources of food supplies. He had given, so Karachan said, a full list of the names of those who were present. I laughed. Most of my conversations with Karachan were conducted in a tone of airy persiflage. 'That beats *The Times*,' I said. 'Believe me or not, as you like, this is another invention of your Cheka.'

'It is true,' he replied. 'We shall publish the letter in a day or two. Fortunately for you,' he added with a grin, 'you do not seem to have been present.'

The story was more or less true. Marchand had thrown in his lot with the Bolsheviks. After the war he returned to France and joined the French Communist Party. He renounced his Communism in 1931.

Karachan also gave me news of the war and of the outside world. The neutral diplomats had issued a violent protest against the Terror, from which I deduced that they were working to secure our release. The Allied forces were making no progress in Russia. The Bolsheviks had registered further successes against the Czechs and the Russian counter-revolutionary forces. On the other hand, the Allies were driving back the Germans in the west. Austria and Bulgaria were on the verge of collapse. He admitted that the Allies might now win the war.

This was good news indeed. It was further stressed by the disclosure of the real object of Karachan's visit. He had come to ascertain my views regarding the terms on which England would be prepared to abandon her intervention and to make peace with Russia. The Bolsheviks were prepared to offer an amnesty to all counterrevolutionaries who would accept the régime, and a free exit out of Russia to the Czechs and to the Allies. Obviously, if the Bolsheviks were ready to discuss peace terms with the Allies, they were not going to shoot me. On the other hand, the Allies were not likely to listen to any proposals of this nature. On the whole, my hopes were raised by this visit. Lenin, Karachan informed me, was now able to sit up and to take nourishment.

The week from September 14th to 21st was wet and miserable, and on two days I was unable to have my daily walk. I still received my daily messages and my daily supply of luxuries from Moura. She sent me, too, a fountain-pen and several notebooks, and I amused myself by writing bad verse and by keeping a strictly non-committal diary of my prison life. I had, however, no more Bolshevik visitors and no news, and, as I was sleeping badly, I underwent a fresh period of pessimism.

Spiridonova, who was imprisoned in the same corridor as myself, I saw often. We never spoke, although we greeted each other solemnly when we passed on our daily walks. She looked ill and nervous, with great dark lines under her eyes. She was clumsily and very carelessly dressed, but might have been quite pretty when young.

Another prisoner, whom I met occasionally on my walks, was General Brusilov. He had had an accident to his leg and walked with difficulty with the aid of a stick. My diary states that he looked 'haggard, ill and very old', and that he had 'a sly, foxy face'. Yet another prisoner was Sablin, the former Soviet Commander, who had played a leading part in the Left Social-Revolutionary attempted coup d'état in July. Good-looking, with an attractive smile and blue eyes, he looked little more than a boy.

The eminence of their prisoners evidently caused some amusement to our guards. One day my sentry piloted me to the shrine where formerly had stood the statue of Alexander II and with pride pointed out to me a sentence roughly chiselled on the side of the huge pedestal. The words, carved by one of our sentries, ran as follows: 'Here the Red Army soldiers of the 9th Lettish Rifles had the honour of walking with Brusilov, Lockhart, Spiridonova and Sablin.' The word 'honour' was in inverted commas. I reflected with grim morbidness that this was the only statue except a tombstone on which my name was likely to figure.

On September 21st Karachan came to see me again. He was in high fettle over the Bolshevik successes on the Volga. The Red Army had captured Simbirsk and Buinsk and was now full of confidence. He brought me copies of *The Call* – a Bolshevik news-sheet, printed in English, which was to be distributed by airplanes among the English troops on the Archangel and Murmansk fronts. It contained a lurid account of the so-called Allied Plot. My name figured largely in it, and to my other crimes was now added the charge of having concocted a false treaty between Germany and Russia as a means of inducing the Allied troops to fight against the Bolsheviks. The account, so the paper said, read 'like a tale from the Arabian Nights'. I pointed this passage out to Karachan and congratulated him on the aptness of the simile. It was a fine example of imaginative fiction. Karachan, who knew the circumstances of my arrest in every detail, smiled blandly. 'Your Government', he said, 'is supporting the war against the revolution. Every kind of irregularity has been committed by Allied agents in this country. You have become the symbol of these irregularities. In a clash between two world forces the individual has to suffer.'

The next day I received a surprise visit from Peters. He brought Moura with him. It was his birthday (he was thirty-two), and, as he preferred giving presents to receiving them, he had brought Moura as his birthday treat. In more senses than one this was the most thrilling moment of my captivity. Peters was in a reminiscent mood. He sat down opposite me at the small table near the back wall and began to talk of his life as a revolutionary. He had become a Socialist at the age of fifteen. He had suffered exile and persecution. I listened only fitfully. Moura, who was standing behind Peters and in front of me, was fiddling with my books, which stood on a small side-table surmounted by a long hanging mirror. She caught my eyes, held up a note, and slipped it into a book. I was terrified. A slight turn of his head, and Peters could see everything in the mirror. I gave the tiniest of nods. Moura, however, seemed to think that I had not seen and

Allied invasion of Russia to suppress Workmens Revolution, and re-establish Tsarism.

Sensational plot discovered to overthrow Soviet government.

Allied complicity in counter-revolutionary plot proved

British diplomat in Moscow discovered at conspirative meeting.—Lavishly distributing bribes. Fabricating forged documents.

The following is a summary of a statement issued by the Soviet government, which discloses a widespread plot instigated by the Allied governments to overthrow the Russian revolution.

On August 14 th. at twelve o'clock, at the private room of Mr. Lockhart, the representative of the British government in Russia, an interview took place between him and a commander of one of the Soviet detatchments in Moscow.

At this meeting it was proposed to organise a rebellion against the Soviet government in connection with the British landing on the Mourman. In order to maintain close relation between the British diplomatic agents and this comm ander of the Soviet troops, an English lieutenant, Sydney Reiley was delegated to act under the allias of «Reis». It was proposed that certain parts of the Moscow garrison should be sent to Vologda to open the road for the English, while the rest of the garrison should arrest the Council of the Peoples Commissioners in Moscow, and establish a military dictatosrhip.

For this purpose on Aug. 14 th. Mr .Lockhart handed 700,000 roubles to his agents. On Aug. 22nd another meeting took place at which 200,000 roubles were assigned for the purpose of arresting Lenin and Trotsky, and members of the Council of Public Economy, seizing banks, posts and telegraphs. On Aug. 28th 300,000roubles was paid over to this commander of Soviet troops who was to go to Petrograd to establish connection with the English military group working there together with a group of Russian counter-revolutionaries.

At the same time in Moscow, meetings under the auspices of the agents of the Allied Powers were held with the object of intensifying the famine. It was proposed to blow up certain bridges on the railways, and wreck food trains, in order that the population of Moscow and Petrograd should become so maddened by hunger as to rise in revolt against the Soviet government.

Letters have been discovered with Mr. Lockhart's signature on official British government paper, delegating this commander of Soviet troops to act on behalf of the British government.

The plot was discovered by the commander disclosing the whole scheme to the Soviet authorities.

Acting on this information the Soviet authorities on the night of Aug. 31st surprised a conspirative meeting at which Mr. Lockhart was present. Although Lockhart was arrested, some of the conspirators escaped and are now at large. They have carried out a portion of the ir plans. Trainloads of food were blown up by them at Voronezh. Documents were seized at this meeting which shows that the intention of the Allies as soon as they had established their dictatorship in Moscow was to declare war on Germany and force Russia to fight again. In order to find a pretext for this, a fictitious treaty between Russia and Germany was concocted which presented the Soviet government as selling the independance of Russia to Germany. This forged treaty was to have been printed and scattered broadcast.

FELLOW WORKERS!

Here is positive evidence of the real purpose for which you have been brought to Russia.

You are being used as the tools of your capitalists who are working here in close unity with the agents of bloodstained Tzarism, for the overthrow of the first Socialist Republic, and the re-establishment of the former reign of oppression.

YOU ARE NOT FIGHTING FOR LIBERTY. YOU ARE FIGHTING TO CRUSH IT.

FELLOW WORKERS !

Be honourable men. Remain loyal to your class, refuse to be the accomplices of a great crime. Refuse to do the dirty work of your masters.

G. TCHITCHERINE,
Peoples Commissarv for Foreign Affaivs.

'THE CALL', A BOLSHEVIK NEWS-SHEET BROADCAST FOR THE BENEFIT OF BRITISH TROOPS AT ARCHANGEL

repeated the performance. My heart stopped beating, and this time I nodded like an epileptic. Fortunately, Peters noticed nothing or else Moura's shrift would have been short. Although he gave me no news about my own fate beyond saying that preparations were being made for my trial, he treated me in every other respect with great courtesy, questioned me several times about my treatment by my sentries, and asked me if I were receiving Moura's letters regularly and if I had any complaints to make. Then, excusing himself on account of pressure of work for the shortness of his visit and promising to bring Moura again, he left me. Moura and I had hardly exchanged a word, but already I felt a new hope. It was as if I had left the world and come back to it again. As soon as they had gone, I rushed to the book – it was Carlyle's *French Revolution* – and took out the note. It was very short – six words only: 'Say nothing – all will be well.' That night I could not sleep.

The next day Peters came again. His second visit explained his first. This time he was accompanied, not by Moura, but by Asker, the Swedish Consul-General, a man of great charm and high ideals, who had laboured night and day to secure our release. Peters went straight to the point. The neutral diplomats had expressed concern about my fate. They had been much perturbed by rumours that I had been shot, that I was being subjected to Chinese torture. He had, therefore, brought the Swedish Consul-General in order that he might persuade himself by the proof of his own eyes (1) that I was alive, and (2) that I was being well-treated. My conversation with Asker was restricted. We had to talk in Russian, and his knowledge of the language was limited. Moreover, he was not allowed to discuss my case with me. Having satisfied himself that I was not being starved or tortured, he managed to say that everything possible was being done on my behalf, and then he left.

On the following morning the Bolshevik Press broadcast a statement that, while the bourgeois Press throughout the world was spreading rumours of the terrible tortures to which I was being subjected, I myself had denied them and had admitted to the Swedish Consul-General that I was being treated with every courtesy.

My interview with Asker was not altogether satisfactory. The fact that he was not allowed to discuss my own case with me depressed me. If I was no longer afraid for my life, the probability of a public trial and of a long term of imprisonment impressed itself more strongly than ever on my mind. My apprehensions were increased by the publication in the *Izvestia* the next morning of the disclosures of Marchand, the French agent. It took the form of an open letter to Poincaré* and denounced in strong terms the counter-revolutionary activities of the Allied agents in Russia. Although my name was not mentioned in the letter and although I had never had any connection with the activities which had turned Marchand against his own country, the Bolshevik Press seized on this opportunity to rake up all the mud they could against me. Once again I was denounced as the instigator of everything true or untrue and as the arch-criminal of diplomacy. I suppose I should have felt flattered. I was by far the youngest of the Allied representatives. Yet I had been singled out for solitary confinement in the Kremlin, and my name had figured in every newspaper as the ringleader of the Allied representatives. Doubtless, the Bolshevik attitude, so different in public and in private towards myself, was determined solely by reasons of policy. I had known them more intimately than any other Allied representative. I had opposed intervention almost to the end. It was necessary that they should do their best to discredit in advance any evidence I might bring against them. The American officials, who were far more deeply implicated in Marchand's disclosures than I was, escaped not only arrest but all abuse. The Bolsheviks knew that President Wilson, who was a historian and who, therefore, remembered Napoleon, was very lukewarm in his attitude towards the Russian policy of the Allies. They were determined to do nothing to prejudice that attitude.

The weather at this period was very trying. There were days when the sun shone and when the temperature was as high as in July. These were days of hope. There were other days when the wind blew and the rain beat down mercilessly on the Kremlin walls. Winter was already in the air, and the cold and the damp added to my depression. My diary tells me that my nerves, which hitherto had stood the strain of these strenuous months remarkably well, were beginning to suffer.

On September 26th Karachan came to see me again. He was, as always, courteous and affable. We had a further discussion about the Allied situation in Russia and the possibility of opening up negoti-

* Raymond Poincaré (1860–1934), three times Prime Minister of France, and President of the Republic 1913–20.

ations for peace. He informed me that the question of my trial had now been settled. It was not to take place. He assumed that eventually I should be set free.

When he had gone, I sat down and translated into blank verse the Tell soliloquy from Schiller: 'Through this deserted valley must he pass.'

Two days later Peters came in with Moura. It was six o'clock on a Saturday evening. He was dressed in a leather jacket and khaki trousers. An enormous Mauser pistol was strapped to his side. There was a broad grin on his face. He told me that I was to be set free on Tuesday. He would allow me to go home for two days to pack. I thanked him, and then he looked at me rather sheepishly, put his hand into his pocket, and pulled out a packet. 'I have a favour to ask of you,' he said. 'When you reach London, will you give this letter to my English wife?' At the same time he gave me a signed photograph of himself and showed me some snapshots of his wife. Almost before I could say 'Of course I will', he drew back. 'No,' he said, 'I shan't trouble you. As soon as you're out of here you'll blaspheme and curse me as your worst enemy.' He seemed incapable of crediting any bourgeois with feelings of humanity towards the proletariat.

I told him not to be a fool and to give me the letter. Politics apart, I bore him no grudge. I would remember his kindness to Moura all my life. I took the letter. Later, of course, I delivered it. Then he began to talk, first, about politics and the plot. He admitted openly in front of Moura that the Americans were as greatly compromised in this business as anyone else. (Since my arrest an American agent had been detected with plans, concealed in a hollow walking-stick, of the disposition of the Red Army.) He confessed that the evidence he had been able to collect against me was not very damaging. I was either a fool or very clever. 'I don't understand you,' he said. 'Why are you going back to England? You have placed yourself in a false position. Your career is finished. Your Government will never forgive you. Why don't you stay here? You can be happy and make your own life. We can give you work to do. Capitalism is doomed anyway.'

I shook my head, and he went away, wondering. He could not understand how I could leave Moura. He left her alone with me.

The reaction was wonderful. Although, except during the first few days before it was clear that Lenin was going to recover, I was not really afraid that I should be shot, the strain had been severe, and I had never been sure that some little straw would not change everything against me. We laughed and cried alternately. Then we settled down to talk. There was so much to tell – a whole month's gap during which I had heard nothing of the outside world, of my colleagues, of Moura herself.

It was an incoherent, disjointed conversation, interrupted by numerous digressions, but little by little I pieced together the whole story. Moura had been in the women's prison. My colleagues and a goodly number of the French had been incarcerated in the 'Butirky'. Wardwell, the American, had been heroic. He had wrung concessions from the Bolsheviks. Daily he had fed all the Allied prisoners and Moura as well with his own provisions. He had not lessened her alarm by telling her that I was to be shot. For ten days there had been great anxiety about my fate. My solitary confinement had baffled the neutral diplomats. There had been a terrible scene between the Dutch Minister and Chicherin, during which both men lost their tempers. The Dutch Minister was persuaded that I was going to be shot and had telegraphed his conviction to London. The British Government had replied with a menacing note to the Bolsheviks. The whole situation seemed hopeless until Lenin was able to take a hand in affairs. After he recovered consciousness, his first remark, it was said, was: 'Stop the Terror.' Gradually the hotheads on both sides cooled down, and out of chaos a scheme had been evolved whereby we were to be exchanged for Litvinov and other Bolsheviks in England. There had been a long hitch before an agreement could be reached. The British Government, who had arrested Litvinov, were not prepared to trust the Bolsheviks. They would not allow Litvinov to leave English soil until I had crossed the Russian frontier. For days the negotiations were side-tracked in this cul-de-sac. I had foreseen this difficulty when I had first read of the proposal in the *Izvestia*. I knew that the Bolsheviks cared little about Litvinov, but much about their own prestige. The only way to deal with them successfully in a matter like this was to take them at their word. They would act up to it. Treated like bandits, they would behave as bandits. I realised that the British Government would prefer the bandit treatment. This was precisely what had happened. Fortunately, Rex Leeper, who advised Mr Balfour during the negotiations, understood Bolshevik psychology. He persuaded Balfour to agree to let Litvinov leave London at the same time as I left Moscow, and Mr Balfour, in face of the opposition of the majority of the Cabinet, took his advice. The Swedes and Norwegians had now taken charge of the negotiations. We were to be allowed to cross the Russian frontier as soon as Litvinov and his party reached Bergen.

During this exciting month there had been one episode in connection with our imprisonment which had made all Russia laugh. When the mass arrest of the Allied representatives began, half a dozen officials, including Hicks and Grenard, the French Consul-General, had taken refuge in the American Consulate-General, which since the rupture of relations had been taken over by the Norwegian Minister. Officially it was now the Norwegian Legation.

The Bolsheviks soon tracked down the missing Allied officials. They wanted to arrest them. At the same time, disturbed by the consequences of their raid on the British Embassy in St Petersburg, they had no wish to create another breach of the law of nations. They would be correct. They would not infringe diplomatic extraterritoriality. But they would force the refugees to surrender by starving them out.

The Norwegian Legation was a large house with a small dower house, where the besieged Allies slept, and a large garden. It occupied the whole space between two side-streets and both sides were entirely exposed to the public view. The Bolsheviks surrounded the whole place with troops, allowed no one to enter the gates, and shut off the water supply and the electric light. Every day half Moscow assembled in the streets to see the fun. But the Allies never surrendered. They took their exercise daily in the garden. Whenever it rained they rushed out with bath-tubs to collect the drops. So far from looking starved, they seemed to have grown fatter. They held out to the end.

The bath-tubs were, in fact, make-believe. The dower house cellars contained the stores of the American Red Cross: bully beef, milk, biscuits, butter, candles, tobacco. In cutting off the water supply the Cheka had forgotten one tap, which was apparently connected with another main. Ample supplies of food, clean and well-furnished quarters, and poker, played by night behind heavily draped windows so as not to destroy the Bolshevik delusion, made the lot of the besieged more comfortable than that of their other colleagues in misfortune.

That night, when Moura left me, I sat up late, smoking and reviewing the situation. After the first joy of relief had evaporated, my feelings changed to a deep depression. My whole future seemed without hope. My nerve had gone. Now that I was to be set free, or rather to be sent out of Russia, I did not want to go. I found myself coming back again and again to Peters's proposal that I should remain in Russia with Moura. I gave it more consideration than the English reader may imagine. It was not so madly impossible as it seemed. Sadoul and Pascal, a young French officer of almost saint-like character, had accepted a similar proposal. There was Marchand. These men were not wilful traitors. Like most of us, they had been influenced by a cataclysm which they realised would shake the world to its foundations. There were moments when I asked myself what I should do if I had to choose between the civilisation of Wall Street and the barbarism of Moscow. Now, however, I was not a free agent. I had become the centre of a miniature world storm – a something over whose body two world systems had been wrangling. I could never be a Bolshevik. At this stage, when the telegraph wires of half Europe had been working to secure my release, I could not forgo my official obligations.

The decision left me helpless and indifferent. Some time before, an American newspaper, in criticising American diplomacy in Russia, had compared the American Ambassador unfavourably with the 'cold, experienced Lockhart with his calculated and relentless pursuit of British interests'. What a satire it now seemed on my conduct. How futile were the personal wishes of the individual in this maelstrom of international conflict.

Moura herself was wonderful. She was ill. She had a temperature of over a hundred, but she made no complaint. She accepted the parting with Russian fatalism. She knew that there was no other way.

For two more days I was kept in the Kremlin. Moura was with me from morning till sundown. Together we packed my belongings: my books, the pack of patience cards, the notes and letters – some of them written on Cheka notepaper – which she had sent me. We talked mainly of the past, avoiding as far as possible all discussion of the future.

On Tuesday, October 1st, Karachan came to see me and to say goodbye. He told me that we were to leave the next day. At three that afternoon I was released and taken back under escort to my flat.

A sentry was posted at the door, and I was informed that I was under 'house arrest'.

The flat was in a sad state. Since my second arrest it had been occupied by a Cheka guard. I discovered that my pearl-studs, my links, my new waterproof and a considerable sum of money had disappeared. The soldiers, too, had drunk all our wine and appropriated our supplies of provisions. In their search for compromising documents they had taken out the linings of my chairs and sofa. They had even probed the wallpapers. Yet in the closed typewriter in my study I found a piece of paper, which had escaped their attention and mine. It bore the words: 'I hereby certify that the firm of . . . is good for the sum of . . .' Fortunately, the secretary, who had been typing, had gone no further.

Although I was not allowed to go out, there was no ban on visitors. That evening Asker came to see me. He had been the most efficient and level-headed of all the neutral representatives. He told me that at one moment I had been in serious danger of being shot. I thanked him as best I could. He was a splendid type of Swede, and to him more than to anyone we owed our release. Wardwell, too, was another whose efforts on our behalf left us with a debt we could never repay. Later, when we returned to England, the British Government conferred the Knighthood of the Order of St Michael and St George on the neutral Ministers who had conducted the negotiations for our release. I was able to secure for Wardwell, who as an American could not accept an Order, a piece of silver-plate with an inscription conveying the gratitude of the British Government for his services on our behalf.

Yet another visitor was Liuba Malinina, the niece of Chelnokov. She informed me that she had become engaged to 'Hickie', who was still beleaguered in the Norwegian Legation. Could I secure his freedom for an hour the next day in order that she might marry him?

I promised to do what I could, and later in the evening, when Peters came in to say goodbye, I put the question to him in the half-joking, half-sentimental way which I knew would appeal to him. He was amused. 'No one but a mad Englishman', he said, 'would make a request of this nature at a time like this. Nothing is impossible to such a race. I'll have to see what I can do.' He did, and 'Hickie' and Liuba were duly married the next day.

The Wednesday of our departure was a busy day. There was a

letter from Peters apologising for the theft of my belongings and
enclosing compensation, which I returned with a polite note of
thanks. There were long conversations with Asker about the control
of British interests and about the protection of British subjects in
Moscow. At six o'clock in the evening the sentry was taken away
from my front-hall, and at 9.30 Asker came with his motor car to
take me to the station. There I found my French and English colleagues, most of whom had been taken straight from prison to the
train. The train itself was drawn up at a siding outside the station.
As I walked down the line, I wondered vaguely whether my colleagues would blame me for all they had endured. Everyone was
strangely silent and subdued. The train was in charge of a platoon
of Lettish soldiers, who were to conduct us to the frontier. Their
presence created an atmosphere of restraint. I think we all felt that
until we were out of Russia we could not breathe freely. There were
a few friends to see us off: Moura, Wardwell, and some Russian
relations of the newly married Mrs Hicks. There was nothing tense
or dramatic about our farewell. There was the usual Russian hitch
about the time of our departure, and we were kept waiting for
several hours. In the cool, starlit night Moura and I discussed
trivialities. We talked of everything except ourselves. And then I
made her go home with Wardwell. I watched her go until she had
disappeared into the night. Then I turned into my dimly lit carriage
to wait and to be alone with my thoughts. It was nearly two in the
morning before our train, with many snorts and several false starts,
steamed slowly out of the station.

The end, however, was not yet. After skirting St Petersburg – the
Izvestia declared that our train had been diverted lest the infuriated
populace should tear us limb from limb – we reached Bieloostrov,
the Russo-Finnish frontier station, on the Thursday evening. Our
rejoicings were premature. There was no Finnish train to meet us.
The commander of our Lettish escort had received the strictest
orders not to allow us to proceed until he had received definite confirmation of Litvinov's arrival at Bergen. There was no news of
Litvinov. There was nothing to do but wait.

These three days at Bieloostrov seemed more trying than my
imprisonment. Now that everything was over, I had given a free rein
to my depression. We were cooped up in a dingy, unheated train. We
had provisions for several days but not for longer. Although I had no

real fears that the Bolsheviks would change their mind and take us back to Moscow, the possibility of a hitch could not be excluded. As the delay dragged itself out, nerves became strained and tempers frayed. There were even hotheads who counselled making a dash by night across the narrow strip of no man's land.

For me personally the nights were the worst ordeal. Now I could hardly sleep at all. I talked with Lavergne and Hicks. Rather feebly we tried to justify ourselves, repeating all the old arguments and consoling ourselves with the reflection that, if the Allies had only taken our advice, they would not have landed themselves in such a mess. I think we all realised that in any circumstances intervention would have been a mistake. We foresaw clearly that we should be blamed and that both the generals and the politicians would shelter themselves behind the excuse that they had been badly informed.

Mostly, however, I walked the platform by myself. I wanted to be alone. I dreaded the home-coming and the questions I should have to face. Fortunately, the weather was fine, and under the starlit northern sky I must have walked for miles. Hope was dead in my heart. I had no illusions about my reception at home. For a few days I should figure in the front page of the news. There would be newspapermen and photographers. I should be received by the Crown Princess of Sweden, by the King, by Mr Balfour. There would be relief at my escape. Had anything happened to me, there would have been unpleasant complications and perhaps some twinges of consciences in Whitehall. Then I should be laid on the shelf. My knowledge, at that time unique, of a complicated situation would be allowed to go to rust. There is no one more quickly neglected than the man on the spot whose policy becomes discredited. And my policy was already discredited in the eyes of both the pro-Bolsheviks and of the interventionists. My future was not pleasant to contemplate, and I subjected my conscience to a severe cross-examination. Months before, when we had had a slight altercation about a question of principle, Moura had described me as 'a little clever, but not clever enough; a little strong, but not strong enough; a little weak, but not weak enough'. Peters himself had described me as the man of the 'zolotaia seredina' – the man of the golden mean – and had despised me. It seemed then, it seems today, a fair definition of my character. And now I had left her. My cup of unhappiness was full.

If these were my inmost thoughts, I had to keep a brave face in public. The piece had to be played through to the end. There were some forty or fifty French and English on the train. We had to keep on good terms with the Lettish commander and endeavour to induce him to expedite our departure. To keep our spirits up, I organised a great series of test matches between the French and ourselves at pitch and toss. We played the series out with the platform for our pitch and with the Lettish soldiers and the Russian station officials as our crowd. They became almost as excited as we did. And, doubtless, to them the sight of a silver-haired French general bending down on his knee on the platform and measuring the distance between the various rouble pieces with a pocket-handkerchief was thrilling. If they thought us mad, they became quite human, and it would have required little persuasion to induce the Lettish commander to take a hand in the game himself. He refused, but there was obvious reluctance in his refusal. Perhaps he was afraid that Moscow might consider his participation unproletarian. England, or rather Scotland, won the series. In my Presbyterian youth I had played the game diligently on the Scottish Sabbath, and, like the curate in the music-hall song, who 'won three out of four 'cause he'd played it before', we were the more experienced players.

The end of the test matches saw the end of our troubles. As we were picking up our coins, the commander came up with a telegram in his hand. Everything was in order. The Finnish train was ready, and we were to leave immediately. He also brought us the Russian newspapers from St Petersburg. They were full of great news. Bulgaria had collapsed and had signed an armistice. Austria was a suppliant for peace. The Hindenburg line in the west had been broken. On my companions the news acted like a tonic. Most of them regarded their departure as a happy release, as a nightmare that had been swallowed up in a glorious morning. They could look forward to the future with a new hope. In my heart there was no elation. My physical body was going forward, but my thoughts were back in Moscow and in the country which I was leaving – probably for ever.

EPILOGUE

That my father was able to produce this book covering manifold world-shaking events in such detail is largely due to his keeping of extraordinarily lengthy diary material from 1915 until a few years before his death. The first brief entry was written on January 11th, 1915, when he was twenty-eight: 'Heard Chaliapin in Boris Godunov.' From then on he wrote copiously. The estimated number of words in the diaries is about 750,000, of which only some 300,000 have been published. The first of these two volumes (1915–38) covers the events of his life and work in Russia before and during the Bolshevik revolution.

For security and personal reasons several passages were not published in *Memoirs of a British Agent*. Some were written in Russian so that my mother would not understand them as they referred to her anger at his affairs with other women, and her increased depression at the miscarriage of her first child. His relationship with Baroness Moura Budberg, whom he met in 1918, continued all his life. Like my mother she became pregnant by my father, but 'Little Peter', as she called the unborn child, was also the victim of a miscarriage. Almost immediately afterwards she repeatedly begged my father in person and in writing: 'Please let us have another "Little Peter".' When shortly after my mother gave birth to myself, Moura became almost suicidally depressed. She emigrated to England in the 1920s but refused to speak to me until I was about twenty years old. However, we did become friendly, especially after my father's death. (In addition to the family funeral, Moura arranged a twenty-four-hour service in an Orthodox church in London which she alone attended.) She also had a big love affair with Maxim Gorky, and in 1988, when Russian television invited me to Moscow for the seventieth anniversary of my father's release from the Kremlin, I was shown a newsreel item covering Gorky's funeral with Moura standing beside Stalin, leading the procession.

Much of the secret work of my father was by no means fully revealed in the book, and some Most Secret material was omitted from his diaries. The references to Sidney Reilly may praise him as a 'master spy' but that is all; there is little word about the activities of Commander Boyce of the British secret service who worked in my father's office.

My personal interest in Reilly began as a teenager when I met several former members of MI5 or MI6 who had been in Russia; my father said little to me about him. Nevertheless, after my father's death, I discovered not only his diaries but masses of documents and letters, including about 150 from Moura. Letters there were, too, from Sidney Reilly. (Much of this material was obviously highly Secret, and as I mention in the Introduction it was subsequently handed over to the Foreign Office.) After painstaking research into the details of my father's joint work with Reilly as revealed in these diaries and papers, I produced my book *Ace of Spies* in 1967, which in 1983 was turned into the highly successful television series *Reilly: Ace of Spies*. As I gained further bits of important information about my father and Reilly, I added them to the numerous editions of *Ace of Spies* since 1967.

Reilly disappeared into Russia in 1925 with the task of getting an anti-Bolshevik revolution underway. At first the Russians claimed that he was shot crossing the border, then later that he was executed in the Kremlin both in late 1925 and late 1927, and there were reported sightings of him in various parts of the world in the 1930s. One item from Russian security-forces archives even alleged to show photographs of him – but they were of someone totally unlike Reilly. It was at this time that Moura wrote to my father after she had visited Moscow: 'R is *still* alive.' In the same letter she expressed the hope that my father was doing well at his work. In World War II, a senior member of the NKVD – the forerunner of the KGB – told the official British Liaison Officer, Brigadier Hill, that Reilly was still alive but retired and living in the country. (As a junior officer in 1918, Hill was associated with my father's work.) All my friends and acquaintances who worked for MI6 and knew Reilly were convinced he had changed sides to save his life and perhaps gain power.

In 1919, Reilly gave to my father a magnificent cigar box with the interior lid gilt-edged. Carved on the inside was: 'To R. H. Bruce Lockhart in memory of events in Moscow in August and September last year from his faithful lieutenant Sidney Reilly.' (Some ten years ago I sold this together with my father's briefcase at Christies for £13,000 but do not know who bought it.)

Against the above, before Reilly returned to Russia, he wrote to my father saying: 'Bolshevism is the nearest approach I know of to a real democracy based on social justice.' 'The Lockhart Plot' – of which the Russians produced three separate plays – became 'The Reilly Plot'! Both Reilly and my father, however, were condemned to death by the Revolutionary Tribunal in December, 1918, if they ever set foot in Russia again.

ROBIN BRUCE LOCKHART

INDEX

Robert Bruce Lockhart is referred to as RBL in subentries throughout this index.